# Gregorian Vision

*Opening a Window to the Thought
of Paulos Mar Gregorios*

**About the Author:** John D. Kunnathu is an educator and an author of several books. Born and brought up in India, he spent almost a decade in Africa and another two decades in the US before he has settled in Kerala, India. His life experiences helped him develop a global outlook, which is clearly reflected in his work. He spreads the message of love and peace. He believes that one can be inclusive of all people in the world while having a firm footing in one's own specific culture. His other major works include

In His Master's Path -- Paulos Mar Gregorios as a follower of Jesus Christ

# Gregorian Vision

*Opening a Window to the Thought
of Paulos Mar Gregorios*

John Daniel Kunnathu

## Gregorian Study Circle
Kottayam, Kerala

## Dedication

To my older brother, George, who introduced Paulos Mar Gregorios to me first

## Acknowledgement

Metropolitan Yuhanon Mar Diascoros has been so kind as to read the manuscript and write a review. Fr. K.M. George kindly wrote a foreword. I am grateful to several other friends and disciples of Gregorios thirumeni for supporting and encouraging me with this work. Fr. Bijesh Philip, Fr. Thomas Ninan, Fr. Ferdinand Pathrose, Dr. Alex Alexander, Dr. M.P. Mathai, Dr. Roy Cherian, Dr. Joseph Thomas, Dr. P.K. George, and Ruben Jacob devoted their time to read the manuscript and make suggestions and corrections. I am grateful to Joice Thottackad for making the arrangements to publish this book.

# Gregorian Vision

Author: John Daniel Kunnathu
Published by: Gregorian Study Circle
©2011 by the Author
Print Edition By Sophia Books, Kottayam  2011
E-Book Edition By Paragon House, USA  2012
Print-on-demand Edition By Createspace, USA 2016

**Contact Info**
Email: Johnkunnathu@gmail.com

# Readers Say ........

Paulos Mar Gregorios remains a great inspiration to me personally. He was a man of great compassion and selfless devotion to making the world a better place. John D. Kunnathu's book will introduce him to a wider audience at a time when we need great exemplars more than ever. **Larry Dossey, M.D**

This book will be a treat for ardent fans of Metropolitan Paulos Mar Gregorios, and it will also captivate readers who know nothing about His Grace. The wisdom of Paulos Mar Gregorios on these subjects will have a life enhancing impact on us. May the legacy of His Grace live forever and inspire us all!This book will educate our faithful on our church and its faith, helping them to live as good Orthodox Christians, striving to deepen the spiritual life and creating a livelier sense of fellowship among them and catering the specific needs of today's world, providing valuable education to confront atheism, secularism, and the challenges in scientific technology and exercising a deep faith in God and His Body.

The Author of this book, John Daniel Kunnathu has devoted his time and energy to compile all the works of Paulos Mar Gregorios into a simple but effective handbook for our faithful. I honestly believe it is a divine call to write this book. More often than not, we have people from cleric rank writing books on spiritual fathers and sensitive subjects like faith, mission of the church, secularism, and etc. His Grace Paulos Mar Gregorios would have been proud to know that a LAYMAN from his church has compiled his work into a good handbook. I write LAYMAN in capitals because it was Paulos Mar Gregorios who started Divyabodhanam, which emphasized on educating the lay people on Theology. I am delighted to give my wishes and blessings to Mr. John Kunnathu. May this book be a success and inspire many of our laymen to write. **Yuhanon Mar Diascoros, Chennai, India**

A long cherished dream of many is getting materialized through this new book on Gregorian thought. This will of course enlighten many in manifold ways.

**Fr. Dr. Bijesh Philip, Principal, Orthodox Seminary, Nagpur**

This book is a proof to how relevant the thought of Paulos Mar Gregorios is to many of the contemporary issues today. For those who have always looked at PMG as a puzzle, or rather as too complicated, this book is where you can start with. I found through this book how unbelievable a person PMG was as a priest and as a Metropolitan of the Indian Orthodox Church, as an ecumenist, as a religious leader, and as a human being...a great effort by John Kunnathu to capture it so meticulously through this book.     **Fr. Thomas Ninan, South Africa**

This is a stellar attempt to highlight the significant contributions of Bishop Paulos Mar Gregorios to foster inter-religious understanding by nurturing pluralism and mutual respect among the various faiths, within the context of his own spiritual and theological identity as a follower of the true tenets of Jesus of Nazareth. All those who admire the life and work of Mar Gregorios will be delighted to read this book.

**C. Alex Alexander M.D., Maryland, USA**

As the subtitle suggests, this book opens a window on the entire thought corpus of the great thinker and theologian of the last century, Paulos Gregorios. It provides a lucid exposition of the profound and sometimes subtle thoughts of Mar Gregorios and hence will serve as a guide to the younger generation readers in particular. A work like this is particularly significant in the present context of the perceived threat posed by inter-religious rivalries.     **Prof. M. P. Mathai**

Dr. Paulos Mar Gregorios was one of the greatest figures in the history of Kerala. I was fortunate to be with him during the last week of his life. Even our dicussions on various philosophical and scientific topics are still fresh in my memory. After this discussion he would leave his personal copy of the book with me. Sometimes he goes through this during our dinner time where our young children were also present. He explains his theories and opinions in such a simplified way that even our children would follow his dialogues. He would comment that "if these children understood what I say I can be sure that I understood what I wrote." I just checked my library and found fourteen of his books, all his personal copies left here for me.

There is no doubt that this work, Gregorian Vision, is one of the best on Dr. Paulos Mar Gregorios. As I have been reading this I was "hearing" Thirumeni's voice explaining to me what each book was about. It brings forty years of memories back alive. The author has clarified several theological issues in a very clear way for the ordinary reader to understand them. I remember Thirumeni was easy to understand when he gives a talk or in conversations. But his books are not easy to read. This book is of great help in this regard. This was the kind of book I have been waiting for. And I think that the author has been faithful the thoughts and ideas of Mar Gregorios.

**Joseph E. Thomas, Ph. D. Chicago, USA**

# Contents

# A Refreshing Journey

Metropolitan Paulos Mar Gregorios has always been a special source of inspiration to many a young person who is intellectually inclined and in constant search for the meaning of life. In the 60s and 70s of the 20$^{th}$ century when there was a global awakening of the youth to the questions of spirituality and transcendence as well as to a new world order of freedom and justice, Mar Gregorios was in the forefront of international debates on such issues as nuclear disarmament, justice to the poor and the marginalized, concerns of indigenous people across the world, apartheid and racist discrimination, interfaith dialogue, ecumenical vision of one humanity and so on. His amazing gift of awareness and articulation of the major political-economic and cultural forces that operated in shaping our contemporary world opened a new window for many young people who were desperately seeking a breakthrough in the hierarchical, authoritarian, power-mongering, militarized, exploitative and oppressive structures of the world in which they lived. When Mar Gregorios brilliantly articulated in public fora his own critical vision of a new world order rooted in his spiritual-theological understanding of the Kingdom of God as portrayed by Christ in the Gospels, people listened with rapt attention. Many young people across religions and ideologies became his admirers and looked up to him for guidance and inspiration. They included Marxists and Buddhists, Hindus and Muslims, Christians and Atheists in the academia and in society at large.

Mar Gregorios also remained a controversial figure and made many enemies as well particularly because of his bold and scathing criticism of Euro-American economic, political and cultural conquest of the rest of the world. He always stood firmly on behalf of the "two-third world" a phrase he deliberately used in place of the regular 'third world". Mar Gregorios was one of the rare leaders who had access to the world behind "the iron curtain" during the second half of the cold war era. His dialogues with the Socialist block was often denigrated and misconstrued by some of his western colleagues and critics. However he always acted with honest courage and carried on the dialogue while firmly rooted in principles of justice and freedom as he learned it from the Gospel of Christ and from the wisdom tradition of humanity.

John D Kunnathu is one among those who found in Mar Gregorios a refreshingly meaningful beacon of life. As he says, his fascination with the personality of Mar Gregorios started when he was still in his teens. He continued his deep spiritual and intellectual interest in the speeches and writings of this extraordinary bishop. Later as he himself matured in age and understanding he became an assiduous reader of the many books produced by Mar Gregorios. The present work in a book review format is the happy result of such a dedicated reading and sustained personal reflection.

One major difficulty encountered by the students of the writings of Mar Gregorios is that he is a polymath and a   polyglot. His thoughts and writings span an unusually broad spectrum of topics from Christian theology to Quantum physics, from Marxian economic analysis to the Buddhist logic of Nagarjuna. Students who are not capable of trotting with ease in these diverse fields of inquiry will fall short of the holistic vision of Mar Gregorios. His important writings like the *Cosmic Man* are profusely interspersed with words and phrases from German and French, from Greek, Latin and Hebrew. To the best of my knowledge no student has yet been able to cope with the demands of this interdisciplinary, broad based and yet precise articulations of Paulos Mar Gregorios.

John Kunnathu has made a sincere attempt to be faithful to the thinking of Mar Gregorios as he analyses and explains book by book and interjects his own reflections. In many places it may be difficult for a new reader to distinguish between the thinking of Mar Gregorios and the interpretation given by the author. Of course John has taken some measure of freedom in interpreting the thought of the master-teacher. This is inevitable in any creative understanding of the writings of great persons.

John Kunnathu's dedication to the thought-world of Metropolitan Paulos Mar Gregorios is admirable. His decision to share with others his own joy and excitement in traversing this refreshing yet intellectually demanding Gregorian landscape is certainly to be appreciated. I wish him well on this rewarding voyage.

**Fr. Dr. K. M. George**

Principal, Orthodox Theological Seminary, Kottayam
24 November 2011 (Feast Day of Paulos Mar Gregorios)

# Introducing my Life-Long Hero

Watching my interest in Paulos Mar Gregorios, I am often asked how I am related to him. I enthusiastically respond that he became a hero to me in my childhood and he continues to be a hero. I have had several heroes since my childhood, but none has stayed a hero to me for such a long time as Mar Gregorios.

When I was in my early teenage, I had a notebook in which I had a collection of the pictures of the great people I admired. On the front page of the book was this favorite verse of mine from Proverbs: *Exalt wisdom; she will exalt you* (4:8). All my heroes in my teenage were those people who exalted wisdom. Paulos Mar Gregorios was someone in my community who exalted wisdom , and I watched with wonder and excitement as he climbed the steps of success and was exalted to become one of the most influential people in the world.

It was from my older brother that I first heard about Father Paul Varghese (previous name). It was in the late sixties, and I was in high school then. My brother happened to see him in an Orthodox Student Movement conference, and later at home he spoke highly of him. We used to subscribe to the Orthodox Youth magazine at our home, and I began eagerly looking for anything written by Fr. Paul Varghese. He usually appeared in a column answering the questions people sent to the magazine. I had to wait until late seventies to read a book by him-- the Malayalam translation of *Joy of Freedom*. I read it with great enthusiasm and wrote a summary of it in the Orthodox Youth magazine under the title, *Our Worship*.

I am fortunate to have meet Mar Gregorios three times. The first was at Kundara in 1974 if my memory serves me right. It was about ten Kilometers away from my home, and I was about 18. Hearing from a friend about his arrival, I went there just to see him and hear his speech. It was Passion Week, and I still remember him talking about Jesus washing the feet of his disciples. He presented it as an example of humility that all people and nations need to follow. I noticed that he had the magic of keeping the attention of the entire audience from the beginning till the end. Not a single sound could be heard from the audience of around 400 people.

The second one was in 1979 or 80. I happened to attend a student conference in Hyderabad. I didn't know Mar Gregorios was the main speaker there, and so it was a pleasant surprise to see him there. He gave a series of lectures on the Kingdom of God. The clarity of his thought made a deep impact on me. It was very different from any other speech or class I had attended. He made sure that the audience understood every theological term he used. He clarified every unfamiliar word he used in his lectures. He presented his thought from simple to complex and from familiar to unfamiliar systematically so that it was a joyful experience to listen to him. While we were going to visit a museum in Hyderabad, I had the opportunity to have a brief conversation with him. I remember asking him what he thought about Universalism, the argument that all people will be saved, and he responded right away that he did not believe in it.

The third time I was fortunate to see him was in 1982, in Kottayam, when Manorama Newspaper organized a symposium and a public meeting to commemorate his 60th birthday. As soon as I read the news of the event in the morning news paper, I hurried to

 catch a train to Kottayam. It was a grand occasion, where I could meet several faces I greatly admired. The symposium was on World Peace. Prof. K. M. Tharakan was the facilitator. The speakers included Dr. M. M.

Thomas, Paulos Mar Paulos, Nityachaitanya Yati, Fr. Dr. K. M. George, Dr. Ninan Koshy, and several other eminent scholars. The public meeting, in the evening, was inaugurated by C. M. Stephen, a Cabinet Minister of the Government of India, and was chaired by C. Achutha Menon, the former chief minister of Kerala. I obtained a copy of *Cosmic Man*, the doctoral dissertation of Mar Gregorios, from there.

After a couple of years I left India to go to Ethiopia as a teacher, and among the few things I took with me was *Cosmic Man*. As I had a lot of free time in Ethiopia, I read this book over and over again. I was excited to know that Mar Gregorios was a school teacher like me in Ethiopia about forty years before. I have had a chance to stay for a few days in a place called Nazareth, where Mar Gregorios was posted as a teacher first. I heard several legendary stories about Mar Gregorios from various people in Ethiopia. I happened to meet in Addis Ababa Ms. Kunjannamma, whom Mar Gregorios mentions in his autobiography. One day, while talking to me casually, an assistant principal in my school (Ethiopian) said to me, "John, do you know, there is a great scholar in India called Mar Gregorios!" He didn't know I belonged to the Orthodox Church in India, and that Mar Gregorios was a hero to me. One day in 1989, I think, I was surprised to see Mar Gregorios on the Ethiopian TV. He was in Moscow addressing an international conference, and on the stage with him was none other than the President of the Soviet Union, Michael Gorbechew, and other prominent figures.

Later in 1992 I came to the United States as a student. I often think that my path in life has been similar to that of Mar Gregorios in that respect. From Kerala he went to Ethiopia as a teacher, and from there he went to USA as a student. But there were important differences too. Mar Gregorios could master Amharic, the language of Ethiopia, in a year, but I could barely understand and utter simple sentences and identify the letters of its alphabet even after eight years of stay.

On Nov 24th, 1996, I was attending a prayer meeting of my parish church in Houston, in Texas. Mathews Mar Barnabas was leading us in the concluding prayer. The phone rang, and a message was delivered to His Grace. Mar Barnabas stopped the prayer to announce: "His Grace Paulos Mar Gregorios, the Metropolitan of Delhi Diocese, has passed away". I couldn't control myself. I forgot where I was, and began to weep. He meant so much to me. He is the one person who has influenced me more than anyone else.

That night I sat down and expressed my feelings in a few lines in Malayalam, and I recited it in our church after a week. It said:

*I am submitting this poem to the memory of Paulos Mar Gregorios, who remained a heroic son to the Orthodox Church of India for several decades, and of whom the church has been very proud of.*

*After fighting for you all day long, here lies your dear son, sleeping, with his head on your lap, O mother, the Church.*

*Rising from the land of Malayalam, your son enlightened the entire world.*

*He proclaimed the good news of Jesus flawlessly to give salvation to the whole world.*

*He traveled all over the world to give you fame.*

*Oh God, Thy dear servant, Mar Gregorios, has shown us the depth, height, width, and length of Thy love to us fully and clearly.*

*Oh God, we thank Thee for giving us this great soul as our shepherd to show us the right path.*

In a few years, I happened to meet a handful of people in Houston who admired Mar Gregorios. Together we decided to celebrate a memorial in November 2000. For this purpose we set up an organization called Gregorian Study Circle, and had the celebration. Soon we started an online group, and people began joining it from all over the world. In 2001 November, there was a memorial celebration in Chicago and another one in Madison in addition to Houston. In 2002, a grand inter-religious seminar was held in Chicago for the memorial.

At present the online group of Gregorian Study Circle has members from around the world. The members include H.G. Job Mar Philoxenos, the successor of Mar Gregorios in Delhi Diocese, Fr. Dr. K. M. George, the successor of Mar Gregorios at the Orthodox Theological Seminary as its principal, Mr. Abraham Varghese, Mar Gregorios' brother in Canada, close friends like Dr. Eapen Cherian and Dr. Joseph Thomas, and Joice Thottackad, the biographer of Mar Gregorios. I feel happy such a worldwide network of the disciples of Mar Gregorios could be formed.

I helped Joice Thottackad put up a website on Mar Gregorios (paulosmargregorios.in) by editing and proofreading the content of the site. I also had the opportunity to collect some of his pictures and make a slideshow of his life, thought, and work. I showed it in and around Houston whenever I had an opportunity. Ruben Jacob, my friend, presented it in some student conferences in India.

The work for this book started as early as 1990 when I wrote an appreciation of Cosmic Man. A few years ago I wrote an introduction to Diakonia, a book by Mar Gregorios, for the Magazine, Sahayatra, published from the Orthodox Seminary in Nagpur. I realized that writing helped me to understand the thought of Mar Gregorios better, which made me write even more summaries and reviews of various articles and books. I am putting this book together with such articles I have been writing.

I intend this book as a window to the thought of Mar Gregorios. People complain that the books and papers of Mar Gregorios are generally too hard to understand. Those books decorate the shelves of a lot of people; mostly they remain unopened. I do not claim that I have adequately understood his works or that I am qualified to explain his thought. But I have made an attempt to understand them by reading them over and over. I see myself as a student of Mar Gregorios, and I am presenting this book as an invitation to all people to join me in this exciting adventure of exploring his thought.

This is also meant to be an inspiration for anyone intending to attempt similar studies on the work of Mar Gregorios.

A word of caution seems to be in order here. Every idea dealt with in this book need not be traced to the thought of Mar Gregorios. Although my intention is to introduce the thought and work of Mar Gregorios, this book also has my own reflection based on his thought. I have divided this book into two parts. The first part mostly introduces and summarizes the thought and work of Mar Gregorios, but the second part is mostly my own reflections and explorations based on the thought of Mar Gregorios.

When I was growing up, existence appeared a very complicated puzzle to me. Reconciling the information I received from my school classes with the information I received from my Sunday school classes was almost impossible. Science and religion appeared like parallel lines to me, never meeting anywhere. It was the thought of Mar Gregorios that helped me to solve this puzzle to some extent. I learned from him that science and religion are not contradictory but complementary. This is just one example of how the thought of Mar Gregorios has provided me with the right guidance and orientation in my life. His thought has helped me to solve many other puzzles I have had about human existence.

Born and brought up in the Orthodox Church in India, I grew up listening to the claim of our religious leaders and teachers that our church is superior to the other churches or may be the only true church. However, I couldn't be convinced easily, for that is what the leaders of any religious community would tell its followers. The irrational adherence to inherited practices I observed in my own community often tempted me to leave it for some other community in which I could observe a lot of vitality. However, I still remain in my own community because of Paulos Mar Gregorios. His explanation of how my church evolved and how its views are different made sense to me.

Each chapter of this book addresses a puzzle about human existence, which explains why the chapter titles are in the form of questions. These are questions that young people often ask. If a young man or woman asked these questions to Mar Gregorios, how would he answer? That is the perspective from which each chapter of this book is written. This book may be used as a study material in youth meetings and at the higher level Sunday school classes.

Paulos Mar Gregorios was someone who transcended his allegiance to his own community and culture and became a world citizen. Staying loyal to his own community, he stretched his arms to embrace the entire humanity. Therefore, while those in the Christian tradition will find it easier to follow the thought of Mar Gregorios, it would not be alien to any member of human race. This book and any work by Paulos Mar Gregorios can be read by anyone with an open mind.

I sincerely hope that this book will be instrumental in introducing the Gregorian vision to the new generation in our world.

John Daniel Kunnathu

November 2011

# Part I:  Taking A Look At The Gregorian Vision

# 1. Why do we Suffer?

Although the approaches to and opinions about suffering vary widely, the fact that we have no escape from suffering remains invariable. Metropolitan Paulos Mar Gregorios discusses this topic in his autobiography[1] in the context of his own suffering. Not only has he clearly explained his view of suffering, but also did he successfully exemplify it in his own life. We will see now his view of suffering briefly and how he evolved this view through his own life experiences.

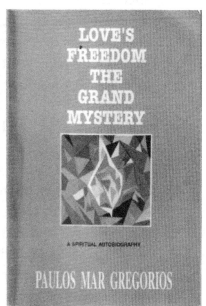

People in general do not care for the meaning of suffering; all they want is to get rid of it. Heaven or paradise or *nirvana* or *moksha* is imagined to be a place or state without any suffering. Some people make use of suffering to elicit others' sympathy. Such people would even pretend to have some suffering in the absence of real suffering.

Sigmund Freud, in his *Civilization and its Discontents*, identifies three causes of suffering:

1.  the superior power of nature, like floods and earthquakes,
2.  the decay and eventual death of our bodies, and
3.  the shortcomings of our social relations and institutions.

The first two he thought were unavoidable, but today we know that much of it can be prevented or avoided. For the third, he offered the remedy of a rational and non-neurotic approach to all questions and eliminating the illusion of religion. This seems too simplistic and adolescent an approach for Mar Gregorios.

Mar Gregorios suggests several other criteria for classifying suffering such as:

1. Suffering voluntarily chosen, such as in asceticism, and in personal sacrifice for the sake of others such as in parental affection;
2. Suffering imposed by other human beings either by mistake or by intention or even because of ignorance;
3. Suffering caused by what previous generations have done to make our inherited physical and social environment what it is;
4. Suffering due to lack and want, including lack of love and care;
5. Suffering induced by compassion for the suffering of others;
6. Suffering brought on by one's own folly;
7. Suffering caused by accidents, natural or otherwise;
8. Suffering caused by the stress and strain of present living;
9. Suffering as anxiety, boredom, and sense of guilt;
10. Suffering due to the social structures of injustice.

Referring to the well-known statement of Descartes, *I think, therefore I am,* Mar Gregorios claims that a slight change such as *I suffer, therefore I am* would have made more sense to common people because one's suffering is his own in a particularly intimate way and he can never doubt it even if others do not quite see it. To support this, Mar Gregorios quotes Milan Kundera's statement in *Immortality* that the universal I is much more a sufferer than a thinker.

Among the Greeks, the Stoics are primarily the ones who dealt with the problem of suffering. *Apatheia* (non-suffering) was a great virtue for them. It was a synonym for *eudaimonia* (happiness) or *eleutheria* (freedom). This term was first applied by Aristotle to things incapable of any experience of suffering. The Stoics applied it as an attribute of God. God cannot suffer, for He is beyond suffering. The ideal for humanity was the same, to be beyond or unaffected by suffering. The Stoics used *apatheia* to denote freedom from all feeling, being unaffected by all that happens. The principle was more clearly explained by the last of the great Stoics, the ex-slave-philosopher, Epictetus (55--135). He believed that our happiness should not depend on things we cannot control. It should depend entirely on one's own self and will. Suffering would then have no power over us. That is freedom and happiness.

Buddhism is primarily a diagnosis and a solution to the problem of *dukha* (suffering). *Dukha* implies unrest, sorrow, discomfort, distress, dissatisfaction, stress, tension, worry, anxiety, unhappiness, pain, anguish, grief, and misery in all their forms. It is the universal condition of all human existence. The root cause of *dukha* is *trshna*, which is desire or craving, lust for experience, greed for wealth, yearning to act and talk, craving for pleasure, power, and domination, and for fame and acclaim. Once desire is gone, suffering ceases and the state of *bodhi* (enlightenment) or *satori* (liberation) is attained. How do we overcome *trshna*? Buddhism prescribes *dharma*, which may be defined as the practice of *vinaya* (discipline) in a *sangha* (community) to overcome desire.

Christianity does not claim to know why we suffer. It does not make any attempt to resolve the issue philosophically. On the other hand, it encourages a Christian to use the suffering that comes in his way for the exercise of self-discipline and compassion. It seems that the development of character happens only in the presence of suffering. Compassion is learned and taught by entering into the suffering of others and by letting others share one's own suffering. Suffering seems to be the way of love. However, suffering does not open the door by itself. The key has to be turned; suffering has to be transmuted by love. Hate and despair can turn it into poison.

A Christian believes that God, who is supposedly free from all suffering, comes and partakes of suffering in Christ, in us, even today. The Christian doctrine of incarnation asserts that suffering is the key to the mystery of existence in this world. Mar Gregorios names it the Grand Mystery.

The solution suggested by our religious traditions to the problem of suffering is to rise above it. An airplane that flies in the air cannot stop a rain, but it can avoid the rain by flying above the clouds. A pilot can see rain negatively as a problem to overcome or positively as an opportunity to become more skillful and gain more expertise. We may not be able to stop suffering, but we can always try to fly above suffering by changing our own attitude toward it.

### The Practical Lessons from Life

Mar Gregorios gives us an opportunity to examine his life of suffering in his autobiography. There we read how he learned the Christian way of dealing with suffering.

As a child in school, he was an object of abuse and mockery by his teachers and classmates. He especially remembers the comment of his Malayalam teacher, Sankara Menon, "How can you shrimp-eating Christians ever learn a literary language like Malayalam?" Being a sensitive boy who did not want to be ashamed of his allegiance to the Christian faith, such abusive comments hurt his feelings. Mar Gregorios also remembers the two nicknames he was given by his classmates: *Manjathavala* (yellow frog) and *Kottoodithalayan* (Hammerhead). Being admitted in the first grade at the age 4, he was small, compared to his classmates, and he was also slightly pale and anemic. That is what made them relate him to a frog. Although he was small he had a longish head, which made him look like a hammer.

Mar Gregorios narrates in detail the incident of how he was bitten by a snake when he was a child. He caught the snake mistaking it to be a fish. Although he was bitten, which caused a bleeding, no venom got into his body. The snake was caught by his older brother and was killed. This incident made him face the possibility of death. As a child he realized how close death always is to all of us.

Mar Gregorios' father was a school teacher, and his monthly salary was Rs. 28 in the 1930s. It was not easy for a family of seven to live on this amount. When he was promoted as a headmaster, he was also transferred to far off schools. He often left home at the beginning of a week, and returned only toward the weekend. On the way to school, he had to cross ferries, which were dangerous in the monsoon season, and there was no way of letting the family know whether he had safely reached his destination. This meant high anxiety for his mother, and he shared her anxiety along with his brothers.

The anxiety and tension led to a catastrophe, which Mar Gregorios describes in detail. Once when his mother was in bed with a high fever, she got up with a great surge of energy, went out of the house, opened the gate, and was talking away quite loudly and senselessly to the passersby. The young Paul could not grasp what had happened. Only after people had forcibly brought her inside the house, did it dawn on him that his most beloved mother had gone out of her mind. She had become mentally ill. Mar Gregorios narrates this incident in his autobiography:

> In her manic phase, she was virtually impossible to control, and was often violent. Quite frequently she would disappear from the house, wander over long distances, and after several days, would return home, distraught and worn out. We never found out how she managed for food on these long wanderings. We supposed that she visited her brothers and other relatives because stories were carried to us from them. Sometimes when she came back, her clothes would be so dirty, giving us the impression that she had slept on the road. Father sometimes beat her up, while we sons watched helplessly or pleaded or struggled to stop him. …… We boys did some minimal cooking, or went without food altogether. My father, a man noted for his integrity and independence, suddenly went sour and sullen, sulky and petulant. Joy had gone from the home and gloom had descended.

There were two things that deeply bothered him in this situation. One was the violence his mother had to suffer from his father, and the other was the intense shame this caused him. He writes:

> Father was cruel when he lost his temper at mother's tantrums. He would beat her up, with the bare hand or with a stick. Mother just took the beatings in her stride, only becoming more and more abusive. And we sons, who loved them both, had to watch this, with mounting pain and frustration. One saw no way out of the suffering. Even today, when I think of it, shudders run up and down my body. The social opprobrium was even worse for a sensitive teenager. Some days, especially

if father were not at home, mother would go and stand on the road side verandah to the south of our house, and would stand there, doing all kinds of pranks and talking all kinds of nonsense particularly when the road on the south of our house was full of children going to school. They were my classmates and schoolmates, and I was filled with shame that they watched my mother in this condition.

Mar Gregorios remembers that at the time of his school final exam his mother was locked up. The two older brothers soon left home finding some job, and the young Paul was left at home looking after his two school-going younger brothers. He completed High school with third rank in Cochin State, but his father couldn't afford to send him to college. Being a very intelligent young man, his father's decision caused so much agony to him. He was only fifteen, so he couldn't be hired for work either. He spent all his time reading and writing. He was fascinated by one particular book: R. L. Stevenson's *Dr. Jekyll and Mr. Hyde*. It was about a scholar-scientist with a split personality, a good man (Dr. Jekyll) who could occasionally turn into a monster (Mr. Hyde) doing wicked things. Mar Gregorios says that his own personality was very similar to the scholar-scientist. In spite of the goodness in him, he knew that a lot of wickedness was lurking underneath all the time. He says that he became addicted to admiration and praise, which he identifies as wickedness. However, he was afraid to be loved. He explains the reason as follows:

> I loved to be praised, but I was afraid to be loved, mainly for fear that I could not take it when the love would be withdrawn. I was once the object of great love and affection from my mother, but its apparent withdrawal as a result of her illness was a trauma that I never got over.

He translated the entire book to Malayalam—a hundred-page manuscript. After a few years, the manuscript was mistakenly disposed off as waste paper by his father, which added to his grief.

At the age of 18 (1940), he got a job as a clerk in a small shipping company with a monthly salary of Rs. 15. After two years, he passed a test of the Post and Telegraph Department and got hired as a clerk. His posting was in Madras with a salary of Rs. 39.

There he became active in the labor union as well as in the Indian Independence movement. In five years, he was transferred back to Ernakulam.

From childhood, he had developed a conversing relationship with God. By the age of 25, he was dissatisfied with his own way of life, and his soul sought a deeper relationship with God. The sudden death of a close friend intensified his yearning for God. He prayed that night:

"Yes, my Lord, I know that I can also die like that. I should change my life and make it bear better fruit. You know I want to. But you also know my friends. They will laugh at me if I become overly pious overnight. I cannot stand that. So long as I live in this society, I dare not repent or change. But I promise you, put me in a brand new environment, and I shall be a different person, totally committed to your obedience, totally dedicated. I promise".

When he placed such a need in front of God, he didn't expect any speedy response. However, the answer came from God the very next day in the form of a Canadian from the Ministry of Education in Ethiopia. Though he was in India to recruit bachelor degree holders as teachers, Paul Varghese got selected as a school teacher in Ethiopia. For Paul it was nothing less than a miraculous intervention by the Almighty.

Saying goodbye to his family, Paul Verghese set off to Ethiopia in 1947. The trip from Bombay to Addis Ababa in a DC-3 Dakota took 18 strenuous hours. Once in Addis Ababa the new recruits had to stay in quarantine for a week, for there was an outbreak of cholera in India. He was posted in a place called Nazareth, a small city about 100km southeast of Addis Ababa. However, regarding his commitment to God he says:

But I had conveniently forgotten my promise to God about repenting and beginning a new life and all that. I taught during the week, and then played bridge incessantly with fellow teachers, sometimes starting Friday evening and stopping only late Sunday night.

Soon he caught chickenpox. The blisters all over the body were cherry-sized, and were excruciatingly painful. New ones kept coming up every day on head, face, chest, on the back, and even on his behind. He could not sit or lie down because of the blisters. He was shut up in his room, and his fellow residents of the house asked him to lock his door and not go out of his room, for fear of giving it to others in the house. No one came to see him, and some food was occasionally slipped in under the door as if he were a convict or a prisoner.

The pain was sharp and intense, and the loneliness was unbearable. When he was thirsty there was no way of asking for a hot drink. He could not wash himself, or even clean his mouth and teeth. Unable to sit or lie down, he paced his room up and down. He felt this was not quite fair on the part of God to put him through all this pain. Like Job, he wanted to ask God for an explanation. At the height of his pain, he sat fiercely on a chair in front of a color portrait of Christ. He started talking to God. He accused God of being cruel and unfair, devoid of compassion, and letting people suffer more than they deserved. He was talking quite aloud, and in the anguish of his pain and loneliness, he threw a stream of abuse at the portrait of Christ. As the torrent of words rose, he blurted out what he knew were insolent words:

"Was your suffering on the cross anything comparable to what I am going through now?"

That stopped the flow of his abusive words. He felt he had said more than what he had a right to say. There was a calm. He writes how he felt then:

The experience that followed is so poignant that I have no words in which to describe it with some sense of adequacy. A voice came, distinct and clear. I cannot be sure that any of our modern equipment could have registered the sound waves that reached my ears and the meaning that hit my heart. I heard those words. I do not know where they came from. I was speaking to God in English, and the reply was also in English. The tone was by no means rebuking or reproving; on the contrary, it was most compassionate and tenderly loving:

"Yes, my son, it was"

That was all it said. But it brought about a total transformation in my condition. My pain was gone, though the blisters were still there. I was wafted up to a higher plane of happiness where pain cannot penetrate. I felt an incredible lightness of body, as if I was being effortlessly lifted up on wings of joy. I bowed my head in humble adoration. I surrendered myself without reservation, into the loving hands of God in Christ. And I said, with deep contrition:

"To Thee, I bow my head, Lord, to Thee I surrender myself. I am Thine. Pardon me my folly, pardon me my insolence. Take me, do with me as it pleases Thee. Break me if need be, but give me grace and wisdom and strength to walk in Thy ways. I love Thee and I bless Thee with all my heart".

The blisters were there, as before. No miraculous healing had taken place. The pain started slowly coming back, but I was a stronger person now and could easily and joyfully take it. The chicken pox took its normal time to heal, but I came out of that sickness radically transformed. I could not share my experience with too many people, but I renewed my commitment many a time those days.

In the next academic year, Paul Verghese was posted in a place called Jimma, a city about 200 km southwest of Addis Ababa. If what he suffered was physical suffering in Nazareth, what was waiting for him in Jimma was extreme mental torture and agony. It was a special school for the young men who had become orphans during the Italian Occupation (1935-41) and had grown up on the streets. The campus with the school and family quarters for the teachers was well guarded with high walls and barbed wire fences. The sixty or so Ethiopian boys were sometimes prone to violence, and some had criminal tendencies. They had grown up on the streets and had taken to petty pilfering, mild drinking, and quick quarrelling. They were not normally allowed to go into town unless accompanied by a teacher; they were virtual prisoners in a barbed wire enclosed compound, with guards at the gate.

Soon the students developed so much respect and affection for Paul Verghese. One day he invited his students to have a tea with him at his residence. Later one of them told him:

"We have something to say to you, Sir. What happened to us today has deeply touched us. This is the very first time that any of our teachers invited us into their home. And you treated us like human beings, not like as if we were thieves and criminals.

It makes all the difference to us. We feel like human beings again."

Paul was moved to tears. It meant so much to his young and sensitive soul. He invited them to come to his residence every afternoon to have tea and to study the Bible. Thus he began a program of daily Bible study, entirely voluntary, friendly, and informal. More than half of the students attended regularly.

The regional director of Education, who stayed on the same  campus, grew jealous of Paul's success in managing the students. He forbade the students from going to Paul's residence for Bible study any more. He spread a rumor that Paul was gay. Soon Paul found that the whole atmosphere in the town of Jimma had changed. Every Ethiopian looked hostile to him, even outside the compound. As he walked along the streets of Jimma, people would point their finger at him and say things to each other. A veil of gloom had fallen over the community; some students often seemed to avoid him. He felt like a battery of persecution had been turned on him. About this period he writes:

Those few weeks were again hell, like the hell I suffered at home in India when my mother went sick. But there was a difference. Spiritually, this was the most enriching experience of my life. For, in the midst of persecution, I could rejoice inwardly. The words of Jesus made fresh sense to me: *Blessed are you when they revile you and persecute you and say all manner of evil against you falsely, on account of me. Rejoice and exult, for great indeed is your reward in the heavenly realms* (Matt. 5:11-12). I understood that Jesus was not talking about any future reward in life after death. The reward or wages can be enjoyed here and now. I was happy inside, and could pray for hours at a time, praising God for being counted worthy of thus experiencing the mystery of rejoicing in the midst of suffering. It was a spontaneous, exhilarating, life-giving joy. It was an experience as constitutive of my spiritual life as the episode in my room in Nazareth, only a few months before. But I wonder if the joy of Jimma would have been possible without the nightmare of Nazareth and the catharsis of encounter with Jesus. In any case, I can testify that during those weeks I experienced simultaneously the depth of suffering produced by mockery, persecution and ostracism on the one hand, and great gushes of spiritual joy welling up within me right amidst all that suffering, especially when engaged in prayer.

Paul was asked to pack his things and report to the office of the Ministry of Education in Addis Ababa. Arrangements were made to terminate his contract and deport him. But miraculously things happened in favor of Paul Varghese, and he was posted in a new place called Ambo, about 100 km west of Addis Ababa

This experience turned out to be a school of prayer for Paul. He spent hours in prayer with a clear and joyous sense of the presence of God. A little suffering for the sake of God had begun to cleanse him. He writes about this experience in detail:

My suffering was beginning to turn the key to the mystery of life. The first important lesson I learned was that to suffer for the sake of truth was not the same as just going through any suffering, for example, the kind of suffering that fell to my lot in my earlier youth in India, or even in Nazareth. To suffer unjustly in the cause of truth, and to be mocked and reviled for the good things you had done, became a most sublimating experience. Of course, faith had to be there to undergird the experience. Equally important was a clear conscience, and not holding a trace of bitterness while one suffered. And the experience of rejoicing in the midst of suffering puts the seal to one's faith in a loving Lord. All doubts vanish, and faith strikes new and deeper roots. To have tasted God's joy-creating love in the midst of pain-creating suffering makes one's faith strong and secure. One finds it easier then to take risks for the sake of obeying God, without anxiety. But one always has to move on.

During the next few decades, Paul Varghese became Father Paul Varghese (1961) and later Paulos Mar Gregorios (1975). He grew to become one of the most influential people in the world. He continued to face suffering in his life in USA, Europe, Africa, and India. His unfinished autobiography has left us so unfortunate as not to be able to know in detail about his further growth during this period.

In a journal entry made in 1993 at the age of 71 from the hospital bed in Germany he says how he suffered from a stroke in an airport:

> On my way from Oxford to Cologne, a mild stroke paralyzed my left side. I am able to sit up with a lot of help (I am still pretty helpless in one half of my body) and operate my Notebook computer with one hand.

He was on his way to Germany for a major conference. Now with the stroke he realizes that he won't be able to play a major role in the conference. However, without any complaint, he accepts it as the will of God. In the airport a lady who was a stranger helped him with his baggage. An elderly airlines staff also helped him with a wheelchair. He writes:

> I thanked God not only for all the help I had received, but also for the fact that ordinary people in the west were still so kind, considerate and helpful to the disabled.

In the hospital bed he continued to type the journal entry:

> Death is no terror. Even the prospect of being a permanent (that is, till the end of this biological life) invalid holds no terror for me if that is what God wills. Whatever happens, He can turn it into the good.

After total and complete surrender to the will of God, he wrote a message for the world:

> I leave this word to all who survive me: Love God with all your mind and all your will and all your feeling and all your strength. Live for the good of others. Pursue not perishable gold or worldly glory. Wish no one any evil. Bless God in your heart, and bless all his creation. Discipline yourself while still young, to love God and to love His creation, to serve others and not to seek one's own interest. Pray always that God's Kingdom may come and all evil be banished from this created order.

About this message to the world, Dr. Joseph Thomas[2], Mar Gregorios' former student and close friend, has commented as follows:

This was what he taught me in Aluva College in 1955, and this was what he taught me in 1993 in Rishikesh at the foothills of the Himalayas. Knowing him personally for forty-one years I know that these words came from his heart and he lived them the best way he could.

On November 19, 1996 when Dr. Joseph Thomas visited Mar Gregorios in Delhi, he found,

Thirumeni was sitting on his chair, wearing the plain white kammeeze of the Orthodox Christian priest. A walking stick, which he had been using for a while, leaned against the arm of the chair. I knew he was ill, but he did not look sick. The usual exuberance and energy was not there, but his face looked bright and serene, and his mind was as sharp as ever.

Dr. Thomas continues to write:

Thirumeni had gone through several personal traumas during his life including his mother's nervous breakdown, his own stroke, post-surgical complications, and cancer! But self-pity  was not one of his flaws, even though now, here he was with 'all of the above' plus fatigue, diabetes and hypertension! Thirumeni's legs appeared to be hurting. He had constant discomfort in his lower legs. I noticed that there were several dark spots on his feet, scars from diabetic sores. He was sicker than he appeared, I thought.

When I watched his defiant struggle against his physical disability, his unceasing striving to learn, think, and write, his incessant campaign for a just and peaceful world, I wondered if he would soon detach himself from all these worldly preoccupations. Maybe he had a different way of dealing with life. 'God gave me this precious life, and I must use every drop of it to my last breath, for His glory.' Like a burning pellet of camphor at the altar of a deity, did he want to burn it all before God with not a trace left?

He reached for his walking stick and struggled to get up from his chair as I watched, keeping my impulse to assist him under firm control. I was not at all comfortable watching him struggle though. "I like to do this by myself," he said, as he dragged his body toward the bed. "My legs don't seem to have the strength to carry the weight of my body." I knew his stoic self resented sympathetic helpers. I ventured to help only when he asked for it. A nurse attended him during the day. His physical capacities had been breaking down one after the other over the past forty months, in spite of his valiant fight against this at every stage. His left hand was paralyzed, and he struggled to prove that he could take care of things with one hand alone.

Dr. Thomas left Mar Gregorios on 22nd, and on 24th he received the news of his passing. In Kottayam,

I stood in line, along with the thousands of other mourners, to touch his feet and get a last glimpse of his face. Caught up in the fast-moving crowd, I got a split-second to look at his face. This was not the face I wanted to engrave in my memory.

**Conclusion**

During the 74 years of life, Mar Gregorios suffered almost everything someone can possibly suffer in a lifetime. As a child he narrowly escaped from death from a snakebite. As a teenager, he suffered intensely due to his mother's mental illness. In Ethiopia as a school teacher, he suffered tremendously both physically and mentally. Later toward the eve of his life, he had a stroke, which paralyzed him, and he also had cancer, diabetes, and hypertension. He had the option to face these sufferings negatively or positively, and he chose the positive approach. True to his own view of suffering, he turned every suffering to a stepping stone to climb higher and higher to greater heights.

# 2. What is the Gospel of the Kingdom?

What is the Gospel of the Kingdom? This question is addressed in the book, *The Gospel of the Kingdom,*[1] a Bible study guide authored by Fr. Paul Varghese in 1967 while he was in Geneva as the Associate General Secretary of the World Council of Churches (WCC). It was published next year by the CLS in Madras as a study booklet of the National Bible Study Program, a joint venture sponsored by the National Christian Council, the Student Christian Movement, the YWCA, the YMCA, and the India Sunday School Union.

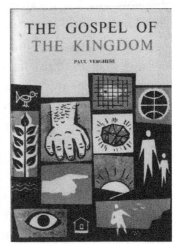

Being one of the earliest and one of the easiest to understand, this book is a window to the vision and understanding of Mar Gregorios regarding the basic questions of Christian faith. He evolved this understanding during and after his studies in US and UK and later during his work in WCC. His participation in the Second Council of Vatican (1962-65) also influenced his evolution of thought. What follows is a summary of the main ideas discussed in this book.

### What is the Christian Gospel?

Christ died for us, and if we believe this, we will escape from hellfire and go to heaven after we die-- this is how a lot of people understand the Christian gospel. However, even a hasty glance through the Bible reveals that this is not the gospel proclaimed by Christ or his disciples.

That the kingdom of God is here is the gospel that Christ proclaimed. People of Israel had been waiting eagerly for the arrival of the kingdom of God. Christ proclaimed to them the good news that the kingdom is already here. That was a good news to the poor, the hungry, the unhappy, and to the oppressed classes of society; not a good news to the rich and the well-fed, those who enjoyed privilege and popularity. It was good news to the exploited, but a bad news to the ones who exploited them. Christ the King came into the city of Jerusalem seated on a donkey. He came healing and serving. He brought joy to the down-trodden and the oppressed, to the lame and the paralytic, to the blind and the deaf. He came as light for the world in darkness, bringing joy and hope.

The disciples of Christ proclaimed the good news that God became man in Christ Jesus. Christ lived among us, died, but rose again. Although this message sounds slightly different from what Christ proclaimed, it was the same as that of Jesus in content. They meant that the kingdom of God was established through the arrival of Christ. The rule of God was fully and clearly manifested in the life and suffering of Christ. God's throne is cross, and God rules with love. As Christ rose again, God continues to rule the world through him. They also acknowledged that this is good news to the poor, the afflicted, the lame, the blind, the oppressed, and to all who mourn.

Those who heard the news could not believe their ears. The message was clear but it was shocking because it differed from two of the popular expectations of the kingdom of God. It was believed that it was entirely up to God to establish the kingdom. It was also believed that the kingdom of God is a world free of pain and suffering. Jesus made it clear that God has already done His part in the establishment of the kingdom, and now it is up to people to accept the kingdom. Jesus also made it clear that pain and suffering are characteristics of the kingdom of God. Blessed are the poor and suffering, for theirs is the kingdom, Jesus proclaimed. The goal of the citizens of the kingdom is not to eliminate suffering, but to use the suffering to grow to the perfection of God. Contrary to the popular expectations, God was clearly on the side of the exploited people, and if you want to be on the side of God, you have to stand with the exploited as well.

But in the course of Christian history, this element of grace to the poor and judgment to the rich became watered down. Also slowly the Christian Gospel became other-worldly. Those who view it as other-worldly do not realize that the other world is the Kingdom which has come to this world though it is yet to be fully manifested. This world and the other world cannot be separated so easily. We perceive the other world differently from this world due to the limitation of our senses. Actually there is only one world, and that is how it is seen in God's eyes. God is already ruling the whole world—both this and the other world, and it is up to us to accept the rule of God and to live according to the will of God.

### Church Continues to Proclaim Gospel

Those who listen to this gospel and decide to stand with Christ and with the poor and the exploited become Christ's disciples, the church. It was about his disciples that Jesus prayed in his high-priestly prayer, *As Thou didst sent me into the world, so have I sent them into the world* (Jn. 17:18). Christ's presence in the world was the same as God's presence in the world, and the presence of the church in the world is a continuation of the presence of Christ. The church continues to proclaim the same gospel to the poor and the oppressed, and it stands on their side.

In Exodus, the Lord says to the people of Israel through Moses: *If you will obey my voice and keep my covenant, you shall be my own special people among all the peoples; for all the earth is mine, and you shall be to me a kingdom of priests and a holy nation* (19:1, 6). It clearly means that the nation of Israel is to serve as a priestly nation on behalf of the other nations of the earth. Israel, without any special merit on her part, is called to a special responsibility, which is not for her own sake, but for the sake of the nations.

However, Israel was not aware of its responsibility during the period of Christ. It was only aware of its privileges. It expected God to protect them and save them. Instead of suffering with God, it blamed God for letting it suffer.

In this context, the early Christian church saw itself as a renewed Israel, which truly understood the original mission for which Israel was called. In the place of the disobedient Israel they saw in the church an obedient new Israel. This idea is clearly explained in the first epistle of Peter. Peter says that the church is called as a royal priesthood and a holy nation (2:5, 9). This epistle is probably based on a sermon preached on the occasion of the baptism of new converts during the feast of Easter. One can imagine the newly baptized men and women, clad in white robes, assembled probably in one of the Catacombs of Rome before sunrise on Easter Sunday. The apostle stands before them explaining to them the meaning of their baptism, and giving them their commission for life in the world. It parallels the Lord Yahweh giving his commission to the people of Israel on Mount Sinai. We are a people gathered from all the nations of the earth, not because of any special merit in us, but by His gracious calling, to a life of close intimacy with God. Our calling is always on behalf of others. A priest is one who intercedes for others and not for himself. And all of us have been by baptism incorporated into the one eternal priesthood of Jesus Christ who intercedes for the whole world. Our priesthood is a part of this ministry of universal intercession.

This idea is echoed in the Book of Revelation as well. The four living beings fall before the Lamb, and they sing a new song: *Worthy art thou to take scroll and to open its seals, for thou wast slain and by thy blood ransomed for God from every tribe and tongue, people, and nation, and made them into a kingdom and priests to our God, and they shall reign on the earth* (5:10). The kingship or lordship belongs to Christ the God-man, which is shared by the church.

Christ describes the qualities of the good shepherd, the real messianic King (Jh.10:1-18). Some of these qualities are to be specially noted as the exercise of our sharing in Christ's kingship.

1. The shepherd knows the sheep intimately, and calls them by name, and the sheep recognize his voice as one that can be trusted, for it always acts in their best interests

2. The shepherd leads the sheep out of the confinement of the sheepfold into the wide open pastures, goes before them, and feeds them.

3. The shepherd stays by the sheep even when the wolves come, face the wolves, and when necessary lays down his life in defense of the sheep.

4. The shepherd tries to bring all the sheep into one fold (where all can be fed by the same shepherd).

We are also called to be a holy nation. *Be holy, for I am holy.* (I Pet.1:16). It involves both a privilege and a responsibility. The responsibility is to grow up by the spiritual milk of the word, to put away all bitterness, resentment, malice and hatred, to love one another earnestly, and to come to Christ and to be built up by His Holy Spirit to become an abode of the Spirit and a holy priesthood, offering up our own lives along with that of Christ on behalf of all men, and to announce by word and deed the marvelous grace of God that has called us out of the deceptive pleasures of this life, into the joyous light of expectant faithful, loving service, and worship (2:1- 9)

The positive elements of holiness are:

1. Hope, looking forward to the coming of Christ, and not to our own success and comfort;
2. Faith, being established solidly in Christ and therefore free from unreliability, dishonesty, anxiety, and deceptiveness;
3. Love, patiently surrendering oneself to others and being actively engaged in their welfare.

**How may we Proclaim the Gospel Today?**

We are initiated into this royal priesthood through Baptism. The crossing of River Jordan marked the birth of Israel. Baptism in River Jordan marked the initiation of someone to the new Israel. The first epistle of Peter makes this clear. *And baptism saves you, not by removal of bodily uncleanness, but the pleading of a clear conscience in the presence of God, through the risen Jesus Christ, who is at the right hand of God, who has entered heaven with angels and authorities subject to him* (1 Peter 3:21). Baptism is initiation into the heavenly community which lives in the presence of God, enabling us to join in the service of God. Chrismation (*Muron*) as an integral part of baptism is anointing them to the priestly, prophetic, and kingly ministries of Christ.

Our ministry of priesthood is on behalf of the whole creation, and not a means of personal salvation which is already given to us as a free gift. The kingly priesthood is a ministry of self-sacrificing service for the kingdom. Our service may be in village work, in urban social work, in teaching, in healing, in building, or in pleading the cause of the poor, in labor union work, or in the ordained ministry of the Church. Whatever be our area of service, we need the same attitude of our master, who came to serve and not to be served.

The royal priesthood is also a ministry of worship and prayer. We need to make the Eucharist the center of our life of prayer. We should not regard the Holy Communion as an occasion when Christ gives us his grace by feeding us. That is only part of the Eucharist. But primarily it is a participation in Christ's eternal act of self-offering on the cross. When the bread and the wine are lifted up and offered to God in Christ, we are offering ourselves, our bodies, our minds, our souls, our abilities and all we have to God in Christ in an act of loving self-immolation to the gracious and loving Father; not to appease Him, but because He is worthy of all, and our gratitude to Him can be expressed in no lesser way.

In the Eucharist we should learn to offer up the problems of our people and of the whole of humanity to God. We have a responsibility to lift up the sufferings and yearnings of those with whom we live and whom we know well. We must feel in ourselves and directly experience the poverty and misery of our people, and must intercede for the poor and the miserable and the oppressed with deep personal concern. Only that way the service we render to our fellowmen will receive the quality of authenticity. The Eucharist is the mode in which the sufferings of this world are linked up with the sufferings of Christ on the cross, through the conscious act of the Church, by the power of the Holy Spirit. But this must become a reality in our worship life, and a reality in our daily life.

Christ is unceasingly interceding for the world, and we should participate in this continuing ministry of intercession, not in order that we may spiritually grow, but rather in order that life and joy may come to the dying and the miserable. As busy students and hard-working people, we may not have long hours to engage in sustained prayer. The tempo of our technological civilization demands new forms of prayer life. From time to time we may say from the depths of our hearts short prayers such as, "Lord, have mercy on the poor", which can be said on any occasion such as when a lecture gets boring, when we have to wait for somebody, or while walking to the college. The content of these prayers should also become concrete whenever possible, like "Lord, have mercy on our nation, and deliver us from famine and from corruption". In the early morning, even while remaining awake in bed, we should lift up our hearts to God in loving, adoring thanksgiving and worship. Only thus can the subconscious mind be cleansed.

Let us use our mind and our imagination to find ways of pioneering in fighting oppression and injustice in our societies. The Christian Church started schools, hospitals, and other institutions which have now become the common property of all -- including those who are not Christians. This is our continuing ministry in the world -- to be pioneers of new forms of good. We are not to imitate the world. *Do not be squeezed into the mould of this age* (Rom. 12: 2). Our task is to get ourselves transformed, and become a transforming influence in society, by demonstrating what the will of God is for our time and place. When there is black-marketing and hoarding of food in our society, as intelligent students and young people it is our job to find means to prevent such acts and to expose those who practice them. If our officials and leaders are corrupt, it is our job to bring the corruption to light. But this kind of destructive criticism may be too easy. We must also show new ways of doing things which change the structures of corruption and oppression, and at the same time inspire others to integrity and self sacrificing service. Creative pioneering is the main vocation of a minority Church.

We need to be ready to accept failure and to lay down our lives with faith, hope, and love. Christians should not be so naive as to think that by our pioneering action, our society will become a paradise overnight. The cross of Christ was apparent failure, ineffective in saving the world. But out of the apparent failure have come the great movements of emancipation and welfare of our day. We should not anticipate either success or general approval, in direct response to our actions. To act in faith is to be despised and rejected and to fail apparently, as part of the calling of the suffering servant (Isaiah 53)

In all things render thanks to God, and wait for his full manifestation. Our job is to work within our mandate, with joy and thanksgiving. His presence, open and unveiled, will also bring the day of final release, final salvation, when the whole earth shall rejoice in the light of God. It is the anticipation of this final, open triumph of God in Christ that makes Christians an extraordinary people who never lose courage (2 Cor. 4:1-11).

To serve these purposes, help to make the Church a creative fellowship, where honesty, integrity and love are the binding forces, and where hypocrisy and mutual competition and deceit no longer rule. *Come to him (Christ) to that living rock, rejected by men but in God's sight, choice precious; and like living blocks of rock be yourselves built into a house of the Spirit, to exercise the holy priesthood of offering up spiritual sacrifices acceptable to God through Jesus Christ* (1 Peter 2: 4 -5)

**Conclusion**

Christ proclaimed the good news that God rules and justice prevails! This was a message of joy to the poor and the exploited, but a message of woe to the unjust. Those who positively responded to this good news immediately joined the side of the poor and the exploited because that was the only way to be on the side of God. The dark powers of injustice crucified Christ, but Christ could not be kept inside the tomb. The spirit of God descended upon the disciples of Christ, who went forth proclaiming the same message of Christ.

The good news of Christ remains as relevant today as it was in the time of Christ. Poverty, exploitation, and injustice prevail all over the world, and the good news of Christ challenges people to join the side of the exploited, and stand against injustice. It is also a call to join the disciples of Christ, get filled with the spirit of God, and proclaim the good news with courage.

# 3. What is our Faith?

The second Vatican Council is probably the single most important event in the history of Christianity in the modern times. It made a fresh look at the faith of the church and its relation with the world. It opened under Pope John XXIII on 11 October 1962 and closed under Pope Paul VI on 8 December 1965. It was held in four sessions between 1962 and 1965. Some 2,500 Bishops took part and the Council produced 16 documents. The Council rapidly became a movement for the renewal of the Catholic faith for a new era.

Father Paul Varghese had the opportunity to participate in the council as an observer and as an expert theologian. In a paper[1] he read at the Hammersmith Christian Unity Conference in 1966, he presented an evaluation of the council. He said,

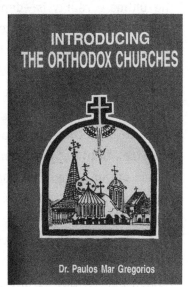

INTRODUCING THE ORTHODOX CHURCHES

Dr. Paulos Mar Gregorios

> "The two most fundamental gains of the second Vatican Council are, first, this incipient re-education of the leadership of the Church, and, second, the dramatic reversal of the negativistic, or anti-non-Catholic trend of development which has characterized Catholic

theology since the Reformation." He also noticed a radical shift in the attitude toward dogmas. "This tentative and cautious approach to Christian doctrine is a welcome return to the Eastern patristic tradition and a healthy sign of vitality in the Western Catholic tradition. Truth cannot be captured in formulae. Words can only point to truth, warn against error, kindle a light in the mind and open it to the truth."

Participation in this historic event was an opportunity for him to clarify the fundamentals of Christian faith, which led him to write several articles on this topic. The book, *Introducing the Orthodox Churches*[2], is a compilation of such articles. What follows is a summary of how Mar Gregorios views the Christian faith.

We are often bombarded with questions about our faith. *What do you believe?* People ask us. Before trying to answer this question, we need to remember that the word *believe* can be ambiguous. It has more than one meaning. Often it means simply holding on to an opinion without demonstrable evidence. All religions have their beliefs and opinions, and we have ours too. But we use the word with a slightly different meaning when we ask *who do you believe?* Here it does not mean an opinion, but trust. Our faith is not an opinion, not one of many possible views; it is an affirmation of how the ultimate reality is—dependable and trustworthy. Our trust is not on the ancient character of our Church or on any dogmas or doctrines. Our trust is in the One True God.

We believe (trust) God, and we also have beliefs (opinions) about God. We believe that God is eternal, self-existent, indivisible, infinite, incomprehensible, glorious, holy, uncreated (not owing his being to something else), all-sovereign, and creator of the whole universe. All things are from Him. We also acknowledge him as the source of our being. One important aspect we believe about God is that God is trinity, which is, God exists as Father, Son, and Holy Spirit.

In spite of whatever we believe about God, we acknowledge that God is beyond all conceptual comprehension not only by human beings, but by any created mind. He is different from the way anything else in creation is. When we say God is one and three, it is not a statement about how God really is, but merely a statement of how God appears to us. The reality of God is beyond our number system. No affirmative statement about God can be true because God transcends our language. Even the statement, God exists, is false because God's existence is not like the existence of anything else.

In spite of the incapacity of our thought and language to reach God, we think and talk about God because our existence depends upon God. We use our best possible similes and metaphors to think and speak about God because the only way we can think of God is by comparing God to what we are familiar with. That is how God becomes a shepherd, a potter, a farmer, a father, a mother, and other similar things we see in our world. The use of *he*, the masculine pronoun, to refer to God does not mean that God is a male. God transcends the gender difference. We use the masculine pronoun because we don't have another appropriate pronoun to refer to God. Even the word *God* can be misleading in referring to God. Usually we name something that we know. But in this case we use this word *God* to refer to something we know nothing about. The word *Theology* is misleading. One may explain it as the study of God (*theos+logos*) like the other sciences, forgetting that God cannot be the subject of any study. Theology is actually the study of our views, beliefs, and opinions of God.

We can know anything about God only through His operations or activities, the energies of God which come down to us through the Incarnate Son and through the Holy Spirit. The Triune God, Father, Son and Holy Spirit, share the same is-ness *(ousia)* that is infinite, eternal, uncreated, and self-existent. The three persons or centers of consciousness act in concord and unison as one being. There is no gap or interval of time or space between the three persons; there is no senior or junior; greater or lesser.

Although God cannot be known conceptually, God can be known in an intimate way by human beings who seek God and live a godly way of life. This is probably what Jesus meant when he said that the pure in heart can see God. The Sun cannot be seen directly with our naked eyes, but we can see the Sun reflected in clear water in a pond or a container. Similarly God cannot be seen or known directly, but can be seen reflected within our own heart if it is kept clean and clear.

About **Father**, the First Person of the Trinity, we know only what the Son and the Spirit reveal to us. All that we know specifically about the Father is that it is from the Father that the Son is born, and the Holy Spirit proceeds.

We believe that the **Son** became a human being, Jesus Christ, and rules the world. All authority in heaven (the world now not open to our senses) and on earth (the world now open to our senses) is given to Jesus Christ the God-Man. Death and Evil have been overcome, but they are still allowed to function, serving Christ's purposes. But they will eventually disappear, and love and life will triumph.

The **Holy Spirit** is Life-giver, Sanctifier, and Perfecter. He is the source of life for all living beings. It is He who makes us God-like by purifying us by effecting forgiveness of sins and, removing barriers between us and God and among ourselves. He works in the Church, through His special gifts, to build up the body of Christ. He also works in the Creation, bringing all things to their fullness and perfection.

While we do speak about these operations of the Father, the Son, and the Holy Spirit, who are not three Gods, but one God, we acknowledge that we know next to nothing about His being as God. It is important for us to confess the incomprehensibility of God. He is not to be discussed or explained, but to be worshipped and adored and acknowledged as Lord of all.

We believe in the **Church**, the community that came into existence as a result of the Son of God's incarnation. This community not only bears witness to Christ, but also is the abode of Christ. Christ dwells in the Church, His body. It is in the Church that the life-giving power of the Spirit is at work. The Church is not simply a community of believers gathered together, but it is a community with the risen Christ as the cornerstone, the Apostles and Prophets as foundation stones, and with all who belong to Christ from Adam to second coming as members. This community, which is one, holy, catholic, and apostolic, spans heaven and earth. A local Church is not a mere part of the church, but it is a representation of the fullness of the Church, especially when the community is gathered together with the Bishop for the hearing of the Word of God and for the Eucharistic participation in the one eternal sacrifice of Christ of the Cross. We remember at every Eucharist the departed as a whole, especially the Apostles, great teachers, and spiritual leaders who have helped build up and protect the Church from error and deviation. We ask the Saints to intercede for us with great joy and with genuine appreciation of their past and present role in the one Church of Jesus Christ.

Of the great Saints in the Church, the first and unique place goes to the **Blessed Virgin Mary**, for she was the first to hear the Gospel of the Incarnation of our Lord from the Archangel, and to receive Him, on behalf of all of us human beings, into her womb. She is the mother of Christ, and thus mother of all the faithful who are joint-heirs with Christ. But she is also the *Theotokos*, the God-bearer, for the one whom she bore in her womb was truly God. For her, Jesus Christ was not an ordinary human being who was then adopted or exalted as Son by God the Father. No, He is the Second person of the Trinity, who dwelt in the womb of Mary without being absent from the "place" of His eternal being. Jesus Christ is now fully God as he always was, of the same being as God the Father. He is also fully a human being, sharing our fallen human nature, but without incurring sin. His humanness and his Godness are inseparably and indivisibly united without change or mixture. One divine-human Christ, one Person, with one united nature and faculties which combine the divine and the human. Our union with this divine-human nature of Christ is what makes us participate in the divine nature (2 Pet. 2:4; Heb 2:10-14) without ceasing to be human beings.

**Salvation** means separation from evil and growth in the good. It means eternal life with true holiness and righteousness. It also means being united with Christ in his divine-human nature, in his sonship, and in his rule over the universe. It means becoming more and more God-like in love, power and wisdom. This is what the Holy Spirit makes possible.

The participation in Christ's body and His being and nature becomes possible by the grace of God and by the Holy Spirit through the **mysteries of the Church** (*roze-d-idtho* in Syriac), which are called Sacraments in the West. Baptism, Christmation, and Eucharist let us experience the eternal and eschatological reality of our oneness with Christ in the Church here and now. Confession-Absolution is for forgiveness of sins. Anointing of the Sick is for deliverance from sin and sickness. Marriage unites Man and Woman in an act of permanent mutual commitment and union, reflecting the Union of Christ with His Bride, the Church, or of God with the new Humanity. Laying of hands is (*hierotonia* or *hierothesia*) for receiving the special gifts of the Holy Spirit for the Bishop as the mystery-presence of Christ, the High Priest and Good Shepherd, with His Church, and for priests, deacons, and deaconesses.

We hold the **Bible** in very high regard. The Gospel is the Word of Life, the proclamation of life and salvation to the world. We hold the Scriptures in the highest respect, and no other writings can have the same standing, for the primary witness to Christ is in the Scriptures. We revere the Scriptures as the inspired Word of God, and all our prayers, as well as the services of the mysteries of the Church are saturated with Biblical reference, and always completed by the public reading of the Scriptures.

**Icons** are important for us. These mediate to the worshipping community the presence of the Saints, and of the saving events of our Lord's incarnate life. We do not make images of the unseen God. We consecrate icons to mediate to us the God-bearing persons and events which have been actually manifested to our senses.

**Tradition** is the life of the Church as a continuing body, with the presence of Christ and the Holy Spirit in it. It is the Spirit that makes the Tradition alive and it bears witness to Christ; it also moves forward in expectation of the final fulfillment. Hence Tradition for us is dynamic. It includes knowledge of Christ, the teaching of the Apostles, the doctrine of the Saints and fathers, the practices of worship developed by the community of faith, its way of doing things and practicing love. Scripture is part of this tradition. Tradition is not just a body of knowledge, but a way of life, worship, and service. It does not mean that we unquestioningly accept all that comes down as tradition. We have to critically examine them as exemplified by Christ. We do not want to nullify the word of God for the sake of traditions. (Mat. 15: 1-14)

Our **worship** as a community is the centre of our life, not our own personal articulations of faith. It is there that the Church, united with Christ, participates in Christ's self-offering for the world. Our daily life flows out from worship and has to be a life of love and compassion, caring for the needy, struggling against evil, and serving the poor.

**Our hope** is focused on Christ's coming again. It is only in that coming that evil would be separated from good, death from life, so that the good can triumph and grow eternally. In that coming there will be a reconstitution of the universe; evil shall be banished, and all things shall be made new. Death and darkness would be finally overcome; light and life and love will triumph. It is our task to bear witness to this final reality, while living it out here and now, as much as we can, though we are overwhelmed by sin and frailty. Let us pray from the bottom of our hearts: Let Thy Kingdom Come!

### What does Orthodox Mean?

Today the word orthodox is used to mean conservative, unchanging, stubborn, or antiquated. But its original meaning was not so. The word was first used in early 4th-century. Those who followed the teaching of Arius used the doxology (*doxa + logos* = word of praise), *Glory be to the Father, through the Son, by the Holy Spirit.* In this, praise was only to the Father, because only Father was believed to be truly God. The Christians who did not follow Arius used the doxology, *Glory be to the Father, Son, and Holy Spirit, one true God*. They called this form of praise Orthodox, meaning the right form of praise (*Ortho + doxa*). Those Christians who used this form of praise became known as the Orthodox Christians.

Later the Latin-speaking Christians under the Bishop (pope) of Rome called themselves Catholic, and the remaining Christians (Greek, Syrian, Ethiopian, Indian, etc.) continued to be called Orthodox. The terms *West* and *East* are used to denote this division.

The West (Catholic and Protestants) and the East (Orthodox), with their differences in language and culture, developed slightly different ways of understanding the basics of Christianity. What follows is a quick overview of the ways in which the West differed from the East.

### Deviation of the West

In the West, St. Augustine (4th century) developed a different view of **God**, according to which, the Holy Spirit proceeds from both the Father and the Son. Later the Nicene Creed was altered by the Catholic Church to include this modification. Moreover, the Holy Spirit was seen as the love that links Father and Son. Such a view of Trinity was offensive to the East, which had developed its understanding of the Triune God over several centuries.

The East had realized that God is incomprehensible, and that God can be known only through His activities (*energia*) in the world. They spoke of God as Trinity only in relation to the world. However, Augustine's was an objective view of God – an analysis of the essence (*ousia*) of God without any reference to the world. This was in fact a very unrealistic and low view of God.

Augustine also promoted a low view of **humanity**, according to which human beings are basically evil, and they are incapable of anything good. The world for Augustine was an evil place, and salvation was escaping from the world and going to the heaven above. Adam's sin was inherited by all humanity, which made all people born with original sin. However, Jesus and Jesus' mother were not born with original sin. The dogma that Jesus' mother was born without original sin is called Immaculate Conception. They added another dogma that claimed that Jesus' mother ascended to heaven just as Jesus did.

The Orthodox fathers claimed that humanity inherited only the consequences of Adam's sin, and not sin itself. Thus no one was born a sinner. However, they fully agreed with Paul that all people are sinners, compared to God.

The Catholic Church promoted a low view of **church**. Church for them is all the Catholics alive in the world now. A local church is incomplete in itself, for it is a part of the global church. Relating to the old Israel in the wilderness on their way to Canaan, church is seen as a community in the wilderness of the world on its way to the heavenly Canaan.

The East views church as the body of Christ, who is at the right-hand of God representing the whole creation, and it consists of all Christians of all times and places. A local church is complete in itself, for it represents the whole church.

The Pope in Rome was seen as the visible representative of Christ authorized to exercise the authority of Christ in the world. The bishops received authority from the pope, and the priests received authority from the bishops. The **lay people** had no authority at all, and they had to depend upon the priestly hierarchy for their salvation and for receiving grace from God. Thus the Catholic Church promoted a low view of the lay people.

The church as a whole was seen by the East as the body of Christ, the eternal high priest. Bishops and priests represent Christ for them in Eucharist. Other than that they do not have any special status before God. The lay people have direct access to God.

**Mission** for the Western church has been to convert as many people as possible into its fold, for joining the church is seen as a means of salvation. "We are saved people on our way to heaven. If you want salvation, join our group." This is what the western church has told people. Thus the Catholic Church had a low view of Christian mission.

Mission for the east is to continue the mission of Christ. It sees church as the visible embodiment of Christ, and it sees the mission of church as the same mission of Christ-- reconciling the whole creation to God. It proclaims the same message Christ proclaimed: God rules. It does not believe in converting people from other communities to the Christian community; rather it believes in converting all communities to God. This was the nature of mission in the original church, in which the non-Jews were not asked to become Jews, but were asked to become a new creation by turning to God.

**Eucharist** is seen by the West as an opportunity for the lay people to witness the crucifixion of Christ, and accept Christ as their savior. It was also a means to receive grace, the divine power. This is a low view of the Eucharist.

For the east, Eucharist is nothing less than Christ standing in the presence of God mediating for the whole of creation. As the body of Christ, church unites with Christ in his self-sacrifice and submission to the will of God.

### The Reformed View

Later there was a reformation in the Catholic Church, which gave birth to the Protestant churches. It began as an attempt to reform the Catholic Church by priests who opposed what they perceived as false doctrines and ecclesiastic malpractice that the reformers saw as evidence of the systemic corruption of the Church's Roman hierarchy, which included the Pope. It was primarily a struggle for freedom. Martin Luther proclaimed freedom by asserting *sola scriptura* (by scripture alone) and *sola fide* (by faith alone). By placing the authority on the scriptures, he was refusing to admit that the church hierarchies and centuries-old dogmas had any authority. When the responsibility was placed on the faith of the individual, he was breaking the claim of the church as a vehicle of salvation.

The reform movement managed to save the world from the corruption of the Catholic Church; however, it is still engaged in its experiments for an alternative. Although Martin Luther and other reformers realized that there was something wrong with the Catholic Church, they couldn't pinpoint the exact problems because they didn't have access to a better model. They were unaware of the Orthodox churches and their faith. If they had been aware, the reformation would have been much easier and meaningful.

### Conclusion

The Christian church of the eastern Roman Empire of the fourth century, with its four centuries of experience behind it, developed a highly sophisticated understanding of the basics of Christianity. The Christian church of the western Roman Empire, which started only by the third century, could not develop such a sophisticated view. Their language being Latin, they could not understand the thought of the Eastern fathers, whose language was Greek. The western Christianity later grew in number and has filled the world, and the eastern Christianity has been ignored until recently. Today the whole Christian world needs to turn to the wisdom of the eastern Greek fathers.

# 4. What did the Church Fathers Teach?

What did the Church Fathers Teach? This is the question addressed in *The Faith of our Fathers¹*, one of the early books by Paulos Mar Gregorios. It was a study guide meant for college students. About this book he wrote in his autobiography as follows: *I wrote brief accounts of the life and teachings of some of the prominent Eastern Christian Fathers, mainly for the use of the Orthodox college students.*

Here I am making an attempt to summarize this book. It deals with the Greek fathers only. I am using another article by Mar Gregorios entitled *The Fathers in the Fifth Tubden²* for information about the Syrian fathers.

**Why do we need to study the Fathers?**

The Bible, the Liturgy, and the Fathers -- these three form a complex unity. None of these can be understood in isolation without some knowledge of the other two. The Bible is essential and primary, but not sufficient in itself. Christianity cannot be understood without understanding the Fathers. These men embodied in their lives and teachings the true elements of our faith. Three aspects characterized the Fathers:

1. A dedicated life with an intense discipline of prayer, worship and fasting,
2. A singular capacity to combine wide and deep secular knowledge with knowledge of the ways of God, and
3. An infinite and active compassion for the poor and the needy and a willingness to serve them.

The same combination is needed in today's world and Church if humankind is to find its way forward. Getting exposed to the personality, life, and thought of some of these spiritual giants of the past will be beneficial to our young people.

The study of the Church Fathers is known as Patristics. Although Protestant churches generally ignore church fathers, many Protestant seminaries provide courses on Patristics as a part of their curriculum. The Orthodox churches and the Roman Catholic Church accept church fathers. However, only a few of them are commonly accepted by all. Some are accepted commonly by the Catholic Church and the Eastern Orthodox churches. Some are accepted commonly by all the Orthodox Churches. The others are accepted specifically by Catholic Church or Eastern Orthodox or Oriental Orthodox churches. Those who are fathers for the Greek and Latin Churches, but who are not authoritative for the churches in the Syrian tradition include Maximus the Confessor, John of Damascus, and much later, Gregory Palamas.

### Who are the Fathers of the Church?

The term *fathers* is usually applied to all the great doctors (*malpans*) and saintly leaders of the Church. For the sake of convenience in study, the Fathers may be classified into four groups chronologically.

1.  The Apostolic and Pre-Nicene Fathers
2.  The Fathers of the three Ecumenical councils
3.  The post-conciliar Fathers
4.  The Monastic Fathers

The Apostolic fathers were direct disciples of the Apostles like Ignatius of Antioch, Clement of Rome, and Polycarp of Smyrna. Among the other pre-Nicene Fathers we include the fathers of the second and third centuries like Clement of Alexandria and Ireneus of Lyons. The group of the Fathers of the Three Ecumenical Councils includes not only those bishops and teachers who took part in the councils but also those who lived and taught during the period 300-450 even if they were not present at the councils. Post-counciliar Fathers lived after the period of councils. The monastic fathers are the developers of the great ascetic tradition of the Church such as St. Antony, St. Pachomius, St. Makarios, St. Simeon Stylites, and St. Ephrem.

## The Apostolic Fathers and Other Pre-Nicene Fathers

The title Apostolic Fathers is often rather loosely applied to the fathers of the period immediately following the age of the apostles, but more strictly, they are the direct disciples of one or more of the Twelve Apostles. They witness to the fact that only a portion of the apostolic tradition was actually written down in the New Testament.

| Name | Place | Time | Importance |
|------|-------|------|-----------|
| St. Clement | Rome | 96 | Bishop, disciple of Paul and Peter |
| St. Ignatius | Antioch | 35 – 110 | Bishop, disciple of Paul, Peter, John. Thrown to wild animals in Rome |
| Hermas | Unknown | 2nd century | Author of *The Shepherd* |
| St. Polycarp | Smyrna | 69 – 155 | Disciple of John, burnt to death at 86 |

The *Didache* (teaching), or to give its full title, *The Teaching of the Lord to the Gentiles through the Twelve Apostles*, is now believed to be a very ancient document, older than several of the books of the present New Testament. The contents may be divided into four parts:

1. The two ways: the Way of Life and of Death (ch. 1-6);
2. A ritual dealing with baptism, fasting, and Communion (ch. 7-10);
3. The ministry and how to deal with traveling prophets (ch. 11-15); and
4. A brief apocalypse (ch. 16).

It says about Eucharist:

On the Lord's Day, assemble together and break bread and give thanks, first making public confession of your faults, that your sacrifice may be pure. If any man has a quarrel with a friend, let him not join your assembly until they are reconciled. So that your sacrifice spoken of by the Lord: "In every place and time offer me a pure sacrifice.

About ministry it says:

Appoint therefore for yourselves bishops and deacons worthy of the Lord; kindly men, who are not greedy for money, men who are genuine and tested.

The Shepherd, authored by Hermas, was one of the most popular books produced in the early Church, and for a time it was frequently quoted and regarded as inspired. The book is a picturesque religious allegory, in most of which a rugged figure dressed like a shepherd is Hermas' guide. It consists of five visions, twelve mandates, and ten parables, and it is characterized by strong moral earnestness. It is primarily a call to repentance and adherence to a life of strict morality, addressed to Christians among whom the memory of persecution is still fresh, and over whom now hangs the shadow of another great tribulation. As a Christian slave, Hermas had been sold in Rome to a woman called Rhoda, who set him free. As a freedman he married, acquired a fortune, and through ill luck had again been reduced to poverty. He was a simple man of limited outlook, but genuinely pious and conscientious.

Among the pre-Nicene fathers there were many great teachers who flourished in Asia Minor, present Turkey. The theology of the universal Christian Church was shaped mainly in three centers -- Antioch, Alexandria, and Asia.

Ireneus from Smyrna was a disciple of Polycarp. He took the Asian tradition to the west by evangelizing France. Ireneus' greatest contribution to our faith lies perhaps in the area of understanding what Tradition itself is. Ireneus has clarified for us the meaning of apostolic tradition as the continuing stream of the mind of the Church. Certain heretics had claimed apostolic succession for their own errors, by pretending that they were the disciples of the disciples of the Apostles. Over against their false claim to apostolic succession, Ireneus lay down the true view of Apostolic Tradition.

We learn from the disciples of the Apostles many things that are not directly stated in the Bible. On many fundamental questions of faith, the Bible used by itself can lead to heresy. All the early heretics used the Bible in one form or another. The Tradition of Christian truth can be found in its fullness only in the Church. No one can simply take the Bible and sit down and construct a faith out of it. What the modern sects often present to us as Biblical truth is little more than their own particular tradition, which may be a local German or American or English or Dutch tradition of a few hundred years old. Only in the Universal tradition of the Church can we see the Bible in its true light and learn the Christian truth. We learn, however, also that the disciples of the Apostles had a very great respect for the Bible, and were very thorough in their knowledge of the Old Testament and the writings of the Apostles. In the Orthodox tradition we have no reason to neglect the Bible. The more authentic knowledge of the Bible we have the more truly Orthodox we become. We learn also, how important the Church, the Priesthood, and the mysteries of the faith (the sacraments) were for the disciples of the Apostles. The denial of these realities and a dependence on the Bible alone (*sola Scriptura*) can be a great error. The faith is truly experienced and known only by membership in the Church, which has a responsible and properly apostolic ministry and a high tradition of the Christian mysteries. Outside that Church even the Bible becomes a snare and a stumbling block.

**Origen** (184—254) was a great Christian scholar of this period. He was the head of the famous Theological Institute in Alexandria in the 3rd century. A prodigious genius of towering proportions, he seems to have written about 3000 books. He was a great Biblical scholar, but freely used allegorical interpretation of the Bible and unbridled philosophical speculation. He is supposed to have believed in metempsychosis (*punarjanma*) and the pre-existence of all souls. He died in about 254. His teaching was condemned as heretical by the Church of Alexandria in 400. The Roman and Syrian Churches agreed with the decision of Alexandria. The Greeks condemned Origen a century and a half later at the Council of Constantinople in 553. The Pope supported this decision. Despite this, it is seen that Anglicans and Roman Catholics cite Origen as authority for certain doctrines. They probably feel that the voluminous contribution of this genius should not be ignored because of a couple of contrarian beliefs he held.

### The Golden Age of the Fathers

The period from the Ecumenical Council of Nicaea (325) to the Council of Chalcedon (451) has been called the Golden age of Eastern Patristic literature. There are many reasons for this flourishing of Christian thought such as never taken place before or after.

Constantine's Edict of Milan placed the Church in a position where it had to take this world more seriously. Today we live in the same situation. It is not sufficient to think about the other world alone. We have to give expression to our faith here and now, in this world. The Church was forced to take an active and responsible role in politics, in culture, and in education because of the Constantinian settlement. Previously the Church could condemn the Roman Empire as Babylon, the harlot, which persecutes the faithful. Now the Empire was in the hands of the Church, so to speak. And it is in the context of this new situation that the Eastern Fathers developed their thought.

At this time some of the most learned of men applied themselves to the clarification of Christian thought. What Origen had attempted and failed in the time of persecution, Athanasius and the Cappodocian Fathers successfully achieved in the age of the Councils, since the debate could be open and public. Origen had nobody to question his views, but the Fathers of the golden age were constantly under fire from heretics and had to sharpen their thoughts on the anvil of controversy.

It can be said that true discussion of the most fundamental theological questions took place for the first time in the fourth century. And by the grace of God, there were a large number of learned and keen minds who could clarify the issues. There were, during this period, some important theological academies which could both produce scholars and debate the issues at the same time. Such schools existed in Alexandria, Antioch, and in Caesaria. Two Syrian schools existed in Edessa and Nisibis. Theology, even in the fourth and fifth century, was mainly a product of Asia and Africa, though most of the writing was in Greek, the *lingua franca* of the empire.

|  | Place | Date | Importance |
|---|---|---|---|
| Mar Athanasius | Alexandria | 296– 373 | Conflict with Arianism |
| Mar Baselios | Caesarea | 330- 379 | Community monasticism |
| Mar Gregorios | Nazianzus | 329- 389 | Established the deity of Logos |
| Mar Gregorios | Nyssa | 335- 395 | Clarified Orthodox faith |
| Mar Ioannes Chrysostomos | Constantin ople | 347- 407 | preacher, liturgist |
| Mar Cyrillos | Alexandria | 378– 444 | Conflict with Nestorianism |

Six of the most important fathers of this period are given in the table above. Taking the entire period from 325-451, the following fathers are also important: Alexander of Alexandria, Mar Didymus the Blind, Mar Theophilos of Alexandria, Mar Eustathius of Antioch, Mar Eusebius of Caesarea, the church historian, Mar Kurilos of Jerusalem, and Mar Dioscorus of Alexandria. In addition to these there were the Monastic Fathers. We are also omitting two great teachers of this period whose Orthodoxy is in question: namely Theodore of Mopsuestia and Diodore of Tarsus.

**St. Athanasius** (296 - 373), one of the most heroic figures of the ancient Church, fought the battle against the heresy of Arius almost single-handedly. He attended the Council of Nicaea (325) as Deacon and Secretary to the then bishop of Alexandria, Alexander. In 328, when Alexander died, he became the bishop, or Pope of Alexandria (the Coptic Church). Because of his opposition to Arianism, he was exiled at least four times from Alexandria. He died in 373 before he could see the final victory of his theology at the Council of Constantinople in 381.

The two main articles of the Christian Faith are faith in the Holy Trinity and faith in the Incarnation of our Lord Jesus Christ, and in both, Mar Athanasius laid the foundation of true understanding.

Athanasius said clearly "God became man that man may become God." Though not a great classical scholar, his knowledge of the scriptures, his clear mind, and his skill in debate made him a formidable enemy of heretics. It is from his works against Arius that we learn what Arius was teaching. His "life of St. Antony" is one of the classics of Monastic literature. But most of his writings were in defense of the teaching of the Council of Nicaea.

**Mar Baselius, the Great** (330-379) is one of the Cappodocian fathers. Cappodocia was a province of Asia (present-day Turkey). His parents lived in Caesarea, the capital of the province. His father had five sons and five daughters. Three of the sons became bishops-- Mar Baselius in Caesaria, Mar Gregorios in Nyssa, and Mar Pathros in Sebaste. The eldest sister of Mar Baselius, Martha Makarina, was a saint and a scholar. She founded monastic communities for women. She was the teacher of her brothers who became bishops. Even as a bishop, says Mar Gregorios, he learned from his sister the great mysteries of the faith.

Mar Baselius studied first from his father and grandmother, who were themselves both great scholars. He then studied in Caesarea, then moved to Constantinople, and finally to Athens, the center of all learning at that time. After completing studies with honors, he returned to Caesarea, and began his career as a rhetorician (secular professor). But soon he awoke as out of a deep sleep. He says, "I beheld the wonderful light of the Gospel truth, and I recognized the nothingness of the wisdom of the princes of this world that was come to naught. I shed a flood of tears over my wretched life, and I prayed for a guide who might form in me the principles of piety."

He was soon baptized, after having been duly instructed by his sister Makarina. He then travelled in Egypt, Syria, Palestine and Mesopotamia to learn from the many monks who lived in these parts. When he returned, he distributed his wealth among the poor (he was a very rich man) and went to solitude for prayer and fasting. Soon others joined him, including his friend and classmate Mar Gregorios of Nazianzus, though only temporarily. The community grew and it became a great spiritual center of Christianity in Asia.

Mar Baselius wrote, in co-operation with Mar Gregorios Nazianzen, the rules for a monastic community. These rules became the basis for all eastern monasticism, and for some forms of western monasticism like that of the Benedictines.

Soon he founded more monasteries, and his sister Makarina started a convent for women across the river from the men's monastery. Together they established hospitals for the sick, nursing homes for lepers, homes for the poor, hotels for travelers and strangers; and the monasteries soon became a spiritual city, where the poor and the destitute praised God for His wonderful ways.

In addition to his great learning and spirituality, St. Basil was, like Mar Athanasius, a man of very great personal courage. He stood up to the Emperor Valens when pressured to support the Arian heresy. When the Emperor sent his Viceroy to threaten Mar Baselius with confiscation of goods, torture and exile, Basil replied that he had nothing to be confiscated except a cloak and a few books, and as for exile, anywhere in the world would be his home. As for torture, he said his body would give up its life at the first blow, and that Modestus the Viceroy would be doing him a favor by sending him off to God so quickly. Mar Baselius said,

Death would be an act of kindness, for it will bring me nearer to God, for whom I live, and for whom I have been created and to whom I hasten.

Modestus was surprised by this bold answer and said:

No one has spoken to me with such boldness before.

Mar Baselius replied:

Perhaps you have never met a Christian bishop before. Fire, swords, beasts and the instruments for tearing the flesh we desire as delights rather than horrors. Afflict us, torture us, threaten, do all you can, enjoy your power, but let the Emperor also know that in no way can you win us over to embrace untruth, though you threaten with the cruelest deeds.

That was the end of the Emperor's opposition to Basil. Both the Emperor and the Viceroy were deeply impressed. On another occasion the Viceroy of Pontus threatened St. Basil, by calling him to court and saying, "I will tear out your liver." St. Basil replied: "Please do, it gives me much trouble where it is."

Mar Baselius established the deity of Christ and of the Holy Spirit. Thus he established the doctrine of Holy Trinity as three hypostases in one ousia. He was also a great monk who laid down the basic principles of community monasticism -- a balance between prayer, study and work and the need to serve one's fellowmen by working with one's own hands. He was a great man, very learned, very aristocratic, who lived in simplicity and poverty. His humility was not on the surface. He was regarded as a proud man, but his heart was truly humble.

**Mar Gregorios of Nazianzus** (329-389)    was one of the three Cappodocian Fathers, a cousin and friend of the other two, namely Mar Baselius and Mar Gregorius of Nyssa. He was also a classmate of Mar Baselius in Athens.

There is a story from his student days in Athens, about how Mar Baselius and Mar Gregorius became such good friends. The students were then organized in regional groupings, and the Armenian students decided to debate publicly with Baselius in order to bring down his pride. Gregorius watched the debate, saw Baselius was winning easily. Gregorius took pity on the Armenian students and took their side in the debate. Baselius was now losing the debate, and the Armenians began to rejoice. When Gregorius saw that Baselius' pride was well broken, he joined Baselius' side, and finally Baselius won the debate. From then on Baselius and Gregorius became bosom pals.

Mar Gregorius' brother, Caesarius was an outstanding doctor, who became the chief physician to the Emperor Constantius. Later he left the Imperial court and joined Mar Baselius and Mar Gregorios in their monastery. It was his presence which made it easy for the monastery to build their first hospitals and look after the sick in the surrounding area.

Mar Gregorius' father was a bishop, one of the last married bishops of the Church. One day when Mar Gregorios was a young man of 29, his own parish people in Nazianzus took him to his own father to ask him to ordain the young Gregory to priesthood.

Gregorius ran away to Pontus, where his friend Baselius was already building his mountain retreat. Some months later he returned to his parish and found all parish people very angry with him. Some accused him of being afraid to accept the priesthood, because he feared the Emperor Julian. Others said he was a coward. Yet others said that he was ambitious, and he ran away because they did not directly make him a bishop. In his sermon explaining why he ran away, he describes the great qualities necessary for a priest. His sermon became the basis for several later books by others on the priesthood and its high responsibility.

Mar Gregorius of Nazianzus as well as Mar Gregorius of Nyssa held that God could not be understood by the human mind or by any other created mind including the angels. God can only be apprehended from what He does. And from what we see as His work in the world, we can see that He is three in one -- the Holy Trinity. Mar Gregorios is called *Theologos* (Theologian) because he showed that the *Logos*, the Word of God, was fully *Theos*, that is, God. He also was a great help to Mar Baselius in proving that the Holy Spirit was also fully God. Mar Gregorius gave final shape to the doctrine of the incomprehensibility of God. He taught also that the Eucharist was a true sacrifice of the body and blood of our Lord and that the Blessed Virgin Mary was the bearer of God Theotokos.

Mar Gregorius was a great poet and a powerful orator. His sermons were ornate in style, but very balanced in theology, and full of biblical allusions. His five theological orations are a masterpiece. Along with Mar Baselius, he wrote the monastic rules for their community. Mar Gregorius was a shy, retiring, and sensitive soul, who ran away from all public praise. The towering figure of Mar Baselius dominated his life throughout, but Mar Gregorius was as profound and clear in his thinking as Mar Baselius. He became Patriarch of Constantinople for a short period during the famous synod of Constantinople in 381. He resigned soon after, returned home to breathe his last there in 389.

**Mar Gregorius of Nyssa** (330--395) was the younger brother of Mar Baselius, and just as learned as his brother. He was born around 330 (may be in 335). He became a rhetorician -- the ancient equivalent of a combined professor and politician. Later he left his profession and entered the monastery of his brother Baselius. Most of his education came from his grandmother and his sister, St. Makrina. He became bishop of Nyssa around 371. This was the time when the heresy of Arius was very strong. Many bishops were the followers of Arius. The Arian bishops opposed Mar Gregorius and deposed him from the episcopate in 376, with the consent of the Emperor Valens.

When Valens died in 378, Mar Gregorius was brought back from exile. He was one of the main drafters at the second Ecumenical Synod in Constantinople in 381. The Emperor declared the faith of Mar Gregorius as the standard by which the beliefs of other bishops could be tested. In his later life, Mar Gregorius travelled widely as a preacher in great demand. His teaching had many fresh and original elements.

Mar Gregorius' teaching does not agree with Augustine's, especially in the matter of original sin. Augustine regards man as basically evil. Therefore without the grace of God, man can do nothing good, and even that which appears like virtue in non-Christians is only a "splendid vice." Gregorius, on the other hand, believes that Man is created in the image of God, and therefore potentially capable of doing good. But he is now fallen in sin. In Christ God has become man so that the power of sin may be destroyed. Christ unites us with himself and fills us into the true image of good. He thus transforms us into the true image of God to become partakers in the divine nature. Man is a sinner, according to Mar Gregorius, but that is not his nature. His created nature is to be like God, capable of all good. He disagrees fundamentally with Augustine who of course did not know enough Greek to read his writings.

Mar Gregorius also teaches that the world is good, since it is created by God. Man is made to enjoy both the earthly beauty and the heavenly joy. Augustine teaches that the world (the city of the earth) is bad, and that Man should love only heaven, the city of God. Mar Gregorius taught that man is made to rule the creation, and that his nature is a kingly nature. He can fully exercise this nature only in union with God. Mar Gregorius welcomed the knowledge, the science and technology of this world, as something good and necessary for man's growth, whereas Augustine was more inclined to despise these things as mere folly before God.

Augustine was afraid of human freedom. He believed that man is fully controlled by God in doing good. Mar Gregorius taught that goodness without freedom was not virtue; that God was totally free, and that man is also meant to be free in doing good. Human freedom needs to develop to its full measure in order that he may really be the perfection of all good.

**Mar Ivanios, the Golden-Mouthed** was also known as St. John Chrysostom. This Prince of Preachers, was born in Antioch. His father was a high army officer in the Praetorian Guard, who died in his infancy. He had an excellent secular education under the great pagan teacher Libanius, who taught also Mar Baselius and Mar Gregorius of Nazianzus as well as the Emperor Julian.

He wanted to become a monk mostly by the persuasion of Mar Baselius. But because he had to look after his sick and widowed mother, he stayed at home and imposed a monastic rule upon himself. In 374 his mother died, and John was now free to be a monk. But the people of Antioch wanted to make him a bishop. But he escaped the pressure and lived as a monk of the very strict order of St. Pachomius. His health was sadly undermined by the rigor of his asceticism.

In 381, he was ordained deacon by Mar Meletios, and was attached to Bishop Flavian of Antioch. He became a very famous preacher during five years in the diaconate. The Antiocheans gave him the name Chrysostomos, which means Golden-mouthed (the same as silver-tongued)

Antioch was full of cruel, quarrelsome, slanderous, gossiping people, many of whom called themselves Christians. The court, the clergy, and the people had all become morally lazy, because their bishops had no great spiritual quality with which to inspire them. They were self-indulgent, luxury loving, and quarrelsome. St. John

Chrysostom's preaching for 12 years as a priest changed the moral values of the city. He preached mainly from the Bible. His homilies on the Bible earned him a title as one of the greatest Bible teachers of all history. He had a great capacity to discern deep spiritual meaning in the Bible and to apply it directly to the practical problems. Mar Ivanios preached also against the economic and social evils of his city. He preached against vice and extortion, corruption and bribery, black-marketing and nepotism. He enjoined the virtues of humility, honesty, simplicity, love, and service.

In 398 he was chosen by the Emperor Arcadius to become Patriarch of the Imperial City, Constantinople. Mar Theophilos, the Patriarch of Alexandria had hoped for this honor, but the Emperor insisted on Father Ivanios. Mar Theophilos consecrated Mar Ivanios, both with equal unwillingness, the former because he hated Mar Ivanios, and the latter because he disliked the honor of the Patriarchate. In Constantinople he found the patriarchal palace very similar to the Imperial palace, full of luxury and corruption. He set himself to cleaning house first. He purged the bishop's house of all the corrupt priests, monks and laymen, and changed it from a palace into a monastery. He then began attacking the corruption in the Government and the Imperial palace. He preached against the personal conduct of the pleasure-loving Empress and the Minister of the Emperor. They became his enemies. All the rich and self-indulgent people of Constantinople became infuriated by his preaching against corruption and injustice.

Mar Theophilos of Alexandria took advantage of all these enmities and convened the Synod of the Oak (403) which excommunicated Mar Chrysostom on 29 charges, almost all of them false. He was soon reinstated by the Emperor, but he continued to incur the displeasure of the Empress. He was again excommunicated, on the charge that he assumed charge of a See when he had been canonically excommunicated. He was exiled and persecuted, and when his health failed, he was made to walk very long distances in severe weather, and he died falling on the road in 407.

Mar Ivanios was not a great theologian, but he was an outstanding preacher and Bible teacher. He was a man of great personal holiness. He, along with Mar Athanasius, are the two most popular Eastern fathers among western people, probably because they are easier to understand than the other more profound fathers. Theologically, his greatest teaching was on the Priesthood. He says clearly that the Priest has been given an authority higher than that given to the angels -- that of forgiving sins, of binding and loosing something on earth and thereby binding and loosing in heaven.

**Mar Kurilos of Alexandria** was born in Alexandria around 378, and must have received an excellent classical education in the Christian academy in Alexandria. The clarity and precision of his mind are quite impressive. He has laid the foundation for our understanding of how the human and divine natures of Christ are united.

In 412, when Patriarch Mar Theophilos died, even though the Government tried to get their own man elected, the people chose Mar Kurilos. The Government chief was opposed to his election, and became his great enemy, but the monks of the Egyptian desert were on his side.

His biggest fight was with the Patriarch of Constantinople, none other than Nestorius. We are just beginning to understand what Nestorians actually taught regarding the Person of Christ. Nestorius taught that Christ was two persons with two natures -- a divine person and a human person. It is quite clear that Nestorius rejected the word *Theotokos* (God bearer) as applied to the Mother of our Lord, which affirms that the child in the Blessed Virgin Mary's womb was God and man from the very conception. It was not that Mary conceived a human child who later became the bearer of God.

Nestorius attacked the word *Theotokos* and wanted to use only *Christo-tokos*, Christ-bearer. It was his attack of the word *Theotokos* rather than his belief in two persons that caused the Church to condemn him as a heretic. Perhaps Nestorius did not fully realize what he was teaching. His rejection of the *Theotokos* formula implied a belief in two persons, though probably Nestorius never actually taught that Christ was two persons. He suspected that those who held to this formula believed that Christ was simply the logos and human flesh without a human soul -- which was very near to the heresy of Apollinarius. Nestorius attributed such a heretical belief to Mar Kurilos of Alexandria. This was a complete misunderstanding. Mar Kurilos believed that the Word of God, the Logos, the second person of the Trinity, assumed unto himself a full human nature with body, soul and spirit.

Nestorius was not a clear thinker. He therefore denied all the sacred teaching of the Church which he could not understand. If he were just a private individual, his unclear teaching could have gone unnoticed. But as Patriarch of Constantinople, he had no right to deny the faith of the Church. Mar Kurilos therefore took the initiative to question Nestorius, and got his heresy condemned at the Council of Ephesus (431) St. Cyril's formula was "God the Logos did not come into a man, but he truly became Man, while remaining God."

Nestorius taught that the Logos "indwelt" the man Jesus. St. Cyril regarded this as too loose a relationship between God and Man in Christ. God did not simply dwell in Jesus as in a temple, but Jesus Christ was God become man without ceasing to be God. And therefore Christ has only one nature, "the one nature of the Word of God Incarnate," which is both fully human and fully divine, but cannot be called two natures, because they have united to form one single divine-human nature of God-in-the-flesh, Jesus Christ. Mar Kurilos knew the distinction between deity and humanity -- the former is Creator and the latter is creature. But in Christ Jesus the Creator has become the creature without ceasing to be the Creator. That is the miracle and the mystery of the Incarnation.

The teaching of Mar Kurilos may be summarized as follows: The nature of Christ cannot be divided into two after the union by Incarnation. The actions of Christ cannot be attributed to two different subjects - one divine and one human. It is one and the same Christ who performs miracles and also hungers and thirsts. The Word of God is hypostatically united to the humanity, which was assumed, and the two operate together, the Word being always the subject.

The controversy between Nestorius and Mar Kurilos was settled finally at the Council of Ephesus in 431 when the teaching of Nestorius was condemned, and he was "dispossessed of all dignity in the Church". St. Cyril is the touchstone of Christology for East and West, for those who in one united divine-human nature. St. Cyril died in 444.

### The Syrian Fathers

| Father | Place | Time | Importance |
|---|---|---|---|
| Mar Aprem | Edessa | 306- 373 | These five fathers are |
| Mar Yakob | Serug | 451- 521 | especially important |
| Mar Balai | Aleppo | -432 | for the Syrian |
| Mar Semavoon Kookoyo (potter) | Antioch | -514 | Orthodox churches. Most of the liturgy |
| Mar Severios | Antioch | 465– 539 | used by these churches has been composed by them. |
| Mar Yacob Burd'ono | Edessa | 500- 578 | Syrian church continued to exist because of him. |
| Mar Yacob | Nisibis | | Known as a scholar and as a saint |
| Mar Yacob | Edessa | 649-708 | Literary works, Bible translation |
| Mar Isaac | Nineveh | -700 | Written on monastic life |
| Mar Barsaumo | | -458 | Monastic life |
| Mar Simeon the Stylite (desthune) | Aleppo | 390-459 | Lived on a pillar |

### The Fathers of the Roman Catholic Church

The Roman Catholic Church defines a Father as characterized by four things -- Orthodoxy of doctrine, holiness of life, the approval of the Church, and antiquity. Some of the fathers are also doctors (teachers) of the Church. They have more than 20 *doctores ecclesiae*. The four most important doctors for the Roman Catholic Church are

Gregory the Great, Ambrose, Augustine, and Jerome. Along with Augustine, Tertullian is regarded as an authority for doctrines of the Trinity and the Incarnation. The universal tradition has not accepted their teachings, and since these men are the sources of many of the errors of western legalistic-individualistic teaching the eastern tradition has been rather careful about not using them as authority for the faith of the Church.

Some of the doctors whom they have recently accepted have always been the formers and shapers of our tradition. For example in 1920, the Pope declared Mar Ephrem as a "Doctor of the Church". He was always a towering figure for the eastern tradition, both Greek and Non-Greek. The particular occasion for the Pope's officially declaring St. Ephrem, as a doctor of the Church was the need to use him as authority for certain doctrines about the Blessed Virgin Mary, which the Catholic Church wanted to declare officially.

# 5. What is the Mission of the World Council of Churches?

After Paulos Mar Gregorios became a president of the World Council of Churches (WCC) in 1983, he felt restless about some of the erratic theological formulations propagated by this organization, and he offered to give a series of lectures to its staff in Geneva to correct those errors. Dr. Emilio Castro, the then General Secretary, welcomed the idea, and Mar Gregorios gave a series of lectures on the theme of *Diakonia*, and later in 1988, five of those lectures were published by the WCC as a book entitled *The Meaning and Nature of Diakonia*[1]. What follows is a short summary of the major ideas discussed in this book.

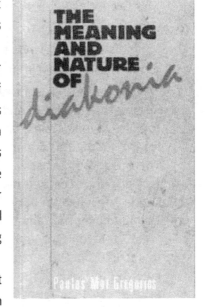

In this series of lectures, Mar Gregorios addresses the question of what the World Council of Churches exists for. An organization can function effectively only if its workers have a clear grasp of the purpose for which it exists. Mar Gregorios argues that the central task of WCC is the upbuilding (*Oikodome*) of the church.

This naturally leads to the next question—what does the church exist for? Mar Gregorios asserts that the church, being the body of Christ, exists to continue the same ministry of Christ. *Diakonia*, the Greek word, means service, and is often translated as ministry in the New Testament. The word Deacon, which means servant or minister, is a derivative of *Diakonia*.

### The Diakonia of Christ

If the ministry of the church is the same as that of Christ, we need to find out what the ministry of Christ is. Reconciling the world to God is the ultimate goal of Christ's *Diakonia*. In order to attain this goal, Christ plays the role of a mediator between God and the world. God is love, and Christ, in perfect unity with God, manifested that love, and offered himself to the world on behalf of God. In response to that self-giving love of God, Christ offered himself as a sacrifice to God on behalf of the world. The role of Christ is traditionally understood in the roles of a priest, prophet, and king. As a prophet, Christ speaks to the world on behalf of God. As a king, Christ rules and takes care of the world on behalf of God. Unlike the other kings, Christ's throne is cross. As a priest, Christ offers himself as a sacrifice to God on behalf of the world.

### The Diakonia of the Church

Mar Gregorios quotes a few passages from the New Testament to assert that the ministry of the church is the continuation of Christ's ministry. Christ sends the church to the world just as he was sent to the world by the Father. Jesus said,

> "As the Father has sent me, I am sending you." And with that he breathed on them and said, "Receive the Holy Spirit. If you forgive anyone's sins, their sins are forgiven; if you do not forgive them, they are not forgiven." John 20: 21- 23.

The mission of Christ was to attack the kingdom of hades, the world of disobedience and death, save people from there, and let them enter the kingdom of heaven, the world of obedience and life. Christ handed over the same mission to his church.

> "And I tell you that you are Peter, and on this rock I will build my church, and the gates of Hades will not overcome it. I will give you the keys of the kingdom of heaven; whatever you bind on earth will be bound in heaven, and whatever you loose on earth will be loosed in heaven". Mat. 16:15-19.

The church as the body of Christ has no other *diakonia* but the *diakonia* of Christ. It stands as the mediator between God and world. On behalf of God, the church offers itself to the world, and on behalf of the world, it offers itself to God. As prophet, the church speaks to the world on behalf God. As king, the church rules from the cross and takes care of the world. As priest, it offers itself as a sacrifice to God on behalf of the world.

The idea that the church is a priest standing before God on behalf of the world is very well reflected in Peter's expression of "royal priesthood". Israel was called to serve as a priestly nation in a community of nations-- a nation that stands before God on behalf of the community of nations interceding for them.

> Now then, if you will indeed obey My voice and keep My covenant, then you shall be My own possession among all the peoples, for all the earth is Mine; and you shall be to Me a kingdom of priests and a holy nation. Ex. 15:5-6

Peter reminds the Christian church that it has the same calling to be a priestly nation. Whenever the church stands before God, it does so on behalf of the whole world.

> But you are a chosen people, a royal priesthood, a holy nation, God's special possession, that you may declare the praises of him who called you out of darkness into his wonderful light. I pet 2: 9

If as a priest, Christ turns to God on behalf of the world, as a prophet, Christ turns to the world on behalf of God. Church continues the same mission of speaking on behalf of God. The protestant churches give this ministry more importance than the others. But we need to remember that only by facing God in silence, we will be empowered to face the world to speak on behalf of God. The prophetic ministry has to happen as a natural outgrowth of the priestly ministry.

As a king, Christ rules and guides his people on behalf of God. Christ preferred to call himself a good shepherd rather than a king. He lays his life for the sheep. It is on his cross that we see the inscription, the king of Jews. Cross is the throne of this king. Church is called to be a good shepherd to the world. Christ lists three qualities of the good shepherd: knows the sheep by name, leads the sheep out to find pasture, and lays his life to protect them.

The church has to care for the people in the world as a shepherd cares for his sheep.

> When the church hates any group of people, be they people of other religions or other ideologies, the church loses its credentials as good shepherd.

Like a good shepherd, the church has to

open doors that confine people in oppression, injustice and exploitation, to lead the nations to where they can find the just societies of green pastures and the still waters of peaceful and secure national and international situations.

The church does not hand out peace and justice to the nations. From a relationship of trust, church should be able to lead the nations away from injustice, war, oppression, exploitation, terrorism, and environmental decay. As the sheep move toward freedom and justice, the wolves come. As the church oppose them, the wolves, the oppressive structures of the world, advance on us to tear us apart. If the church takes up a fight with the wolves, it will lose much of its privilege and power. Therefore, most of the time, the church, like a hireling, flees for life, hypocritically leaving it to God to bring justice and peace in the world.

However, the church will be able to perform this *diakonia* of Christ only when it becomes fully one with Christ. Only as the church approximates Christ's personality will it become truly one and fully participant in Christ's ministry. The Holy Spirit is guiding the church into all truth and to full obedience. The unity of the church is a primary aspect of that personality, and division in the church is a denial of Christ-likeness. This is where the relevance of WCC comes in.

Until the church becomes fully one with Christ, the *diakonia* of the church cannot be the same as the *diakonia* of Christ. Christ's ministry remains wider and ranges farther than the ministry of the church. The church cannot claim monopoly of Christ or his ministry until it becomes fully one with Christ.

**Our Erroneous Ways**

Using the *diakonia* of Christ as a model, we can figure out where we have gone wrong. It seems we are mistaken in our very goal. Christ's *diakonia* is to unite the world to God. We seem to have a very selfish interest of gaining salvation for ourselves. We are not concerned about our fellow beings and the rest of God's world. We don't manifest the love of God to the world. On the other hand, we hate people of other religions and ideologies. We struggle and fight for our own existence and our own rights, but never raise a finger for the poor and the oppressed, and for the rights of the people who are denied basic human rights.

*Our Priestly ministry*: We pray to God only to gain something for ourselves. We don't sacrifice ourselves to God on behalf of our fellow beings.

*Our Prophetic Ministry*: We have become unable to speak on behalf of God to the world. We only condemn and judge the world.

*Our Kingly Ministry*: We rule the world from thrones, and not from the cross. Instead of being a good shepherd to the world, we have become a hired servant, unconcerned about the sheep. The world no longer trusts us, nor does it respond to our voice. We don't open the gates to liberate people from the captivity of exploitation and oppression, and we don't lead them to the green pastures of a just, free, secure and peaceful life. We are unwilling to oppose the wolves of oppressive structures for fear of losing our own privileges and power.

Mar Gregorios cites a number of references and incidents to illustrate the failure of the church.

In the first lecture he refers to the incident of John and James bringing their mother to recommend for special power and privilege for them. Their ambition is to be seated at the right and left of Christ when he assumes power. Based on this incident, Mar Gregorios makes this observation: Nothing has been as divisive of the churches as the ambitions, the jealousies, the power struggles among the Christian workers and leaders.

As an example of the suffering servant in the second Isaiah, Mar Gregorios, with no hesitation, shows before us a non-Christian.

Gandhi walked into the village of Noakhali, where Hindus and Muslims were shooting and stabbing each other, in 1947. Clad in loincloth, without sleep and without eating, with just the old man's walking stick in his hand, this frail and fragile servant walked into Muslim homes and Hindu homes, saying to Muslims: "I am a Hindu; kill me if you want to kill a Hindu, but do not kill others." To the Hindu household, brimming with the same passionate and murderous hatred as the Muslim household, Gandhi walked in and said: "I am a friend of the Muslims; kill me first, but do not kill others."

Then he continues:

Christians, I must say to the shame of my own community in India, should have seen, but did not acknowledge, their Lord as the Suffering Servant, in this exceptionally free and dedicated *non-Christian*, who held to the truth as his breast-plate and manifested the love of God in laying down his life that others may live. Draw what lessons you can from this episode of a man of another faith fulfilling the role of the Suffering Servant in our time

As an example of how the present-day Christian mission has become a means of exploitation and oppression rather than a means of liberation, Mar Gregorios draws before us a picture of the modern international aid empire.

It uses aid to capture markets and to exploit people in such a way that many times more than the aid flows back to the aid-giving economy through unjust trade relations.

**Conclusion**

The church, the body of Christ, continues the same ministry of Christ as priest, prophet, and king. The ministry of WCC is to build the church.

# 6. Why do we Need a New Civilization?

At the eve of his life, Paulos Mar Gregorios had a clear vision of a new civilization, and as a skillful engineer, he mapped its foundation. The details of his plan can be read in his work in the nineties. An excellent summary of this plan was presented by him in a talk at the Parliament of World Religions in Chicago in 1993. It is entitled "Towards a New Enlightenment" and it is published in the book *Religion and Dialogue*[1]. Here I am making an attempt to summarize it so that the readers will be encouraged to read the work of Mar Gregorios, and to share the vision of the new world. Mar Gregorios begins with an analysis of the foundations of the present civilization in our world. After pointing out the widening cracks in its foundation, he presents the framework of a new civilization.

### The European Enlightenment

The western dominant civilization began in Europe in the 18th century with a movement called European Enlightenment (EE). Mar Gregorios praises it as the most significant development of the last millennium, and advises us to be thankful for the great contributions of EE.

> It is hard to imagine what a miserable place the world could have been if EE had not happened. Humanity would have been disintegrating through ignorance and squalor, thorough plague and pestilence, through disease and natural disasters, through starvation and epidemic. The EE has given to us modern science and technology, the institutes of democratic polity, systems of education, healing, information-gathering, transport and communication, without all of which six billion people could not have lived on this planet. P.109

Although we have to acknowledge and be thankful for all these good things we have received from EE, we can't ignore the one huge drawback it has, which makes the continued existence of the humanity impossible. It is true that it helped us see a part of the reality clearly, but in that process, it made us blind to the rest of the reality. It is a light which is so bright that it makes us blind.

Like bright sunlight that shuts out the night sky with its myriads of stars and millions of galaxies. If we lived 24 hours a day by the sunlight, who would know that the reality that the sunlight revels is only a billionth part of the gigantic universe? What we see so clearly by the modern science makes us blind to the mighty mystery that lies behind and beyond what we see and hear.[P.109]

EE has such a drawback because it has its foundation upon secularism. Mar Gregorios defines secularism as

An ideology which believes that the world open to our senses and our instruments is the only world that exists, and that meaning has to be found in that universe without reference to anything outside of or transcending our field of sense-perception and our rational mind. [P.102]

The first manifestation of EE was the French Revolution of 1789, which publicly repudiated God and religion. Its two prevailing manifestations today are liberal Humanism-Secularism and Marxism-Socialism. Both of them see science as the principal way to vision and meaning. Both say "In science we trust", and regard religion as something that belongs to the childhood of the humanity.

Modern science was created by putting together the Empirical Aristotelianism of Bacon and the logical Platonism of Descartes, and it now takes over the structure of authority from religion and philosophy. It created a new world-- a world that is

subject to human reason and human technological manipulation. In that the ruling authority is the secular-scientific ideology, which throws into margin not only religion, but also art and literature, poetry and philosophy. [P.104]

As a result, the human race now lives in the untruth, caught in the darkness of evil, and dying and killing each other. We pray the Vedic prayer from the bottom of our hearts:

➤ Asato ma sat gamaya -- lead us from untruth to truth
➤ Thamaso ma jothir gamaya - lead us from darkness to light
➤ Mrithyor ma amrutham gamaya - lead us from death to life

### The Buddhist Enlightenment

EE can be understood better in the light of the Buddhist Enlightenment (BE). The concept of enlightenment is important in all religious traditions, but Buddhism made it its central concept. Buddha means the enlightened one. Prabuddhatha (enlightenment) is a state of being and consciousness. The Buddhist enlightenment is similar to EE in many aspects, but different in certain crucial aspects.

Both were reactions against misuse of authority by the dominant religion—Brahminism in India and Christianity in Europe. They also repudiated the authority of the accepted scriptures. Both appealed to the human being to stand up in defiance of authority and to think and act for oneself. Both were exhortations to a new way of understanding the nature of the reality and the human mechanism of knowing. Both were regarded Godless by their opponents. Both sprang from deep socio-economic changes.

But unlike the EE, the BE provides a trans-sensual and trans-conceptual vision of the Infinite Whole, transcending the subject-object dichotomy. EE relies on the senses and conceptual thought for its vision, and subject-object dichotomy is always maintained. BE transforms and heals the human person by putting an end to suffering and desire, by generating a sense of co-being, compassion and friendship for all reality, and by making him/her unpretentious, humble, non-domineering, and capable of transmitting peace, joy, and meaning to others. However, EE gives knowledge-derived power over the object and impels the desire to possess, manipulate and dominate. It gives power to produce goods – both that are necessary for humans and much more that are not only unnecessary but also harmful to all life on earth. It makes war and violence more sophisticatedly destructive.

### The New Enlightenment

Now Mar Gregorios tells us that the need of our world today is a New Enlightenment (NE). NE needs to be created taking the best aspects from the BE and EE, and avoiding their harmful aspects. It may begin with a few pioneering individuals as in BE, but it has to become a mass movement that spreads like fire as in EE. NE will be grounded on a three-in-one perception of reality:

1.  the transcendent un-manifest reality (God/ Brahman/ Allah/ Buddha nature/ Tao),
2.  the manifest reality (world/universe)
3.  the human entity which participates in the above two realities , with the mediatorial task of manifesting the un-manifest in the universe, and leading the universe to the un-manifest.

In this perception of reality, the universe is the body of the humanity, and we are supposed to take care of the universe just as we take care of our own body. The dichotomy of manifest and un-manifest exists due to the limit in our power of perception. However, from the perspective of the un-manifest, such a dichotomy does not exist. Thus what appear three to us is one in reality. Mar Gregorios claims that such a perception of the reality will have earth-shaking consequences in the various areas of our life.

**Politics and religion:** In NE, a state will not be a sovereign power, but the enabler of the local community; not as a dividing boundary but as a unit in a global community. Instead of separation of religion and state, there will be the right relation of religion and state. The problem of multiplicity or religions will be avoided by adopting the policy of democratic pluralism in the polity. The religions will occupy a central role in the state, competing each other in serving the whole community in spiritual and moral creativity. In NE no one will speak of foreigners and aliens, but only of neighbors and friends. In NE politics will not be for opportunists, but for sages, for men and women of wisdom and maturity.

**Education:** The purpose of education will not be to run the machinery of economic production, but education will be a genuine search for meaning and fulfillment.

**Healing:** Diagnosis will not be to detect the defects of the body, but to detect the arhythmias in the functioning of the human person and society. Therapies will be more human and spiritual directly related to the transcendent and to the society.

**Economics:** Its focus will be away from commodities, and closer to right relations of humans among themselves, to the environment and to the transcendent.

# 7. Why do we Need a New Worldview?

Why do we need a new worldview? This is the question addressed in *Human Presence*, the most well-known book by Paulos Mar Gregorios. What follows is a brief account of the context of writing this book and the major ideas discussed in it.

### The Context

In 1979 the World Council of Churches called a world conference at the Massachusetts Institute of Technology in USA. The topic of the conference was *Faith, Science and the Future of Humanity*. Attended by about 500 physical scientists, and about the same number of social scientists and theologians, this conference was chaired by none other than Paulos Mar Gregorios. The conference, which preceded five years of preparation, lasted seven days. Mar Gregorios later looked

back at this memorable event and wrote in his autobiography that it was a major turning point in his own thought-life. He wrote,

"I had occasion to work with many world thinkers on the issues relating to modern science as our chief way of knowing, and to modern technology as our principal tool for transforming society and environment." [1]

Mar Gregorios authored three books in connection with this

conference.
1. Science and Our Future[2]
2. Human Presence[3]
3. Science for Sane Societies[4]

Science *and Our Future* was written in preparation for the conference. It was a combined work with contributions from several Indian scientists and thinkers. Mar Gregorios was the primary contributor and the general editor of the book.

The dramatic context of authoring *Human Presence* is found in the autobiography as follows:

> In 1978, as I was chairing the Preparatory Committee for the WCC's famous World Conference on Faith, Science and the Future, I was infuriated by a book by one of my Committee members giving the Christian theological basis for an approach to the Environment problem. It was much too Calvinistic and hardly Christian from my perspective. The best I could do to respond was to sit in the Gregorian Library in Rome for three weeks and produce The Human Presence, giving an Eastern Orthodox Christian approach to the same problem. It has been one of my more successful books in terms of sales and reviews. The chapter on "Mastery and Mystery" has been widely quoted.[5]

Once the conference was over, Mar Gregorios took time to put down his own thoughts on it, which was published as *Science for Sane Societies*.

During the cold war, the US, Soviet Union, and other nations amassed nuclear weapons as much as to destroy all life on earth several times over. When the extreme danger intrinsic to nuclear war and the possession of nuclear weapons became apparent to all sides, a series of disarmament and nonproliferation treaties were agreed upon between the United States, the Soviet Union, and several other states throughout the world. Many of these treaties involved years of negotiations, and seemed to result in important steps toward creating a world free of nuclear weapons. Behind the peace that the world is enjoying today is the influence of organizations like WCC and the dedicated work of numerous humanitarians like Paulos Mar Gegorios. The primary purpose of the conference in USA in 1979 was to make the world aware of the existential problems facing humanity and to seek solutions. It was an opportunity for the best scientists and theologians in the world to come together and find ways to save life on this planet. It was like a meeting of some physicians to diagnose the illness of the world and to prescribe a remedy. Being the principal organizer and coordinator of this conference, the primary responsibility to guide the conference in making the right diagnosis fell on Mar Gregorios. He presented his views of the illness of the humanity, its diagnosis, and its treatment in *The Human Presence*.

### A Chariot Running Amok

In the preface, Mar Gregorios uses the metaphor of a chariot running amok. It keeps moving, but without any clear and specific guidance or purpose. It is already out of its right path and almost about to fall headlong into a deep trench, from where it may not recover. The chariot is our civilization, and the charioteer is the humanity. Mar Gregorios classifies the existential problems faced by humanity into three groups:

1. The poverty of billions of people perpetuated by economic injustice and exploitation. We failed in producing essential goods and distributing them equally. This makes us fight and even kill each other to possess the resources.

2. A sense of meaninglessness and boredom among the affluent, raising fundamental questions about the values of the consumer society and the civilization based on it.

3. Challenges to human existence posed by scientific-technological culture such as resource depletion, pollution, possible nuclear war, and possible misuse of artificial gene mutation.

Why can't this driver drive the chariot in the right direction? There is a problem with the vision of the driver. There is a dense fog, and something has gone wrong with the eyesight as well. Due to the poor vision, this driver doesn't even realize that his chariot is running amok, and a catastrophe can happen any moment. If the driver can rub his eyes and regain some clarity of vision, he may be able to bring the chariot back to the right path. Mar Gregorios sees the conference of 1979 and his books as a part of humanity's attempt to regain some clarity of vision. Today as I am writing this, and as you are reading this, we are also engaged in humanity's attempt to gain some clarity of vision.

In order to stay on the right path, the driver needs to know where the chariot is in relation to the path and the surroundings. The humanity needs to have a clear vision of where it stands in relation to the world and to God. The primary problem is with our worldview. The driver may be able to realize the problem with his present vision if he can remember how his sight was earlier. Mar Gregorios' going back to the vision of the fourth century fathers is such an attempt. In Human Presence, Mar Gregorios gives us the opportunity to compare our own worldview with that of the fourth century fathers, especially of Gregory of Nyssa.

### The Origin and Development of the Current Worldview

Like the ancient three-tier-worldview of heaven, earth, and hell, the classical western worldview is also a three-tier one with God, Humanity, and World. At the lowest level is the world or nature, an order with its own constitution. Above it is the humanity, creating culture and history through its actions. The top level is one of super-nature, grace, and revelation. Thus this structure may also be named nature-culture-grace. There is something seriously wrong in the way the relationship between these levels is viewed. These three levels are viewed as antagonistic to each other rather than as an integral system. This is the root cause of the present existential problems of humanity. Such an antagonistic worldview has led to our recent thoughtless exploitation of natural resources and to our unhealthy competition for the resources amassing weapons of mass destruction.

It is not very easy to trace the origin and development of this alienating worldview, but one may identify its roots in Augustine and in Thomas Aquinas. By 17th century, it evolved further into a "scientific" two-tiered worldview with man manipulating an objectified nature —mechanistic and materialistic. No more super-nature was in the picture.

There have been two major admirable attempts recently to develop an alternative worldview. One is process theology, based on the philosophical thought of A.N. Whitehead (1861- 1947). The other one is the view of Teilhard de Chardin (1881- 1955). Both of these views try to rectify the defects of the classical worldview, and present a much better and constructive view of the world.

### The View of Gregory of Nyssa

The best alternative to the classical western view can be found in the classical Eastern Orthodox view as seen in Gregory of Nyssa. Gregory was very much familiar with the pre-Christian classical Greek views such as platonic and stoic. It is possible that Gregory came to know Platonism through Plotinus, later known as neo-Platonist. The stoics saw the world as a living being with God as its soul. Plato saw our visible, changing world as an expression of the invisible, changeless world. Although Gregory derived valuable insights from them, he did not accept them as such. He modified their worldviews with Christian insights.

Unlike the western view, Gregory saw all that exists as one integral system. The created existence depends upon the uncreated existence and exists within it. Humanity exists as an integral part of the created existence like a fruit to a plant. Humanity is as integral to the world as the brain or heart is to the body. Humanity along with the rest of the world is the visible image of the invisible God. According to this view, the glory of God has to be expressed in the world, especially in humanity. This view is opposed to the western view that humanity's glory is opposed to the Glory of God.

Nature, Humanity, and God are not three distinct realities with a space-interval between their boundaries. Humanity is part of the nature from which it cannot turn away from as long as it needs space to exist, and as long as it needs to breathe, eat, drink, and eliminate waste. God is not a reality with precise physical boundaries. God is the reality which sustains both man and nature, and it is through man and nature that God expresses himself.

Mastery of nature for oneself is the Adamic sin of refusing our mediating position between God and nature. The mastery of nature must be held within the mystery of worship. Otherwise we lose both mastery and mystery. We may give nature as our extended body into the hands of the loving God in Eucharistic self-offering. This is the mystery of the cross. Christ gave himself, with humanity and nature, to God in self-denying love, and thereby saved humanity and nature.

This tradition set by Gregory of Nyssa continued with sages such as Dionysius, the Areopagite, in the fifth century, Maximus, the confessor, in the seventh century, and with Vladimir Solovyov in the 19th century.

### We Need to Create New Worldviews

Old worldviews need to be replaced with new ones. Creating new images or worldviews is the art of iconopeia. Mar Gregorios cites Olivier Reiser as an excellent image maker. He brings a lucid mind and an encyclopedic knowledge of science, religion, and art to the task of making images of the future. In his *Cosmic Humanism*, he advances the hypothesis that human beings are the embryonic cells of an emerging world organism. He conceives the planet earth as a psychosomatic creature with an organized humanity forming its brain cortex. Reiser proposed a global picture language and a global communication medium using an artificial sea of electricity enveloping the globe. Reiser's cosmos includes a manifest universe and an unmanifest universe. Nature has a double-layer structure. The upper level, consisting of material objects, energies and forces, is the manifest layer accessible to our senses. The lower layer, consisting of electric and magnetic fields, remains unmanifest. This picture of cosmos is different from the ones of whitehead and Teilhard Chardin, which lack such an unmanifest level.

### We Need to Address Ethical Questions Anew

We need to identify good from what is not good. We also need to know why we have to do good. These questions can be adequately answered only in the background of a worldview. Ethical questions cannot be considered without ontological questions. Examination and evaluation of worldviews is the primary task of Ontology or Metaphysics.

The present ethical rules are very much individualistic. Let us consider the Universal Declaration of Human Rights as an example. It speaks about the rights and freedom of human individuals, but not about societies. Education is oriented toward the development of the personality, not toward the development of societies. These ethical guidelines are the product of the worldview of western liberalism, according to which the world is made of individual human beings exploiting nature. Ethical guidelines are lacking in relation to human communities, nations and to humanity as a whole. We need to evolve better and more comprehensive ethical guidelines based on better worldviews.

The holders of power in the present system, eager to maintain their privileged position, resist any change to the present system. Instead of establishing justice, they create institutions of charity, by which they help the poor while keeping them in poverty. Often churches become instruments of such exploitation.

A new view of life and a way of life cannot be developed by individuals living separately, but by a community of mature, capable, and charismatic people who live together for a few years. The members have to be from diverse national, religious, and cultural backgrounds. They need to engage in serious study on the problems that confront humanity, embody a new spirituality with transparency to the transcendent and to each other, evolve a style of life with simplicity and spontaneity, and participate fully in the life and struggles of the community around.

**Conclusion**

Paulos Mar Gregorios was making two pleas through *The Human Presence*. One, make a correction in our worldview, and two, make a global community effort to develop a way of life based on the corrected worldview. In the present popular worldview, there is no God, and nature is treated as an object humanity can manipulate. We need a worldview in which God, humanity, and nature are integrally related. Based on this new worldview, a new civilization needs to be built. Such an attempt needs to begin with a community of pioneers who will test this worldview in their community life. They must have the courage to face the Cross from the beneficiaries of injustice.

# 8. What is Wrong with our Healthcare System?

We often think very highly of the modern western medical system, but Paulos Mar Gregorios was a little hesitant to do so. Although he was well aware of its contributions, he was not blind

toward its inability to deal with humanity's health-related problems adequately. Mar Gregorios had a very clear view of how the medical system can be transformed. His views on this topic were put together in a book, *Healing- A Holistic Approach*[1], published in 1995. Here I am making an attempt to introduce some of his major views on this topic.

Although a very large amount of public funds is now devoted to medical education and educational institutions, at present it hardly reaches a fifth of the world's population. Modern medicine is a profit oriented industry that only makes money if people get and stay sick. The occurrence of hospital-induced diseases is on the rise. Antibiotics are increasingly becoming ineffective because bacteria are developing resistance to antibiotics. Cattle are often fed with chemicals and treated with antibiotics, and all these chemicals and antibiotics reach the body of human beings through milk. In its present state, it is unaffordable for most people, unacceptable in terms of the damage it does, and undesirable in terms of its over-mechanization in both diagnosis and therapy. Western Medicine needs a radical transformation to be able to cope with the healthcare needs of today's world.

## In Search of the Root Cause

What is the very root cause of the ineffectiveness of the western medical system? A medical treatment is a solution to a health problem. If the solution is not satisfactory, the problem will remain as such. In order to solve a problem, primarily we need a good diagnosis of the problem. If the diagnosis is wrong, the problem remains unsolved. Mar Gregorios argues that there is something basically wrong in the way the western medical system does the diagnosis.

Imagine that a sick person visits a doctor. The doctor examines him. He compares his pulse rate, breathing rate, temperature, and other information with those of a healthy person, and makes a diagnosis. Let us say he has a temperature of 104° F. The doctor decides that he has a fever comparing it with the ideal temperature of 98.6° F. In order to make such a diagnosis, the doctor must know that the ideal temperature is 98.6° F. If a doctor thinks that the ideal temperature is 104° F, he will not think that his patient has fever. Mar Gregorios argues that like a doctor who doesn't know what the ideal temperature is, the western medical system doesn't know what the ideal health is. If it has a distorted view of health, how can it correctly diagnose ill-health?

The view of health of the western medical system is a part of the distorted and disintegrated mechanistic worldview of the western civilization.

Tom Heuerman[2] gives us a beautiful account of the nature and evolution of the mechanistic worldview. Europe witnessed in sixteenth and seventeenth centuries a mighty cultural movement called the enlightenment, which radically altered the existing worldview. An organic and living world was replaced by a machine-like world. Galileo Galilei, Francis Bacon, Rene Descartes, and Isaac Newton were the leaders of this movement. They pictured the world as a mechanical system put in motion by God and operated by exact mathematical laws. Knowledge of the laws and the initial conditions of the system enables a scientist to predict accurately what the system would do and where it would go. The world became almost like a clock— running for ever without any purpose. Humans could detach themselves from the universe and observe and gain knowledge of its workings. Ethics, spirit, values, quality, and consciousness were marginalized. The only things that mattered were the quantifiable, and the knowledge of science was certain and absolute. People used scientific knowledge to dominate and control nature. When our worldview became mechanistic, our life also became mechanistic. The way a machine works became the ideal for factories and workers. Creativity was replaced by routine and control. We are supposed to act like machines and we are treated like machines. Human feelings do not matter --machines don't have feelings.

The western medical system views a human being as a machine. A machine is self-contained, may be related or unrelated to other machines. It is not alive and it does not evolve. It does not have feelings or consciousness. If something goes wrong, a mechanic can fix it by replacing a part or by tightening a screw. The physicians and other healthcare workers in the western medical system view themselves as technicians of the human body. If there is a broken bone, they carefully place the broken parts together to enhance healing. If there is an uncontrolled growth inside the body, they cut open that part and remove the growth. If a tooth gets decayed, they replace it with an artificial one. They have drugs for every identifiable illness, which go inside the body and do chemical changes.

Well, aren't they doing an excellent job? Yes, they are! But they can do an even better job if they change the way they see a human being. Instead of a machine, a human being needs to be seen as a living, conscious, evolving being integrally related to other human beings, to the nature, and to God. Thus health will be seen not just the health of the body but of the whole human being and of all his relations. This is often referred to as the holistic health. Holistic deals with the whole, not just with a part of it. Our medical system is not holistic; it treats mainly our body, seeing it as a machine.

## In Search of a Solution

Our medical system came to have a mechanistic view because our worldview itself became mechanistic. We can have a holistic view in the medical system only if we have a holistic worldview. Are we evolving such a view? Yes, we are.

Fortunately, from the middle of the twentieth century a new worldview began to emerge mainly due to the developments in Physics and Biology. We may call it organic worldview or ecological worldview. The world is no more a machine but a living being in this view. The world is no more building blocks put together but an integrated whole connected by a web of relationships. We can no longer stand apart and observe and control the world; we are one with it. From certainty and prediction we are moving to uncertainty and probability.

Tom Heuerman concludes:

> The universe of the emerging worldview is an alive and undivided whole created as one entity with its elements interconnected, interrelated, and interdependent. All betterment flows from the totality as the diverse parts interact and organize together in patterns that balance and sustain the essence of the whole. The potential for change is unlimited and uncommitted. This is a universe of spirit, purpose, meaning, and mystery.

David Bohm, the eminent physicist, has developed a holographic view of the universe. A hologram is a no-lens photography in which each part is a representation of the whole. A hologram is a product of two light waves colliding, while the universe may be a product of several energy waves colliding. A hologram is static, while the universe is dynamic.

This view is close to the traditional Asian religious understanding of reality! According to the Hindu notion of *maya*, the present perception and experience of *samsara* (world) as a flowing reality, is the joint product of a certain *vikshepa* (projection) of *maya* (power) by *Brahman* (Ultimate Reality) and the veil of *avidya* (ignorance) brought to perception by the human mind. According to the Buddhist concept of *pratitya-samudpada* (conditioned co-origination), our perception of reality is the joint product of the conceptually indescribable reality and our own mental sensory equipment. In the Chinese tradition *tao* (order) and *te* (power) together constitute cosmic reality, which includes the human reality. In the Eastern Orthodox Christian tradition, this world is a projection of God's *energia*. It is God's will, wisdom, and word that keep both the universe and humanity going.

All that exists is one integrated whole, but for convenience we may see them in four separate levels. Paulos Mar Gregorios presents this four-level world neatly as follows.

At the lowest level we have inorganic matter-energy, that is, bundles and packets and waves of energy expressing itself in numerous forms -- the elements, their compounds, and things made of them, forces which we see as light and sound, heat and electricity, magnetism and gravity, and the strong and weak forces that hold matter together or make forms of matter-energy interact with each other, including nuclear power.

Continuous with this inorganic level is the organic or bio level. We say continuous because the line of demarcation between a crystal or radioactive element on the one hand and a protein molecule or virus on the other is not so absolute or clear. In general terms, however, we see the distinguishing mark of life as homeostasis or the capacity to maintain certain internal constants in the face of a wide range of external pressures, such as maintaining a constant temperature within the body despite fluctuations in the environmental temperature. Our knowledge of this level is far from satisfactory. We have seen what difference a little discovery about genes and their structure can make in our over-all perspective.

Continuous with the organic level is the third level—of consciousness. Consciousness may be defined as an internal apprehension of external reality Consciousness is difficult to conceptualize or study objectively. We distort consciousness when we make it an object.

There is a fourth level about which we know even less. We could call it the cosmic level or the transcendent level. This level is the one least understood or even accepted by modern science. Attempts have been made to conceptualize how the four levels work together through pseudo-sciences like astrology. Carl Gustav Jung suggested synchronicity as a scientific principle which shows how the micro reflects the macro at any given moment. Art, poetry, and religion are better able to deal with this level than science.

Sickness may be seen as malfunctioning at the first three levels. However, today's medical and surgical therapy usually pays attention only to the first and second levels. Today we are moving towards including the third level in diagnosis.

Dr. Deepak Chopra suggests similarity between quantum events and mental events. He suggests that each cell is intelligent, and that human intelligence is like a field propagating its influence over a large expanse of space and time, and the body is a web of such fields rather than molecules organized in space. Every particle of living matter is in touch with every other, so that life as a whole is an intricate cosmic system of interacting fields. This means that the human system is a subsystem of all that exists and is integrally related to it. Disturbances in that integral relation are the diseases. Restoration to the ideal relationship to the whole is healing. The whole is the source of healing force— the same source from which matter, life, and consciousness originate.

We need a new medical system in which we see matter, life, and consciousness as a single continuum. It means that pharmacology should be seen as only one element in the healing process. A caring community must be recognized as a healing force. Faith healing needs to be given importance. The society needs to be restructured to make social relations holistic, and the human environment needs to be life-supporting. Medical practitioners have to break out of their self-image as technicians and become warm human beings. Often by a caring touch, they can communicate confidence, warmth, support and understanding. When a healer prays for the sick placing the right hand on the head, healing energies transfer through the touch.

Almost any form of meditation will have healing effects. Yoga is a combination of exercise and meditation. Meditation helps us to overcome our mental chatter, which is the root of much ill-health. Good meditation decreases the restless alpha waves and increases the quiet beta waves, and also synchronizes the hemispheres of the brain. However, we should not develop meditation into a religion, for it is nothing but an exercise of our mind for concentration. We need to climb higher using it as a stepping stone.

**Conclusion**

The modern western civilization, which provides the ideological foundation to the life of humanity in our world, views the world as a machine. Our healthcare system understands health, illness, and healing using this metaphor of machine. In order to evolve a new healthcare system, we need nothing less than a new worldview—one that sees the world as an evolving, conscious, living being. It is already emerging, but it needs active and conscious support and promotion to take roots.

# 9. What is Wrong with our Education System?

What is wrong with our education system? This question was addressed by Paulos Mar Gregorios primarily in the context of independent India. There emerged three distinct views of education in the independent India— of Gandhi's, Nehru's and Tagore's. Nehru's view has been accepted by India. Mar Gregorios asserts that it has been a wrong choice, and he proposes Tagore's view as the ideal.

### Diagnosing the Illness

A society functions with its own way of life, which includes its common views of life, languages, ways of dressing, eating, politics, economics, healthcare etc. A society always consists of children and adults. Adults are the citizens, the ones who run a society, and children are the ones who get trained to become citizens. Education is the process through which the children learn to become citizens in a society.

But a society may have basic defects in its view of life and in its way of life. Such fundamental defects of a society cannot be corrected by changing its system of education. What is needed in such a situation is a re-education by the whole society—a renaissance or a reformation. If a society has an ill-performing education system, it could be a symptom of an underlying sickness of the whole society, and its solution will be the treatment of the whole society rather than treating the system of education.

Inaugurating the International Ecumenical Assembly of Christian Universities in 1995, Metropolitan Paulos Mar Gregorios argued that the current problem with the education system is not something that can be corrected by making some modification within the system, but something that calls for a correction in the view of life of the whole society. The ill-performance of the education system is a symptom of an underlying illness of the society. Therefore, its solution is not to treat the education system, but to treat the entire society. He said:

I have come to realize that educational reform is rather futile, unless it is an integral aspect of social reform. The idea that educational reform can precede social reform and can even engineer social change has proved to be largely a false assumption. I myself have learned to focus on social reform as the larger matrix in which educational reform has to seek its place.1

An example will clarify this idea. Let us say you go to an eye doctor because you sensed an unusual pain and irritation in your eyes. The eye doctor checks your eyes thoroughly well and lets you know that the problem is not with your eyes at all. If the problem were with your eyes it could be easily corrected by changing your glasses. But you have an underlying problem. So now you go to a general doctor to find the underlying problem, and she finds that you have diabetes. The irritation and pain you felt in your eyes was merely a symptom of diabetes. So the solution is to treat diabetes.

The current major problem with our education system cannot be solved by making some adjustments within the system itself. Adding or changing the educators or materials or facilities or methods is not going to make any change at all. The current illness of the education system is a symptom of the underlying illness of the society as a whole, and it needs a solution at that level.

### Educational Reform in India

India was tremendously influenced in the last couple of centuries with two cultural currents from the West-- liberal humanism, and Marxist socialism. The Western liberal education had a direct role in initiating and advancing India's struggle for development and justice. The Indian elite such as Raja Ram Mohan Roy, Dayananda Saraswati, and Debendranath Tagore were ardent social reformers. Their will to reform found expression in Western style societies and movements—Arya Samaj, Brahma Samaj, Servants of India Society, and Indian National Congress. Tilak, Gokhale, Vivekananda, and Gandhi were organizers of social reform movements the like of which were not seen in India before the Western impact.

This early movement was an attempt to integrate western ethics into an Indian religious framework and to universalize Indian religion. Ram Mohan Roy, for example, stood for an upanishadic universalism not only for Indians but for all humanity. It was with Jawaharlal Nehru that the secular and socialist ideas unrelated to the religious framework became pervasive in Indian elitist thought. For Nehru, the springs of motivation lay, not in the religious and cultural heritage of India, but in the European struggle for emancipation from ecclesiastical control of thought and from feudalist and capitalist oppression. Also the liberal-humanist and the Marxist-socialist streams of thought merge in Nehru. Out of this merging originated two different streams in the quest for a reawakened India-- the vision of Nehru and Gandhi of India's future. There was so much in common between the two visions which enabled them to co-exist in the Indian National Congress. However, there were extremists on both sides. The secular-Marxist ones later separated to form the Communist Party of India. Some religious extremists separated to form groups like the Rashtriya Svayam Sevak Samiti. But the vast majority remained with the Indian National Congress. Within the Congress itself, however, the Gandhian vision and Nehru's vision uneasily co-existed, the latter predominating.

### Gandhi's Vision

The Gandhian vision, inheriting the original upanishadic universalism, consisted in a Ramarajya, which was anti-industrialist, anti-urbun, but not anti-capitalist. Capitalists like Birla and Tata were regarded as allies who would hold properly in trust for the people, providing funds for humanitarian purposes. Simplicity of life, an agrarian-rural setting with a minimum of factories and cities, primacy of the spiritual, uplift of the downtrodden, work-based basic education-- these were some of the features of the Gandhian vision. Coming in the tradition of Ruskin, Tolstoy, Rousseau, and Thoreau in the West, the Gandhian vision had much in common with the counter-culture syndrome in America and other Western countries.

### Nehru's Vision

Nehru's vision was openly committed to the urban industrial culture based on Western science and technology. Ideologically anti-capitalist, though unable to free itself from dependence on capitalist wealth and power, the India of the five-year plans had as her objective the raising of the GNP, catching up with the West in its ever-expanding production and consumption, increasing educational and health services, and better distributive justice through graded taxation. While giving encouragement to art and music, dance and drama, literature and sports, the Nehru vision had but limited interest in either the spiritual heritage of India or in a coherent vision of man and the meaning of his life. In agriculture, as in industry, in education as in research, our inspiration as well as ideas came from the West, whether socialist or capitalist. This vision of Nehru has dominated India.

### Tagore's Vision

Rabindranath Tagore showed a third way to which India paid but very little attention. He was willing to use Western insights, but he wanted a radical reorientation of our educational system. His basic thesis is a distinction he makes between the scientific attitude to life, which he describes as an attitude of objectifying everything and bringing it under control, and the unitive approach, which seeks a vital, non-objectifying relation to reality. Tagore argued that joy was more important than power. And joy comes from union, not from knowledge or control. Tagore accused the Christian West of not really coming to terms with Christ's teaching on fundamental unity. The Western style of education, according to Tagore, alienates us from reality and creates ghettoes of the mind, full of parochial prejudices, national chauvinism, and acquisitive greed.

He saw the Western form of education as enslaving, and denying us true knowledge. Tagore accused the West of exclusiveness --it fell upon the resources of other people, and it was cannibalistic in its tendencies. Tagore did not reject scientific development, or material progress. He wanted a higher standard of living for people than existed in his times. He saw clearly that the Western method of education would maintain inequalities, and was incapable of achieving development, or political freedom. He believed that political freedom does not give us freedom, when our mind is not free. He was willing to assimilate Western science and knowledge within an Indian cultural and educational framework that would deliver us from poverty and ignorance.

Tagore believed that education should be rooted in our own cultural traditions. It is like a tree which has to stay rooted in the soil in order to be free. He believed that the medium of instruction must be one's own mother tongue. He placed great importance on children learning in a natural environment, and said that nature herself was our greatest teacher. The process of education was seen as one of self-discovery and free creation. It should incorporate the act of playing, and the joy that playing brings. Education should be linked to working, and learning a craft. The school should be integral to Society. Education should enhance not only intellectual skills but also emotional skills. Education should also involve spiritual or religious education, which raises us to the awareness that we are an integral part of cosmic infinity. Education should also lead to the brotherhood of mankind.

### The Chinese Educational Reform as a Challenge

Mar Gregorios presents Chinese educational reform as a challenge to India. The Chinese educational system, under the leadership of Mao Tse Tung, introduced sweeping changes based on a clear ideological vision.

China began her experiments in 1958 with Marx's idea of a part-work and part-study education, not based in the schools, but in the factories themselves. But it proved to be a failure by 1962. In 1964 the scheme was reactivated with renewed vigor in integral relation to what was happening in the society around, especially in communes. In 1966, the Great Proletarian Cultural Revolution exploded with earth-shaking force. The masses, led by the army and the young people, took over their own education. All students, beginning with senior middle school, were now required to spend a year or two among the workers, peasants and soldiers, in the factories and communes. There they were to be educated in the three primary principles of Chinese education: the class struggle, the struggle for production, and the promotion of scientific research and inventiveness. University entrance was no longer on the basis of academic merit. That criterion led to the shocking fact that even in the mid-sixties, the Shanghai Music Institute had some ninety percent of its students with a bourgeois origin.

The examination system was abolished both for entrance and for graduation. The Cultural Revolution forced the university students to return to the factories and communes for a year or two. Readmission to university reduced enrolment to about a third of what it was before the Cultural Revolution. Students were readmitted on the basis of their social attitudes, their capacity for productive work, and their scientific inventiveness and initiative as demonstrated in the years in the communes and factories.

Chinese education is no pale imitation of the West. It has its own vision, dynamic, cultural roots, and particularity. Chinese education abandoned all foreign stereotypes, and was based on bold, independent thinking coming out of the experience of working class youth engaged in productive labor. Manual labor was accepted as a normal part of education for teachers and students alike.

### Developing a Plan for India Today

Mar Gregorios asks India to refrain from imitating the West. India should not imitate the Chinese either. India needs her own pioneering. There are some things which India can learn from the Chinese, not as models for copying, but as principles of fairly universal relevance.

India should learn that reforms will not come from Governmental planning, but only through nation-wide cadres, ideologically oriented, strictly disciplined and coordinated, democratically organized, from a mass-base. Mass social education is the context in which a new educational system and new types of educational institutions can take shape. Education should develop a pattern that is related to primary relations of economic production and distribution which teaches the dignity of labor, promotes creativity and inventiveness in science and technology, and generates new altruistic social attitudes among the masses and their leaders.

In the context of the disillusionment of the West with an urban-technological culture's incapacity to save man, we can see a new vision coming out of the depths of our own rich past. We should learn from the Chinese experiment all its valid lessons without being blinded by inherited prejudices. We should continue to make use of Marxist social analysis in so far as it has been confirmed by experience. We should continue to learn from the patterns of implementation of national plans in the Soviet Union and in Tanzania. We can still use our Western-acquired secularist liberal humanism for an evaluation and criticism of our value-system.

Mar Gregorios points out three things as high priorities in India:

1. The relation between mass education and institutional education should be further studied, and a new national scheme for both has to be envisaged and implemented through a huge nation-wide network of disciplined and trained voluntary cadres.

2. We should, as a nation, take a fresh look at our theoretical assumptions about what kind of a society we should plan for in India. Here we should look at our own three options--the Nehru, Gandhi, and Tagore visions. We should also look at the Chinese, Cuban and North Korean experiments at social reconstruction. We should examine the experience of the bourgeois West, which is raising new questions about the validity of science and technology as a way of man's relating himself to nature in the context of problems like resource depletion, urban agglomeration and environmental pollution. Only on the basis of a more adequately clarified vision of what it means to be human today in India can we proceed to a genuine program of educational reform.

3. We need to make institutional education directly linked to the primary relations of production and distribution. The question is not that students should leave their institutions in an occasional sortie to a neighboring village. What is demanded is that a village's or a factory's primary relations of production and distribution become the milieu in which education takes place. The village or the factory itself becomes the school rather than an isolated school building. The students live in and participate fully in the agricultural and industrial activities of society and get their training there.

## Challenge to the Christian Educators

Addressing an international conference of Christian educators, Mar Gregorios challenged Christians to join hands with the followers of other religions like Islam, Judaism, Hinduism, Buddhism, Jainism and Taoism to challenge the secular assumptions of our civilization and the European Enlightenment which created it. We should not be browbeaten by intellectuals and misdirected political leaders who advocate and propagate secularism as an unquestionable dogma and a panacea for all our social ills. A Christian University which challenges this dogma is likely to be mercilessly persecuted. But if Christians cannot risk some persecution for the sake of truth what authenticity can their faith have?

Some bold and imaginative steps need to be taken to break the monolithic dominance of western culture in higher education. This is not simply a question of having a Department of Religions in each Christian college and teaching a few courses on Asian religions. The whole perspective of higher education at all levels has to shift from the mono-cultural to a multi-cultural and multi-religious perspective on reality. Secularism should also be recognized as a religion among the others. Philosophy should find a new role in the University curriculum -- not just "modern" philosophy, which is under constraint to repudiate all tradition and traditional or contemporary religions. It should be a philosophy which can help the students ask the basic questions about the meaning of life, the nature of reality, the transcendent foundations of the manifest universe, fulfillment in life, the nature of our relationship with each other and with the universe in which we exist and so on. The university should not provide ready-made answers to these questions, but it must help the student to ask these questions without embarrassment and to find their own personal answers. But a philosophy which is dry, academic and unproductively conceptual will not do the job. The university should enable cohesive religious communities to co-exist, interact and learn from the worship and practices of other religions and ideologies.

We cannot just bring back traditional religion in the university curriculum in the pre-Enlightenment form; not even in the form in which religion is in the curriculum of many western and other universities. We cannot just reverse the process of secularization and restore the pre-Enlightenment curriculum. The religious context in the university should be as inclusively pluralist as possible. It cannot be abstract or academic religion, reduced to so-called teachings or philosophies. It should be the interacting confluence of various religious communities committed to faithful practice of their religion.

# 10. Can we Know the Truth?

Can we know the truth? This is the question addressed in the book *Quest for Certainty*[1], one of the early books of Paulos Mar Gregorios. It is an excellent introduction to the development of epistemology in the west.

### Context of writing the book

Paulos Mar Gregorios refers in his autobiography to the role he played in the philosophical arena in India as follows:

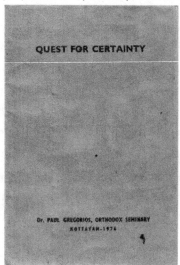

I was elected Vice-President of the Kerala Philosophical Congress in 1968. In 1975, we were able to host the annual session of the Indian Philosophical Congress and to chair the Reception Committee. My association since 1974 with Indian philosophers in the Indian Philosophical Congress and in the Indian Council of Philosophical Research has been a major factor in the growth of my understanding and awareness of the great and rich Indian philosophical heritage. Later on, I was elected as General President of the Indian Philosophical Congress, founded by Rabindranath Tagore and S. Radhakrishnan some 80 years ago. It seems I was the first and only Indian Christian to adorn that post. The honor was hardly deserved, but some of my friends in the Indian Philosophical establishment thought that the General Presidency should not be given only to members of the majority community.

In preparation for the Alwaye Conference of the Indian Philosophical Congress, Mar Gregorios authored a brief introduction to modern European philosophy, and it was published with the title, Quest for Certainty, Philosophical Trends in the West, by Orthodox Seminary, Kottayam in 1976. What follows is a very brief summary of this book. I am writing this to encourage others to read the book and study the topic further.

### An Introduction to Epistemology

We want the truth about our life and about this world. Philosophy is the branch of knowledge specialized in the search for truth. But how do we know truth? This question is addressed in the branch of philosophy called epistemology. Episteme in Greek means knowledge. In this book Paulos Mar Gregorios tells us the story of the western philosophy's search for truth. Intended for the Indian readers, he clarifies some of the western philosophical concepts using Indian terms.

◆ pramanavichara -- Epistemology
◆ Pramanas – measuring sticks
◆ Pratyksha –sense perception
◆ Anumana – inference/reason
◆ Sabda—scripture/tradition

In India we have sought truth using three pramanaas—pratyksha, anumana, and sabda. The west also used these three until recently. The modern western philosophy, however, is characterized by its quest for certainty eliminating the third pramana, the sabda.

### Quest for Certainty in Europe

In the medieval Europe, sabdapramana, consisting of scriptures, traditions, dogmas, canon laws and moral rules, was considered the ultimate authority of truth. When it was overthrown by the Protestant reformation, there was nothing to replace it, and a wave of uncertainty swept over Europe. Europe began a quest for certainty, which was voiced first in Rene Descartes, a French philosopher. He suggested reasoning as the primary source of knowledge. He asked to doubt everything and look for the foundational knowledge. For him the one idea that is the most foundational was: I think; therefore, I exist. The British philosopher John Locke and the Scottish philosopher David Hume continued the quest emphasizing the role of our senses in acquiring knowledge.

While Descartes held Anumana as the primary source of knowledge, John Locke held pratyaksha as the primary source.

Immanuel Kant, the Prussian philosopher, sought to bridge the rationalist and empiricist traditions in epistemology. He did so in response to the skepticism of David Hume, whom Kant said had awakened him from his dogmatic slumbers. Kant agreed with the empiricists that concepts without perceptions or experiences are empty. Concepts or ideas alone cannot constitute knowledge. Innate ideas do not constitute knowledge. There must be experiences for there to be knowledge. However, Kant also agreed with the rationalists that perceptions without concepts are blind. Merely having experiences also does not constitute knowledge. There must be some way in which the mind organizes or structures experience for there to be knowledge.

The **Kantian** starting point provides the basis for several influential schools in contemporary western Philosophy. Three of the most important among them are Neo-Kantianism, Phenomenological systems, and existence philosophies.

The **neo-Kantians** such as Cohen, Natorp, and Cassirer correlate the Kantian philosophical system with the current knowledge in natural sciences.

As envisioned by Edmund Husserl, **phenomenology** is a method of philosophical inquiry that rejects the rationalist bias that has dominated Western thought since Plato in favor of a method of reflective attentiveness that discloses the individual's "lived experience." Brentano was another influential phenomenologist. Max Scheler's philosophy is a phenomenology of feeling—of love and hate, of sympathy and empathy, and of taking interest. It is a vast enterprise of seeing life whole. His was no mere intellectual quest, but a search for a way of life.

**Existentialism** is a term applied to the work of a number of philosophers since the 19th century who, despite large differences in their positions, generally focused on the condition of human existence, and an individual's emotions, actions, responsibilities, and thoughts, or the meaning or purpose of life. Existential philosophers often focused more on what they believed was subjective, such as beliefs and religion, or human states, feelings, and emotions, such as freedom, pain, guilt, and regret, as opposed to analyzing objective knowledge, language, or science. Mar Gregorios prefers to call them existence philosophies because they are not systematic philosophies to be called –isms.

Martin Heidegger was an important thinker of the twentieth century. He radicalized Husserl's Phenomenology, and went beyond Scheler's creative drive to pose the question of *Being* in a comprehensive way. He was not satisfied with the mathematical rationalism of Husserl or the comforting idea of scheler that the human community of love was the heart of reality. Heidegger's was an appeal to the depths, to abandon the common-sense standpoint from which the mystery of being must remain concealed. Heidegger invokes the ancient mystical principle that Being is avachya or ineffable. Man must stand reverently before Being and let Being do the talking; and when he is able to listen to this silent speech, there is not much left for man to say. Because being is unknowable, certainty is impossible.

Karl Jaspers tries to describe in philosophical language how to live one's life. No objective understanding of the nature of man is possible. There are many other philosophers such as Sartre and Marcel in the list of existence Philosophers. Existence philosophies are generally individualistic and ahistoric, and this kind of philosophizing is very much on the wane.

**Structuralism** as a scientific method of Philosophy-Anthropology is a swing of the pendulum to the opposite pole of existence philosophies. Its concern is with the systematic structure of human language and culture, and its methodology is mathematical-cybernetic. Ferdinand de Saussure laid the foundations of structuralism in the Geneva school of Linguistics. The most famous thinkers associated with structuralism include the linguist Roman Jakobson, the anthropologist Claude Lévi-Strauss, the psychoanalyst Jacques Lacan, the philosopher and historian Michel Foucault, the Marxist philosopher Louis Althusser, and the literary critic Roland Barthes. As a quest for certainty it is a painstaking enterprise that seeks to maintain the whole in relation to the parts and understand the parts in relation to the whole.

**Modern empiricism** is very different from the original empiricism of Auguste Comte (1798 -1857). According to Auguste Comte, all human thinking evolves through three steps: religious, metaphysical, and scientific. Modern empiricists are much more modest in their claims. The Vienna Circle, Frege, Whitehead, Rudolf Carnap, Bertrand Russel, and Ludwig wittgenstein are among the modern empiricists. According to them the subject of Philosophy is not Reality itself, but statements and ideas about reality that are made by sciences. Where Kant based certainty on the analysis of knowing process, the new empiricists based their certainty on the right use of language. Mar Gregorios asserts that a linguistic analysis cannot be the basis for certainty or as criterion for truth. All scientific language is an artificial construction, a structure we impose on reality as a hypothesis. Science usually does not abandon one theory even when there are cases which falsify it, until it has found a better one.

**Pragmatism** is related to empiricism in some ways. It was the American professor, C.S.Peirce , who used the term Pragmatism as a philosophical term. William James and John Dewey used the term as a way of thinking—testing the truth or untruth of a statement in terms of the experiential or practical consequences. Everything is to be understood in terms of human purpose. For Peirce, Pragmatism was a theory of meaning. For John Dewey, it was a theory of truth. Pragmatism remains the major unsystematic and often concealed philosophical assumption behind a great deal of our current ordinary thinking. Everything is to be judged by its cash value in terms of experienced pleasure or utility. Pragmatism continues to be the most influential philosophy wherever American influence spreads.

It is necessary to distinguish between **Marxian thought** in Marx's own writings and the Marxist thought which was developed later. Karl Marx, though philosophically trained, did not aim at philosophical consistency. Loren Graham, an American philosopher of Science, gives a summary of the development of philosophy in the post-Stalinist Soviet Union as follows:

> Contemporary soviet dialectical materialism is an impressive intellectual achievement. The elaboration and refinement of the early suggestions of Engels, Plekhanov, and Lenin into a systematic interpretation of nature is the most original creation of Soviet Marxism. In the hands of its most able advocates, there is no question but that dialectical materialism is a sincere and legitimate attempt to understand and explain nature. In terms of universality and degree of development, the dialectical materialist explanation of nature has no competitors among modern systems of thought. Indeed one would have to jump centuries to the Aristotelian scheme of a natural order or to Cartesian mechanical philosophy to find a system based on nature that could rival dialectical materialism in refinement of its development and the wholeness of its fabric.

Graham summarizes the dialectical materialist view of nature as follows:

> All that exists is real; this real world consists of matter-energy; and this matter-energy develops in accordance with universal regularities or laws.

Dialectical materialism has thus managed to combine a realist epistemology, a matter-energy ontology, and a process philosophy of change. Man is part of nature, and the whole of nature with man in it is involved in the dialectical process of change.

Moving to the Western Europe, one finds some intellectual activity in Marxist thought, especially in France and Italy. France is in some sense the motherland of Socialist Philosophy, but French Socialist thought was never necessarily linked to the working class. A more orthodox dogmatism and a less closed Marxist liberalism can be seen in French Marxism.

One can see the development of a neo-Marxism, which pays tribute to Marx but takes the liberty of forming an eclectic system which they call free and post-Marxist. It seeks short-cuts to paradise which can attract only student radicals. It draws inspiration from china and the thought of Mao.

In Marxism, one has to wait for some upheaval like the Second council of Vatican. If there is a reconciliation between china and Russia, as is quite possible, Marxism may prove again to be a vital force in world affairs capable of generating a powerful culture and with it a powerful philosophy.

The most fashionable thought in the western thought today is in the field of **perception and consciousness** studies. The Brazilian anthropologist, Carlos Castaneda's books document phenomena and experiences with his Guru, the Yaqui Indian medicine man, Don Juan of Mexico. What he experiences cannot be explained by contemporary science. J.C. Pearce argues that the Western or the so-called scientific cosmos is only one possible construct, and others may be just as valid. New developments in Brain Biology and the neurology of meditation techniques point to the same conclusions. Several scientists have come to the conclusion that human brain is the locus of evolution now, which is not merely biological but bio-cultural.

Developments in Parapsychology, despite certain frauds and set-backs, are being taken seriously. If scientific perception gives access only to a fragment of the spectrum of reality, then other ways of gaining access to the other aspects of reality have to be explored. The quest for certainty by objective techniques was a fond hope of the west. It gave us a kind of science and technology. Now we need to have a new global effort by putting together our different *sabdapramanas*, to get all our *pratyaksha* and *anumana* to help in a critical evaluation of the various traditions, and to renew our varied approaches to reality.

The names of Thomas Kuhn and Karl Popper stand out in recent western **philosophy of science**. They represent two sides of a debate on the nature of science: normative view and cumulative view.    According to normative view, science advances by extraordinary leaps of research, not by ordinary scientific research. The cumulative view holds that science advances by ordinary research along two lines—a horizontal level of developing better instruments and techniques of measurements and observation, and a vertical level of making the theory better conform to available data. While the cumulative view emphasizes objectivity, the normative view emphasizes subjectivity.

### Conclusion

How am I related to others? How is humanity related to the rest of the reality? How is appearance related to the reality? Science has no answers to these questions. There seems to be no path to certainty through the analysis of the knowing process or through seeking assurance about the infallibility of the process. There are primordial answers offered in various cultures and religions. The best we can do is to examine as many answers as possible and come to our own decision. Still we would have to wait for the gift, for ultimate knowledge seems to be both a decision and a gift.

## A list of the philosophers/ writers mentioned in *Quest for Certainty*

| Philosopher/writer | Lifetime | Nationality |
|---|---|---|
| Althusser, Louis | 1918 - | French |
| Barthes, Roland | 1915 -1980 | French |
| Brentano, Franz | 1838 -1917 | German |
| Carnap, Rudolf | 1891 -1970 | German |
| Cassirer, Ernst | 1874 -1945 | German |
| Castaneda, Carlos | 1925 -1998 | Peruvian American |
| Cohen, Hermann | 1842 -1918 | German- Jewish |
| Comte, Auguste | 1798 -1857 | French |
| Descartes, Rene | 1596 -1650 | French |
| Dewey, John | 1859 -1952 | American |
| Foucault, Michel | 1926 -1984 | French |
| Frege, Gottlob | 1848 -1925 | German |
| Graham, Loren | 1933 - | American |
| Heidegger, Martin | 1889 -1976 | German |
| Hume, David | 1711 -1776 | Scottish |
| Husserl, Edmund | 1859 -1938 | German |
| Jakobson, Roman | 1896 -1982 | Russian |
| James, William | 1842 -1910 | American |
| Jaspers, Karl | 1883 -1969 | German |
| Kant, Immanuel | 1724 -1804 | German |
| Kuhn, Thomas | 1922 -1996 | American |
| Lacan, Jacques | 1901 -1981 | French |

| | | |
|---|---|---|
| Lévi-Strauss, Claude | 1908 -2009 | French |
| Locke, John | 1632 -1704 | British |
| Marcel, Gabriel | 1889 -1973 | French |
| Marx, Karl | 1818 -1883 | German |
| Natorp, Paul | 1854 -1924 | German |
| Pearce, J.C. | | American |
| Peirce, Charles Sanders | 1839 -1914 | American |
| Popper, Karl | 1902 -1994 | British |
| Russel, Bertrand | 1872 -1970 | British |
| Sartre, Jean-Paul | 1905 -1980 | French |
| Scheler, Max | 1874 -1928 | German |
| Whitehead, Alfred North | 1861 -1947 | British |
| Wittgenstein, Ludwig | 1889 -1951 | Austrian |

# 11. What does it Mean to be Free?

Fr. Paul Verghese (The earlier name of Paulos Mar Gregorios) was invited by the Lutheran seminaries in the United States to give the Hein Lectures in 1968. The lectures were put together to publish the book, The Freedom of Man in the United States. Later the material of this book was modified and expanded for the situation in India, and was published as Freedom and Authority in 1974 by CLS and ISPCK . In the foreword, he admits that he was inspired for this book by the students, the Blacks, and the women, who are leading the movement for human liberation. He admits his debt to St. Gregory of Nyssa, from whom he learned the meaning of freedom. He is grateful to Nicholas Berdyaev and

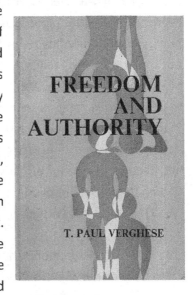

Vladimir Lossky for leading him to Gregory of Nyssa. He admits that he learned the art of thinking primarily from his western teachers, but the content of his thought primarily came from his own eastern tradition.

In the preface to the Indian edition, he rightly points out that Indians today lack the ability of systematic thinking. We read a lot, and we quote freely, but we rarely do our own original thinking either in sciences or in theology. But he also admits that it might be a good thing that we don't go to the other extreme of spinning out a new theology that goes out of fashion soon. We need some concrete person or institution that materializes the thinking before we can make a judgment. He points out the example of the Marxist parties in India. People are not attracted to Marxism as a way of scientific thinking. Only when the party materializes the Marxist ideas into proximate and manageable goals, the people get attracted. Similarly, the Christian church in India needs to become a community that materializes the Christian faith into proximate and manageable goals. This book, he claims, makes an attempt to present the Christian faith as a coherent set of ideas, and also makes an invitation to try a community life based on it.

In the introduction, he states a major human existential problem as it was clearly visible in the second half of the twentieth century-- the crumpling down of the authority structures. The human community has been held together by authority structures, but today they are falling apart, which threatens the very existence of humanity. Children don't obey parents, wives don't submit to their husbands, and employees don't submit to their employers. Students disobey their teachers, laymen do not obey their priests, and even soldiers defy the commands of their officers. Command has become the least effective way to make others do one's will. Church dogmas were blindly believed, but not any more.

Our world has witnessed in the modern era several movements of freedom:

1. Political decolonization. 1500 million people all over the world broke their political chains and marched ahead with a new confidence.
2. Movement against white superiority. The awakening of negro self-consciousness in the Afro-American people.
3. Revolt against socialist Dictatorships. Countries are gaining freedom from socialist dictatorships.
4. Revolt against ecclesiastical authority. Catholic bishops and theologians are openly encouraging disobedience to papal authority.
5. Revolt of Youth against the authority of the older generation.
6. Revolt of Women against male authority

### The Diagnosis

How do we diagnose this situation? Mar Gregorios asserts that there is no need for alarm. Humankind is going through severe pain, but this is not due to any illness. This is merely the birth pangs that would give birth to a new humanity. He further claims that the central element of human evolution is a dialectic between authority and freedom. Humanity grows by discarding freedom-hampering authority structures, and by developing freedom-fostering authority structures. This understanding presupposes three assertions:

1. Man is basically good by nature
2. Real good happens only in freedom, for forced good is not good.
3. The combination of freedom and good, which may be called love, develops only in the structures of a freedom-fostering human community.

Authority and freedom look like opposed to each other. When someone exercises authority, someone else might lose freedom. But it is not so simple as that. We have to ask which authority and which freedom.

Authority can be coercive (arbitrary) or persuasive. Coercive authority disregards the freedom of others, but persuasive authority regards the freedom of others. The authority of parents over children, teachers over students, pastors over parish people, and a government over the citizens needs to be persuasive, not coercive. Whenever some pressure is applied on human will, it reacts to that pressure. Human will always revolts against coercive authority. What kind of authority is God's? Is it coercive or persuasive? In the Old Testament we see a God who is more coercive than persuasive. But the God and father of Jesus Christ is more persuasive than coercive, whose example Jesus Christ asked us to follow.

Freedom is the power to think, feel, speak, and act following one's own will. If someone prevents me from following my own will, I don't have freedom. If I make someone follow my will, he/she is a slave to me. A master exercises coercive authority upon his slave. A slave is not allowed to follow his own will. If he does, it is considered a crime in the system of slavery. In an ideal healthy community, every human individual has freedom. However, one's freedom is limited to his/her own life. One has no freedom to interfere in the life of another person. The freedom to live is a privilege of every human individual. Along with that every human individual has the responsibility to let others have the same freedom. There is no privilege without responsibility.

When we have the freedom to live, and when we let others have their freedom to live, we create rules and willingly submit ourselves to them. Road rules are excellent examples. Where there are road rules and where people strictly follow them, people have the freedom to travel around with very few casualties. A society cannot function without rules. In an authoritarian society, someone creates and enforces rules on the rest of the people. In a democratic society, all people participate in the creation of rules, and all people willingly submit to the rules. Let us imagine heaven, the ideal world. Are there rules there? Yes, there are rules, for without rules no society can function. However, all people willingly and habitually create and follow the rules, and it makes life smooth and joyful for everybody. In contrast, hell may be imagined as a place where no one follows any rules. In heaven, the ideal world, all people are mature, free, and responsible, but in hell all people are immature, bound, and irresponsible.

Our real world is a mixture of both kinds of people. There are mature and immature people, responsible and irresponsible people, those who choose good, and those who choose evil. The presence of good and evil in our world presents an excellent opportunity for people to grow in freedom, maturity, and responsibility. People lack such an opportunity in heaven and in hell, and so there is no opportunity to grow in either of those places.

God is free, and out of his freedom flows only good; no evil. God has granted freedom to humankind-- the right to choose good or evil. Until humankind attains the maturity and perfection of God, humankind will continue to make wrong choices. There might be free beings elsewhere in the universe and also in other dimensions. Our religious traditions call them angels and demons. They also have the freedom to make choices. Thus though good originates from God, evil originates from the wrong choices of the free beings in the world.

So what is our present situation? We are naturally good, and created free. However, we need to grow to maturity-- as perfect as the heavenly father is perfect. We are always surrounded by evil tempting us to choose evil just as Adam and Eve were tempted to make the wrong choice. Jesus himself was not immune from such temptations. He was tempted by Satan to make wrong choices. Nobody is free from such temptations. We have to consciously overcome the temptations and make the right choices as our Lord did. If we do not fall to the temptations of evil, then we will be attacked by the evil forces in various ways. Temptations are internal, but such attacks are mostly external. We need to stand with God and face the powers of evil in our everyday life. Life is a battle with evil.

Augustine, a fourth century father of Latin Christianity, asserted that mankind is basically evil, and so we are not capable of making any right choice at all. Pelagius, a contemporary of Augustine, revolted against this view by going to the other extreme. He claimed that mankind is in a position to easily choose between good and evil. He did not see the power of evil that surrounds us. Along with a low view of Man, Augustine also promoted a low view of this world as well by holding an other-worldly view. The western Christian world, which includes catholic church and protestant churches, still suffers from these distorted views of Augustine. Backed up by political power, the western Christianity spread its influence throughout the world in the past few centuries, and even the eastern Christian churches were not free from their influence.

## Attempts to Regain the Original Christianity

So what exists as Christian church in the world today is mostly a distorted version of the original Christianity. As stated by Mar Gregorios, "Official Christianity sounds ludicrously unintelligent and seems utterly unappealing to the moral conscience of mankind, even to many who have not yet given up their Christian faith." There have been several attempts in the modern world to bring Christianity back to its original form. Although none of them has had the power to achieve the goal, they are treated sympathetically by Mar Gregorios. Five of those attempts are listed in the first chapter:

## 1. Secularization and Pragmatism

Begun as a revolt against ecclesiastical control, secularization has developed as a religion with its own worldview, according to which the world that appears to our eyes is all that exists, and man is in control of this world with no one above him. Secularization and Pragmatism, its twin sibling born in America, support and reinforce each other. According to pragmatism, usefulness to us determines the meaning and value of everything.

## 2. Ontological disillusionment and Existential stance

When secular and pragmatic philosophers refused to deal with the ultimate questions of existence, and set a limit to their quest-- to what we observe or what is useful and relevant to us, philosophers like Husserl and Heidegger stayed in ontological quest asking basic questions of existence. Husserl's quest was for intellectual certainty through careful mapping of the whole region of consciousness. Heidegger seeks the nature of 'being'. Truth for him is an unconcealed relationship between the knower and the known; not a correlation between fact and proposition. Truth is also the knowledge of things in their totality of relationships, the knower included in the whole. Some other philosophers who are under the umbrella of existentialists, such as Kierkegaard, are anti-intellectual and anti-system.

## 3. God's death and hermeneutical quest

The Death of God movement in theology was to reform Christianity. In Nietzsche's words, "God as the declaration of war against life, against nature, against the will to live! God-the formula for every lie about the 'beyond'!" It is this God Nietzsche's madman pronounced dead.

The mainstream theology proceeds within narrow and manageable confines. Instead of considering questions on being, it explores questions like who was historical Jesus, and what is the canon within the canon for interpreting the Bible. This hermeneutical quest is no likely to yield answers to the fundamental questions about human existence.

## 4. The Future of Belief and Belief in Future

The Future of Belief is a book by Leslie Dewart which made a minor storm in Catholic circles. He de-supernaturalized God by liberating God from the Greek conception of God. Mar Gregorios suggests that his criticism of classical western theism would have been enriched by a knowledge of the Greek fathers' views.

A spatially transcendent God , which is quite difficult for western thought, is replaced by a temporal transcendent God. This idea originally came from The Principle of Hope, a book by Ernst Bloch, a German Marxist philosopher. Jewish messianism is the influence behind his thought. The German Theologians like Moltmann, Pannenberg, and Metz, and the American Theologian Harvey Cox are Blochists. Unlike Bloch's view, the Christian hope is based on the Cross and Resurrection, which makes these theologians re-establish the belief in resurrection as a historical event.

### 5. Liberal Humanist and the New Marxist

Humanism believes that the full development of man is possible and is to be striven for. Economic development is regarded by most as the first stage of development. But ideas differ as to the next stages. Liberal Humanist is committed to the unity of mankind and faith in the future of man. The future of man is conceived in simple terms-- cultured, secure, with a pluralistic and permissive social structure. Marxist humanist comes in as a critic of liberal humanist and as a pioneer pointing out that the Liberal humanist's ideas only help to give the glow of morality to a corrupt and dehumanizing system. European Marxists emphasize that man was the cental concern of Marx and so anything that dehumanizes, whether in Communist countries or in the west, is an enemy of Man. Later Marx went to the extreme of denying the authoritarian God to affirm Man.

### The Features of Authentic Christianity

The primary distortion in Christianity, separation of knowledge from life, started as early as second century with Irenaeus. In taking a stand against Gnostics such as Basilides, Cerinthus, and Marcion, who claimed the authority of a secret tradition from the apostles, Irenaeus produced a different set of propositions as inherited from the apostles. Thus the seed sown by Irenaeus further grew up with Origen, who said, "the teaching of the church handed down in unbroken succession from the Apostles, is still preserved and continues to exist in the churches up to the present day, we maintain that that only is to be believed as the truth". The Christian faith has been reduced to a set of doctrines. Origen further claimed that a few doctrines were left behind unclarified by the apostles for the later theologians to work on.

The Cappadocian fathers, however, asserted that the knowledge of God is depended on ethical maturity. There is no way of knowing God apart from living a Godly life. Holiness is not a matter of ethical purity; it involves transfiguration of the very being of man into the likeness and image of God. Among the Cappadocian fathers, it was Gregory of Nyssa who presented this thought most systematically.

For the Stoics, who saw God as the soul of the world, God could not be independent of the world. But God is fully transcendent and free of the world for Gregory. Manicheeism held that matter existed eternally alongside God, and was the source of evil. But for Gregory, the material world exists within God, for matter itself is spiritual (a form of energy as we would say). Being the image of God, Man has to be free like God. Evil has its source in this freedom. Gregory also held that evil, as the absence of good, has no ultimate reality. It is in the struggle against evil that man develops his freedom and becomes mature.

Gregory's thought may be compared to Indian thought especially with Sankara's Advita Vendanta and Ramanuja's Vishishtadvaita. Ramanuja's thought is similar to the Stoics in viewing the Cosmos as the body of God. For Sankara, the Cosmos is Brahman misunderstood by avidya. For Gregory, seeing from the perspective of the cosmos, it exists apart from God, and it comes into being from the will of God. However, seeing from God's perspective, nothing exists apart from God, who is infinite. Gregory views the difference between the creator and creation as follows:

creator's being is self-dependent, but creation's being is dependent on God. Also creator's being is no need of a becoming, but the creation's being is in a state of becoming. For Gregory, man's existence in time is not a mere illusion or a dream, but of eternal significance. But for Sankara, the historical existence makes no difference to the jivatma.

## The Way Forward

What lies ahead in our way toward genuine freedom? We have to really make the trip in order to find out. Only a few guidelines about how we may make the trip is possible.

1. The king needs to be replaced with shepherd. The king uses coercive authority, but the shepherd uses persuasive authority. God needs to be seen as a shepherd rather than a king. All the shepherds in the world in all walks of life, including governments, receive their authority from God, the real shepherd, and they need to learn to use persuasive authority. They need to become good shepherds as Jesus describes in John 10 by caring for the sheep and by developing a warm and a healthy relationship with them.

2. Attempts to grasp the ultimate reality need to be abandoned. Any attempt to conceptualize it leads us to frustration. We need to maintain right relationship with the ultimate reality. Being far beyond our power of comprehension, the ultimate reality needs to be praised and adored.

3. A positive and appropriate attitude needs to be developed about our tradition, the path we have already covered. We need to acknowledge our past, with its successes and failures, in order to make a victorious journey forward. We need to become aware of the common heritage of the humanity as a whole. Openness to future without sufficient awareness of the past is superficial. Loyalty to the past tradition without openness to the present or future prevents us from moving on.

4. Discipline needs to be developed with the awareness that if you need to get freedom, you have to give freedom to others. No

privilege without responsibility. People should willingly take part in creating laws and also should willingly obey those laws.

These principles need to be experimented in the laboratories of communities, so that once they are proved to be successful, they can be followed by the human community as a whole. An experimental community needs to be ecumenical with people of various races, of various religious traditions, and of both sexes. Tagore's Shantiniketan, Gandhi's Sabarmati Ashram, and Aurobindo's Ashram are examples of community experiments in India.

# 12. What is Monasticism For?

Metropolitan Paulos Mar Gregorios speaks about monasticism in three of his most important books: *Freedom and Authority (p. 136-162), Human Presence ((p. 106-111),* and *A Light Too Bright, The Enlightenment Today (p. 223-236).* Fr. Paul Verghese was invited by the Lutheran seminaries in the United States to give the Hein Lectures in 1968. The lectures were put together to publish the book, *The Freedom of Man* in the United States. Later the material of this book was modified and expanded for the situation in India, and was published as *Freedom and Authority* in 1974 by CLS and ISPCK. In 1979 the World Council of Churches called a world conference at the Massachusetts Institute of Technology in USA on Faith, Science and the Future of Humanity. Attended by about 500 physical scientists, and about the same number of social scientists and theologians, this conference was chaired by none other than Metropolitan Paulos Mar Gregorios. The conference, which preceded five years of preparation, lasted seven days. *Human Presence* was authored by Mar Gregorios as a preparation for the conference, giving the Christian theological basis for an approach to the Environment problem from the Eastern Orthodox perspective. *A Light Too Bright, The Enlightenment Today,* first published by the State University of New York Press in 1992, is an assessment of the values of the European Enlightenment and a search for new foundations. All these three books speak about a new civilization that needs to be built based on a new worldview in the place of the present decadent one. Such an attempt needs to begin with a community of pioneers who will test this worldview in their monastic community life. What follows is a summary of what Mar Gregorios speaks about this monastic community experiment in these three books.

In addition to these three books, a short article on Monasticism in Malayalam entitled "*Sanyaasajeevitham Enthinuvendi?*" was also found in the collected works of Mar Gregorios --*Sneham, swaathanthryam, puthiya maanavikatha* (p. 628-631). This article originally appeared in a souvenir of The Bethlehem St.Mary's convent in Kizhakambalam in 1971. Mar Gregorios speaks about the meaning of monasticism in this article.

Mar Gregorios presents before us the basic principles of monasticism citing examples from the pre-Christian Qumran monasticism and from the fourth century Christian monasticism. He also makes an evaluation of the modern monastic movements in India using the basic principles. Finally he presents before us a detailed plan of a new monastic movement that can experiment a new worldview that can become the foundation of a new civilization.

### The Early Christian Monasticism

Monastic lifestyle was in existence even before Christ as evidenced in the Qumran communities. The life and teachings of John the baptist and Jesus Christ were very much influenced by the Qumran communities. Christian Monasticism developed later as a movement in Egypt in the fourth century. We will see the characteristics of this early Christian monasticism as explained by Mar Gregorios.

One characteristic of early Monasticism is its anti-clerical temper. The Qumran monks were opposed to the temple and priesthood in Jerusalem. The Christian monks in the fourth century Egypt were laymen, and they were opposed to becoming a priest or a bishop. Another characteristic of Christian monasticism was spiritual athleticism. Influenced by the stoic ideal of apatheia, they strove to keep passions under control. However, the primary characteristics of Christian monasticism was its struggle against the devil and its eschatological orientation.

The Devil is non-being. Jean Paul Sartre explains in his *Being and Nothingness* that it is possible to exist without being. The devil's basic characteristic is to lie and hate, which is the opposite of truth and love. Mar Gregorios quotes Paul Eudokimov, who describes three manifestations of the devil: parasitism, imposture, and parody. The devil lives as a parasite on the being created by God. He dissimulates the divine attributes, substituting equality for resemblance. He also parodies the creator, and constructs his kingdom without God. The Qumran monks and the Christian monks engaged in a battle against the devil in his own territory, symbolized by deserts and jungles. Evil for the church fathers was not a philosophical problem but a real one. They fought evil in one's own self and then in their society. Christ himself modeled this pattern in his life. He fought the devil in private with fasting and prayer before he went public. Even during his ministry, he spent his nights in prayer to gain the power to combat evil during the daytime. If we go to fight with the devil outside us before overcoming him inside us, we become tools in his hands.

Eschatological orientation was another characteristic of Christian monasticism. It refused to identify the kingdom of God with the earthly kingdoms. When the church was free in the fourth century, it was widely believed that the kingdom of God had already realized. The empire of Rome was believed to be the Kingdom of God, and the pope of Rome claimed to be the representative of Christ. The monk protested against this view, pointing to the transcendent kingdom, whose values were not comfort, wealth, or popularity, but love, joy, peace, patience, and simplicity.

### Indian Christian Monasticism

Mar Gregorios rightly points out that the Christian monasteries (ashrams) in India were patterned after the Hindu Ashrams such as Shantiniketan of Tagore, Sevagram of Gandhi, Aurovile in Pondicherry by Aurobindo, Ramanashrama in Tiruvannaamalai by Ramana Maharshi, Ramakrishna mutts, and Theosophical Society in Adayar.

The Christian Ashrams that sprang up include Christukula Ashram in Tirupattur by Dr. E.F. Paton, Christa Sishya Ashram in Tadagam near Coimbatore by Bishop Pakenham Walsh, CPSS Ashram in Poona by Fr. Jacob Winslow, Bethel Ashram in Tiruvalla, by Sisters Edith Neve and Rachel Joseph, and Kodaikanal Ashram Fellowship by Dr. Keithan. These Ashrams began and grew around a non-Indian personality, and therefore, they failed to take root in the Indian soil. Moreover, they lost their vitality with the disappearance of the charismatic non-Indian leader.

However, Christavashram at Manganam, Christa Santhi Sangh in Khatmandu, and Christa Panthi Sangh in Sihora are of Indian origin, with the initiative of Syrian Christians with Anglican or Marthoma church affiliation.

These ashrams couldn't be successful because they couldn't create genuine corporate community and because they were operating with the western evangelical theology and with activism based on that. Mar Gregorios observes that Indians, especially the Syrian Christians in India, are poor at creating genuine community. They either blindly follow a leader, or they quarrel with each other as individualists. The western Christian monastic movement in general has been declining due to a major reason -- the monks and nuns have begun to feel that they have been exploited as cheap labour by the church.

Mar Gregorios further observes that the Christian ashrams in India are severely handicapped in their intellectual limitations as well as in their lack of access to the depths of the Christian spiritual tradition. There had been few among the monks with the intellectual capacity to unravel either the Christian thought or the western secular thought. Other than having some knowledge of English, they had no access to the continental European or other non-English ways of thinking. Indian Christian monasticism hasn't produced any substantial Christian literature of any kind. Mar Gregorios feels that the Syrian Orthodox church of India is responsible for this situation. It still remains closed to the truly creative and dynamic depths of the oriental Christian heritage. Syrian orthodox church had not produced any theologian competent enough to appropriate the depths of the eastern tradition and communicate it to the others.

Mar Gregorios concludes his survey of the Indian monasticism suggesting that we need to learn from its successes and failures, and using the lessons, we need to reinstate a new kind of Ashram.

## The Monastic Experiment Proposed by Mar Gregorios

We will explore the proposal of Mar Gregorios under the questions why, who, how long, what, and how.

## 1. Why do we need a new monastic community?

Mar Gregorios lived in a world that witnessed so many freedom struggles. He saw that a new civilization was emerging in which people will have freedom. However, he humbly withdrew from providing a design of the new civilization. He said:

> If the essence of free humanity could be put down in words before it actually comes into existence, then it would be neither free nor therefore human. For man's authentic existence has to be lived out first before it is described. (Freedom .. p. 136)

That is what the early Christian monks did.

> The monk did not peddle a pot of message, but by severe contempt of the values of a smug society he paved the way for a new world, built on discipline and self-control. (Freedom ...p. 136)

Mar Gregorios invites the laymen and laywomen of the present time to become the monks of this era. They have to show contempt of the values of a decadent civilization by creating a new one in daring and pioneering.

In the new civilization, the arbitrary authority (like that of a king) will be replaced by persuasive authority (like that of a shepherd or a parent). The persuasive authority of a self-sacrificing leader needs to be experimented in monastic community.

Our decadent civilization in its quest for certainty tried to conceptualize what ultimately exists, but failed miserably. As Gregory of Nyssa has shown, the true being of all that exists is nothing less than the dynamic will of God, which we cannot conceptualize. We can approach God only in worship and adoration which uses the whole body, of things and actions, of emotion and will, and of trans-conceptual expressions. Such a holistic approach to the transcendent needs to be experimented in the monastic community.

Today in our decadent civilization, each race, sect, linguistic group, and nation defends its own tradition over against those of the others. Humanity can develop a new vision and create a new civilization only if it develops an awareness of its common heritage. We need to unite our traditions and hold them together with their successes and failures as our common heritage. Although we need to be fully open to the common heritage, we have to stand firm within the community and its tradition within which we were born and brought up. The new monastic community has to experiment this.

Growth of humanity in freedom requires disciplined community life. It begins in one's own family for all people where they learn self-control and develop conscience. The training continues in school, church, etc. A monastic community has to be an ideal community that makes sure that its members are given the best training for them to grow in freedom. At this point Mar Gregorios deals in some detail with the question of the repression of our passions. He agrees with Marcuse that a mere repression of passions cannot give us victory over passions. He calls for a balance between the reality principle and pleasure principle as expressed between social control and personal initiative, work and play, labour and leisure, prayer and humour, study and artistic creativity, fasting and feasting, and mutual acceptance and honest criticism. They will learn strict and joyful self-control of the instinctual drives, without which there is no freedom.

The monastic setup with its rules and regulations constitutes the structure of monastic life. However, we need to remain vigilant lest the structures we create enslave us. Once a structure serves its purpose, we need to discard it, and we need to create another one that suits the purpose. The scriptures, the rituals, fasts, liturgical year etc. are raw materials for building structures. A structure is like a wooden frame necessary or making reinforced concrete. Without such a frame the concrete cannot take the desired shape. Once the concrete gets solidified, the frame is of no use. Scriptures or traditions are not necessary for a full-grown saint, but they are necessary during the growth process. The long-term goal should be the ultimate freedom of man in history when all people have become free and mature needing no structures, all people fully committed to the welfare of all, and all people using their disciplined power, love and wisdom for the whole of humankind.

### 2. Who should be the participants?

In Freedom and Authority (1974) Mar Gregorios called for an Ashram that has all the three sections of Christianity-- Orthodox, Roman Catholic, and Protestants. It should have members from India as well as from abroad (p 160). He further says that the community has to be international and interracial (p147). There could be celibate communities and married communities within the same complex. They will have a leader on a rotation system. In Human Presence (1978), Mar Gregorios calls for an interdisciplinary, intercultural, interreligious community of mature, capable, charismatic people. (p.106). He suggests that Christians may take the initiative to create such a community, which should be open to others as well. It is possible to create subcommunities within the community to accommodate people of various religious traditions. Maximum variety with maximum community should be the ideal. Mar Gregorios explains why the community needs to be multireligious as follows:

> The community could be multireligious in its composition, and part of the community's program will be to foster the higher elements in each religion and to promote respectful mutual understanding among the religions and the secular people. Its handling of the religious life of the different groups within it as well as its devising some common forms of worship and ritual could make a major contribution to the life of the larger society. (A Light Too Bright p. 229)

### 3. How long should they stay together?

Mar Gregorios suggests that there needs a core group with lifelong commitment , and others with a short-term commitment of at least three years (Freedom ... p147). He suggests five to ten years as the time period such a community may exist (Human presence p78)

## 4. How should they live?

They will evolve a healthy community life with simplicity, doing manual labour, not fearing poverty, open to the cultural and religious sensitivities of others, and open to the world outside. They will have a meaningful spirituality as the basis of this lifestyle with prayer, meditation, worship, and sacraments, with loving service with self-sacrifice, overcoming aggressiveness and acquisitiveness, and by being transparent to each other and to the transcendent.

The community and its members should be free from attachment to property. Our identity should not be based on what we have but on what we are. It is not enough to have everything in common for the community members, but the community may not own its means of production. Just as private ownership is limited, privacy itself should be limited in community life. It is absolutely necessary to have a private realm for meditation and prayer. Jesus, who spent several hours in private prayer before he went out to the public, needs to become our model.

Mar Gregorios suggests that the approach of the early monks in their battle against the Devil needs to be emulated in our times as well.

> The monastic community proposed here has tobe aware of an evil will in the universe which desires our non-being. We have to fight against it. (Freedom.... P.158)

He also suggests that their example of fighting the devil within oneself before fighting the devil outside must be strictly followed. We should not jump into social activism before we attain freedom within ourselves.

## 5. What should they do?

They need to engage in serious and informed study and reflection on the problems that confront humanity today. They also need to participate fully in the life and struggles of the community around them, taking an active role its political, social, religious, and cultural life.

The community must be actively engaged in production such as agriculture, industrial, and diaconal, which include health, education, welfare, communication, art, music, research etc. The production should be oriented to serve others, and not accumulate profits. All members should participate in the productive activities, but no one should be required to spend more than four hours a day on such activities. The community needs to find new ways of doing agriculture, industrial production, and diaconal activities-- new ways of educating people, new ways of caring for their health, new art, music and literature related to the contemporary human situation, new and inexpensive professional services easily accessible to the poor. The community would also engage in research on the structures of exploitation and injustice in society. Mar Gregorios gives a strict warning regarding the activities of a monastic community as follows:

> The community's activities will have to come from its own deep convictions, but not    for the sake of feeling missionary or effective. Such actions will be authentic actions    springing out of the true being of the community, even if they fail to achieve anything. (Freedom .. P. 162)

## Conclusion

In a letter to his friends in 1969, Fr. Paul Verghese expressed his wish for a monastic life:

> I need to withdraw for a while to a disciplined community of solitude, reflection and prayer. I see quite clearly that overcoming self is the greatest victory a man can win. I also see that I myself am not making much progress there; neither do most of the people I see around me in the world. The toughness of a disciplined and strong human will is the ingredient without which there cannot be any real salvation for society or individual, and that will can be shaped best in a modern monastic community.

Although Mar Gregorios had this intention deep down in his mind, never had he had a chance to materialize it. Therefore, though he clearly presented a plan for a modern monastic movement, it is yet to happen. Let us hope and pray that someone will have the vision and the will to take initiative to materialize this vision of this great soul.

# Part II: Reflecting On The Gregorian Vision

# 13. What is the Christian View of God?

By the word "God" I mean the ultimate reality or what really exists. But we can never know what really exists as it is; we can know only how the reality appears to us. Although there is only one absolute reality, it appears differently according to the context. The same God appears in various forms to people in different times and places. How God appeared to the people who produced the Bible is the subject-matter of this chapter. I begin explaining how a God-view is different from the real God, and then I explain the purpose of a God-view in human life. Then I trace the evolution

of the Christian God-view as presented in the Nicene Creed from the traditional Jewish God-view.

I am primarily indebted to the work of Metropolitan Paulos Mar Gregorios for this study. In his *Cosmic Man*[1], he has presented the view of the Greek fathers, especially of Gregory of Nyssa. His *Human Presence* also deals with God-Man-World relationship. Although I am indebted to him for the basic insights, the details are mostly from other sources. Also I take the responsibility for any factual errors, logical inconsistencies, or any naive opinions.

However, my immediate inspiration for this study was Prof. Gregory J. Riley's excellent study of this topic in his book, *The River of God*[2]. How the Christian God-view as presented in the Nicene Creed evolved is the topic of this book. Using the three metaphors of river, of genealogy, and of evolution, he traces the evolution of Christianity. This approach doesn't entertain any claims of superiority to any form of religion. It places a specific form of religion in a time and place, and traces its genealogy backward and forward. A form of religion is not necessarily of more quality than its parents or its siblings, and the survival of a form is not always due to better quality. Although I fully agree with Riley on these main points, I differ from him in a number of details such as how a second person was added in the Trinity.

### The Distinction between God and God-Views

Before proceeding to this subject, it is essential to clarify further the distinction I have made here between God and God-views.

What is real appears real in most of the situations. When the reality appears to us as it is, we use the categories of true and false to speak about it. Walking along a path at day time, a snake frightens us. In this situation, that we saw a snake is true, and that we saw a rope is false. We can talk in terms of true and false because the reality is fully known in this situation. We use factual statements to speak about the known reality.

But there are situations in which the reality remains unknown. Walking along a path at dusk, we may get frightened at a piece of rope mistaken to be a snake. The reality that it is a rope is unknown in that situation, and the reality appears as a snake. The ancient story of the blind men examining an elephant also illustrates this distinction. Four different people perceived the same animal in four different ways, and arrived at four different conclusions of what it was. The same animal appeared in four different ways to them. Every day we see the sun rising and setting. Our scientists discovered that this is an appearance. The reality is that the Sun is stationary in relation to the earth; it appears to go around the earth because of the earth's rotation. In situations where we know that the reality remains unknown, we cannot use the categories of true and false; we use the term *absolute truth* to denote the unknown reality, and *relative truth* to denote the appearances. We cannot use factual statements but only opinions when we speak about relative truths.

Something appears to us differently from its reality due to several reasons: The first is a limitation of our senses. It takes a while to realize that all that glitters is not gold; our eyes lack the ability to penetrate the surface and see what is underneath. It is darkness that makes us mistake a piece of rope to be a snake. We see the world through the five senses in their limited capability. If their capabilities vary, or if the number of senses varies, we will perceive the world very differently. For example, if our eyes are as powerful as a microscope, we will see all the microbes all around us all the time. Or, what if we have a sixth sense that can sense the video signals that are broadcast from the TV stations? A second reason would be the perspective, the angle we perceive something from. The Sun appears to rise because we perceive it from the surface of the earth. If we perceive it from the space, far away from the earth, we won't see it rising or setting, but staying stationary. A third would be the distance from where we view something. Travelers in a desert see a lake from a distance, but coming closer they realize that it was nothing but a mirage, which is an illusion created by light refracted by hot air. A fourth reason would be a pre-conditioning of our mind. If we see ten ornaments in a row made of real gold, our mind will easily assume that the eleventh one would also be made of real gold. Thus, depending upon various factors, appearance may vary from reality.

The ultimate reality is unknown; therefore, how we perceive it is how it appears to us. The absolute truth about the ultimate reality is unknown; therefore, what we have are relative truths. The Greek fathers of the Eastern Christendom made a distinction between the essence (*ousia*) and the expression (*energia*) of God following the categories of the classical Greek philosophy. They argued that the essence of God can never be understood; only the expression of God in various ways can be understood even partially by us[3]. According to Vedas, the ancient sacred scriptures of India, Brahman, the one absolute reality, which is unknowable, appears to people as countless gods, who are of diverse character, abilities, and powers. Here, I am using the word "God" to mean the ultimate reality. In its popular use, this word usually means how the ultimate reality appears to us rather than how it really is.

### The Purpose of a God-View

It is possible to have three views regarding the existence of God and our need to imagine God:

1. God exists and we can know God, so there is no need to imagine God.
2. God doesn't exist, and so, only our imagination of God exists, which, of course, is not only useless but also misguiding.
3. God exists but we cannot know God, so we need to imagine God.

According to the first view, the reality exists and we don't need to imagine it because we can comprehend it as revealed to us in the Sacred Scriptures. In revolt against the naivety of this view arises the second one, which goes to the other extreme of denying the very existence of the reality. According to this view, there is nothing behind the appearances, and what we call the reality is nothing but our imagination. Those who hold this view may want to explain to us how an appearance can exist without something to appear. According to the third view, the one which makes sense, the reality exists, but we need to imagine it because we cannot perceive or comprehend the reality as it is.

Whatever we imagine cannot be the real God; however, we still need to imagine God. Let me try to illustrate this idea. When we make a trip, there is a destination we can always see ahead of us. When we continue to move on, the destination we see will also move forward ahead of us. Though this visible destination leads us forward, the ultimate destination remains invisible till we reach there. The human quest for the ultimate truth in life is like such a trip, and its ultimate destination is the ultimate reality or God, who remains invisible. But at every point in this journey, we need a visible destination ahead of us to lead us forward. This visible God, definitely not the real God, helps us to move on in our journey.

In this journey, visible does not mean visible to the eyes, but to the inner eye. We begin this journey as young children seeing God in our parents. As we continue our journey and grow up, we see God in the heroes we admire. As time passes, we outgrow our heroes, but still we need to see something as ultimate in life so that we can keep moving on and growing. We face the temptation to accept pleasures, wealth, and power as our gods. Many of us continue to move on in this journey identifying them as false gods because they do not help us grow in our humanness. A successful life is a journey that keeps on attaining higher levels of humanness by visualizing a God that leads the way. Our visible God also undergoes transformation as we grow in our humanness.

The story of a civilization is also the story of its God that leads its way. In the Bible we see the growth of a civilization; they visualized their God at each stage of their growth. When they were slaves, God was their deliverer. In the desert as nomads, God became their guide, provider, and warrior. As settled farmers, their God assumed the role of a feudal lord who provided them with the land, rain, and other facilities for farming. Eventually as they evolved into a kingdom, their God became a king with an army of angels.

Such a history of God can be traced in the life of any individual or community. God is always there to assist us in varying forms according to our needs. That is how God appears in our sacred scriptures as a shepherd, a mother hen, rock, fire, father, king, potter, sun, and light. Although no image of God can fully represent God, every image serves its purpose in its own context. A context involves some people, a place, a time, a way of life, and the kind of living conditions. An image which is useful at a time may not be so at a different time. One that is useful at a place may not be so at a different place. An image in which a set of people see the ultimate reality could be a worthless thing for another set of people. This calls for creativity in the use of images. Meaningful and successful life would require abandoning outdated images and creating or adapting new ones.

In this respect, an image is very much similar to a word. A word is an audible or a visible medium that represents an idea or thought. An idea is represented by different words in different languages; similarly God, the ultimate reality, is represented by various images in various cultures. A word loses its original meaning as time passes, and acquires new meanings; similarly, an image of God loses its original connection with its meaning, and acquires other meanings. Every religious reformer has tried to bring back the original meaning of the images in a culture or to create some new images. For example, Jesus was accused for subverting the traditional images of his culture; but he asserted that his intention was not to subvert them but to establish them with their original meaning.

One often wonders what might be the most suitable image of God for us. I think it is safer to be creative and flexible, and choose the most suitable image according to the context rather than sticking to the same one. I have had to change my image of God numerous times as I have grown up. In each juncture in my journey, I choose an image of God that appears to be the ultimate to me, and it helps me to deepen and expand my vision of life, and continue my journey with an increased ability to love God and my fellow beings. In choosing the most suitable image of God for our world, we may use a similar criterion – does it help the well being and growth of the humanity? Jesus saw God as a king to the world, and as a father to the human beings. Christianity saw in Jesus God's image. However, the adoption of each image depends very much upon the receptivity and according to the level of awareness and the need of an individual or a community.

A healthy existence is of supreme importance and of primary concern to us. Our healthy existence means our existence in right relationship with all that exists. This is called *shalom* in the Jewish tradition. In the Christian tradition it is more commonly known as the *Kingdom of God*. Shalom became *salaam* in the Islamic tradition, and the very name of the religion, *Islam*, is a variation of salaam. *Loka samastha sukhino bhavanthu* (Let the whole world exist in peace and joy) is the ultimate aspiration in Hindu tradition. The word *shanti* occurs as the synonym of *shalom* in the eastern religions. Thus all religious traditions have within them a deep yearning for the well being of all that exists. The well being of humankind by maintaining right relationship among themselves, with God, and with the environment is the one purpose for which all the religions ideally exist.

Imagine for a moment that you have got hired for a job into an organization. You are assigned a specific role with some specific responsibilities. First you will be given an orientation, which helps you understand what the organization does and what exactly you are supposed to do. You need to know the vision and mission of the organization, the people you work with, and what is expected of you. The better you know your organization, the better you will be able to perform in your role. I have used this example to refer to a huge organization, or better say organism, which is our world itself. At birth, we become parts of this huge organization. Our home, schools, and colleges give us some orientation to live our life as a part of the world. We slowly develop a view of life, which helps us live our life. As we grow in wisdom, we assimilate the principles, laws, and forces that govern the world, and develop healthier relationships with our fellow beings and with the world as a whole.

As there are people at various levels of intellectual, emotional, moral, and spiritual growth in the world at any time, there cannot be a single God-view that fits all. For example, an adult's view has to be different from a child's view. St. Paul admits that when he was a child, he thought like a child, but once he became an adult, he began to think like an adult. The best God-view for a child might be a father-like God sitting on a throne up in the sky. But once the child grows, he/she grows in understanding as well, which enables him/her to realize that the God in the sky is just one view of God. Any attempt to forcefully standardize the God-views is therefore counterproductive. Although I appreciate the content of the Nicene Creed, I do not appreciate the way in which it came into existence. The councils debated on the right beliefs, and those with political power won. Those who disagreed were branded heretics, and were excommunicated. People must have absolute freedom to formulate their own views of God. No social structure should prevent people from their God-given freedom to seek God for themselves.

All God-views are our creations. We create the God-views as stepping stones to our own growth. The world exists on God, but our religions exist on our God-views. By religion, I mean a way of life we create based on a God-view. God cares for human existence, but not for the existence of any religions. It is God's will that we exist and grow to our maximum potential, and we must have the freedom to employ the means to grow. Religions are our creation, and we have the responsibility to make use of them appropriately.

Christianity was born when Jesus revolted against the religious establishment of his land. The existence of religion became more important for them than the existence of mankind. Their God-view became more important than knowing the real God. The means was given more importance than the goal. The ritual rules were treated with more importance than the moral rules. It was in this context that Jesus declared that Sabbath was made for man, and not the other way around.

A new view does not replace an old one in the minds of all people; therefore, the older views exist side by side with the newer ones. Even when those who accept the new view accept it with their conscious minds, the older views linger longer in their subconscious minds. It is like we still say the Sun rises and sets even though we know that it stays stationary in relation to the Earth. Even after the geocentric worldview came into existence, the three-storied worldview continued to exist. Although Einstein's worldview has replaced the Newtonian one, we still use the Newtonian one for most of the practical purposes. The newer God-views have always existed side by side with the older God-views. With such a mindset, we will be able to appreciate the stories of God walking among men even when we realize that no one has ever seen God. We will also be able to enjoy the psalms written in the background of a three-storied world, and take part in the Good Friday celebration commemorating the victory of the prince of heaven over the god of death.

Having a variety of God-views is similar to having several medical systems such as Ayurveda, Homeopathy, Naturopathy, Acupuncture, Chinese medicine, and English medicine. In spite of such diversity in diagnosis and treatment among these different systems, they all have the same goal—help regain health. If the goal is clear in mind, there will be a healthy competition among them as well as a cooperation to learn from each other. This is true for religions as well. If the goal is clear they will cooperate to learn from each other, and they will engage in a healthy competition to serve humankind. If the medical systems take care of our physical health, the religions take care of our spiritual health. In the ancient world, when a human being was not compartmentalized into body, mind, and soul, an illness was seen as that of the whole person. That is why Jesus is presented as someone who could cure the illnesses of body, mind, and soul. He could cure not only the illnesses of individual human beings, but also the illnesses of communities.

Almost all religious traditions unanimously assert without the slightest doubt that we need to know God for our healthy existence. We will have healthy existence when we willingly submit our will to the will of God because it is the will of God that ultimately governs the world. In order to willingly submit our will, we need to love God, and in order to love God, we need to know God. We, human beings, cannot have any *conceptual knowledge* of God. However, we need to know God like the sheep know their shepherd. Here, the word "know" means the ability to identify the godly way of life, and distinguish it from the ungodly ways of life. Let us call it for convenience a *functional knowledge* because such knowledge helps us to function. A healthy existence demands a God-centered life rather than a self-centered life. In the statement "God must be our God", the first God stands for what is really ultimate, and the second God stands for what appears ultimate to us. It is very important for our healthy existence to know what is really ultimate so that we can avoid the temptations from what appears ultimate to us such as wealth, popularity, and pleasure.

At the same time it is important to realize that we can never know the ultimate truth of God conceptually, so that we can refrain from fighting with each other in the name of God. The difference among religions is not in knowing God but in knowing about God.

Our knowledge about God is reflected in our God-views. The purpose and function of a God-view is to help us know God. God-views vary from religion to religion, from time to time, and even from person to person. A God-view may be evaluated using this criterion—does it help us to know God, love God, and surrender our will to the will of God so that we can have a healthy existence? Any God-view that promotes the healthy existence of humankind must be supported and strengthened. But any God-view that prevents a healthy existence must be rooted out from our minds. Knowing God is above our religious differences—it is the same across the religions. Whether you are a Hindu or a Muslim or a Christian or a follower of any other religion, you can know, love, and surrender yourself to God in the same way regardless of your religious difference. This can be compared to the way we use language. Whatever language we use, we communicate the same kind of information almost in the same way. A religion is like a language. Using it as a tool, we can know and love God, and surrender our will to the will of God.

**The God-View of Traditional Judaism**

The ancient Jewish civilization saw the whole world as a single God-centered system. The hymn of Creation, in the first chapter of the Book of Genesis, gives us a beautiful picture of the God-centered world. The world is a farm, and God is a farmer there. The farmer arrives at a chaotic and disorderly world, and converts it into an orderly and beautiful place. The whole is made of its component parts, and the parts together make the whole. A whole day is made of its parts, the day and night. Earth is made of its parts—land, sea, and air. Plants grow on the earth, birds fly in air, fish swim in water, and animals walk and crawl on land. Human beings rule all other beings on the earth. All these parts constitute the whole, referred to as the 'World'.

Existence of the world depends upon relationships. There are dependent relationships between parts of the whole, and between parts and the whole. There is a relationship between land and sea, between day and night, between male and female, and among human beings. All relationships are governed by laws and agreements. Any action by a part affects the whole. Therefore no relationship can exist if laws are broken. Thus laws are essential to the existence of the world.

> Praise him, sun and moon. Praise him, all you shining stars. Praise him, you highest heavens. Praise him, you waters above the skies. Let all of them praise the name of the Lord, because he gave a command and they were created. He set them in place for ever and ever. He gave them laws they will always have to obey. Psalm 148: 3-6

Laws for the world are created and established by God. As a Law-giver, God is a king, and the world is God's Kingdom. This metaphor became popular probably when the Jewish people experienced a Kingdom under David and Solomon. God appoints people under Himself hierarchically to rule representing Him. Thus God appoints the Sun to rule the day, and the moon to rule the night. Human beings are appointed to rule all other beings on the earth.

All beings in the world have to follow the laws for the world to exist in harmony. All beings are God's servants, who normally obey God's laws unquestioningly. As the psalmist sings:

> Thou hast established the earth, and it abideth.
> They continue this day according to thine ordinances:
> for all are thy servants. Psalm 119: 90-91
> He makes the clouds His chariot;
> He walks upon the wings of the wind;
> He makes the winds His messengers,
> Flaming fire His ministers. Psalm 104: 3-4

All inanimate things and most living beings are programmed to obey the laws, for they do not have the option to disobey. The sun and moon, land and sea, plants and animals— all are God's servants.

However, human beings, created in God's own image and likeness, are not programmed to obey the laws. Endowed with free will, they have the option to disobey. Unlike the other beings, the human beings have to willingly choose to surrender to the laws. They have the option of denying the laws or obeying the laws. Although they are not programmed to obey the laws automatically, they are programmed to understand the laws and grow infinitely. They have to learn to obey the laws willingly as they grow up. This special relationship between God and human beings is expressed in another familiar metaphor-- God as father and human beings as God's children. Although God is a king to the whole world, God is a father to the human beings.

This relationship is very well illustrated in the story of Jonah. All the servants of God in the story obey God unquestioningly. God commands the wind to blow on the ship that carries Jonah, and later a big fish to carry him to Nineveh. Still later, God appoints a plant to give shade to Jonah, and the next day, God appoints a worm to attack the plant. All these are God's servants, and they do not have an option to disobey (Jonah 1:4, 17, 4:6, 7) However, Jonah has the freedom to disobey because he is not a servant to God, but a child of God. He is not programmed to obey automatically, but he is programmed to learn and grow. That is why God teaches him an important lesson. Jonah has the opportunity to grow, but the servants of God do not have that opportunity.

In the story of Adam and Eve, we see an example of how human beings refuse to submit to the laws. God is like a feudal lord in that story, and Adam and Eve are like tenants. They can live there and eat from there. They are responsible to take care of the garden. But they are not supposed to eat from one tree, which belongs to the Lord. They choose to break the law when they eat from the forbidden tree. When law is broken, relationships are also broken. Breaking a law is a mistake and it has far-reaching consequences. Being God's children, they always have the option to correct the mistake. However, Adam and Eve do not correct their mistake. Without taking the responsibility of their mistake, they place the blame on others. They don't apologize for their mistake.

Whenever a law is broken, the whole world suffers its consequences. This places a huge responsibility upon human beings. Although human beings are not programmed to obey the laws automatically, they are programmed to learn and discover for themselves the importance of laws, and the need to obey the laws. If they see God as an unfriendly power that forces laws upon them, they tend to disobey the laws. However, as they grow to see God in friendly terms, they begin to obey the laws willingly.

Thus it is love toward God that makes people obey God willingly. A law obeyed willingly ceases to be a law. Jeremiah differentiated the old covenant from the new one as follows.

"This is the covenant I will make with the people of Israel after that time," declares the LORD.

"I will put my law in their minds and write it on their hearts. I will be their God, and they will be my people." Jer. 31:33

The old was external – written on stone tablets, but the new one is internal – written on the walls of the human heart. A law coming from within is no more a law, but one's own will and desire. Love is the last thing that can be compelled on anyone by law. People can be forced to pretend love, but real love that springs from the heart cannot be forced upon anyone by law. If not by law, how can people be made to love God and their fellow beings? Jesus answered this question. He showed people a God who loves them unconditionally. He said, "Love your enemies, for God, your Father, loves His enemies. God gives rain and raises his Sun for both righteous and wicked people" (Mat. 5:44-45). This understanding that God loves us even if we hate God makes us love God willingly. In order to willingly surrender our will to God's will, we must have wholehearted love toward God. Such love to God springs from our heart only if we have a strong conviction that God loves us unconditionally.

This idea is represented very well in the Lord's Prayer, the one prayer most of the Christians pray several times a day. In this prayer God is the king of the world, but a father to the human beings. God's will, the laws that govern the world, must be done for the world to exist. Human beings have to consciously submit themselves to the will of God while the rest of the creation is programmed to follow the will of God.

In its most general application, the word Law means the law given by God for the whole world to exist. In a limited sense the same word was used by the Jewish people to refer to the first five books of the Bible because those books represented the law of God for them.

Later in the Jewish history, this concept of law was represented by another term—wisdom. The wisdom of God is the source of the Law upon which the world exists. In Proverbs we see wisdom personified, and is called a craftsman of the world (Prov. 8: 22-31). For Jesus, the will of God is probably synonymous with the Law of God. The Kingdom of God for Jesus is where the will of God is done. That is why Jesus claims that the Law of God won't change even if the sky and earth pass away. The same concept was also represented by the term, God's word. In the Hymn of Creation in Genesis, God creates the world with a command.

> Your word, O LORD, is eternal; it stands firm in the heavens. Your faithfulness continues through all generations; you established the earth, and it endures. Your laws endure to this day, for all things serve you. Ps. 119: 89- 91

A similar idea existed in the Greek Philosophy, especially in Plato. Plato believed that it was an emanation of God that created the world. Plato called this emanation Demiurge, which means craftsman. Philo, a Jewish Philosopher who lived in Alexandria at the same time Jesus lived in Palestine, found Plato's worldview very appealing and very similar to the Hebrew worldview. Philo preferred the term Logos for Demiurge. The term Logos has its own history starting from Heraclitus, another Greek philosopher. By Logos Philo meant the sum total of all the fundamental principles and laws upon which the world exists.

**The Christian God-View**

This idea appealed to the community that created John's Gospel and it was adopted wholeheartedly. The relation between God and Logos is related to father-son relationship by John's gospel. The father creates everything through the Son. The father cannot be known; only through the Son can we know the father. Even Logos can be known only through the world, in which these principles and laws become visible. Thus the idea of logos was a natural development from the Jewish idea of God's law, which governs the world. Here I am differing from Prof. Gregory J. Riley who argues in his popular book "The River of God" that the idea of logos was created anew as a necessary link to connect the transcendent God with the material world in the geocentric worldview.

The community of John's gospel further asserted that in the life and work of a fellow human being in Palestine they could see the full embodiment of Logos. This man, Jesus, revealed Logos through his life and activities. John's gospel reminds us of the Book of Genesis. In Genesis we read how God creates the world by uttering a series of commands. On the last day of creation, God creates man in His own image. John's Gospel echoes the Genesis Hymn of Creation, but makes some fine distinctions and adaptations based on the changed worldview. Accordingly, God creates everything through Logos, and in Jesus they could see the visible image of Logos in the full measure. This reminds us of how Paul relates Jesus to Adam in the Epistle to Romans. Adam was created as the visible image of the invisible God to represent God in the world. However, Adam became irresponsible. Instead of doing the will of God, he followed his own will. On the other hand, Jesus followed the will of God unto death, and thus stayed responsible to his calling as God's image and representative.

Thus in Jesus, the community of John's gospel sees the inauguration of a new humanity that deviates from the destructive path mankind has been following. Presenting himself as a role model, Jesus invites others to join him in revealing Logos in their lives. As more and more people joined the movement of Jesus, it became a dynamic mass movement that had the power to determine the future of the world. It proved that following the example and leadership of an individual, a community could become the embodiment of Logos. An invitation to join this community of Logos is the good news of John's Gospel. It is an invitation to follow the path of light leaving the path of darkness. It is an invitation to follow the path of truth and honesty leaving a life of lie and dishonesty. In short, it is an invitation to live a meaningful life as the very embodiment of Logos.

## The World-in-God View

Depending upon how the relationship between God and world is understood, our view of God can be one of the following:

1. God-in-World view
2. God-and-World view
3. God-is-World view
4. World-in-God view.

In God-in-World view, the world is larger than God, and God is a part of the world. In God-and-World view, God and world exist side by side independent of each other. God-is-World view does not differentiate between God and world; they are one and the same. According to the world-in-God view, God is bigger, and the world exists within God.

God-in-World view is the most popular view irrespective of culture and religion. It is illustrated by various metaphors in the Bible. If the world is a kingdom, God is like its king. If the world is like a farm, God is like its farmer. If the world is like a family, God is like its father. Although this is the most favorite view and an easy-to-conceptualize one, it is contradictory to our sense of logic and rationality. How can God, the creator of the world, be a part of the world? If God is a part of the world, God must be a subject of study under Science; however, God is not a subject of study under any branch of science. Thus this view always brings religion into confrontation with science.

In God-and-World view, God and world exist side by side, independent of each other. God might have created the world at the beginning, but now it exists by itself without depending on God. A literal interpretation of the metaphor of creator-creation is what lies behind this view. It sees the world as a machine that works by itself once its creator set it to work. Thus this view makes God unnecessary for the world to exist. This view might be considered a stepping stone to the God-is-World view. From a God-and-World view one will move to a God-is-world view. Moreover, God cannot be infinite according to this view, for God ends where the world begins. This view also comes into confrontation with science as it does not agree with our rationality.

The God-is-World view equates God with the world. Atheism, Materialism, and pantheism are just variations of this view with slight differences in details and emphases. This view's God is bigger than the God of the God-in-World view. In the God-in-World view, God is only a part of the world, but in this one, God is as big as the world itself. But by equating God with the world, it makes itself not only a useless view but a very harmful one. In effect it negates God's existence, and as a result, we are without a God. This is the dominant view in the modern world today. What we call secular societies function with such a worldview. This view probably evolved in revolt against the naivety of the God-in-world view and the God-and-World view. It has successfully overthrown the first two views from all the significant places in our life such as politics, science, and education. However, organized religions, which are still dominated by those views, are still around, and are powerful. God-in-World view and God-and-world view are clashing with God-is-World view for dominance all around the globe. Today the human race is under the peril of annihilation due to the devastating effects of these destructive views and the clashes between them. These three views need to be replaced by the World-in-God view if the humanity wants to survive.

The World-in-God view corrects the fallacy of the first three views. Though it affirms God's existence as in the first two views, it does not share their naivety. Because it is fully rational and logical, it does not clash with science. The world, which exists in the limits of time and space, must derive its existence from something that exists beyond these limits. God has to be beyond the limits of time and space, and hence, God cannot be in the world as a part of the world. Existing beyond the limits of time and space, God is infinite, and the world must be within God. As God is beyond the limits of time and space, God is beyond our thought patterns as well, which makes God entirely incomprehensible to us. As this view does not claim any knowledge of God, it does not come into any confrontation with science. Thus science and religion make a united front with the World-in-God view. This view further claims that the world appears to exist within God as we view from our perspective, but viewed from God's perspective, nothing exists apart from God. There is continuity from God's side, though there is discontinuity from our side.

Anyone or any community that honestly seeks God will pass through the first three views before settling down in the last view. The first two views are popular among those who understand the scriptures literally. A realization of the naivety of these views usually leads to the God-is-World view. It takes another enlightenment to move on to the World-in-God view.

Although the World-in-God view was implicit in Jesus' teachings, the first successful attempt to state it explicitly was made by the fathers of the Eastern Christendom in the first few centuries after Christ. What follows is how I understand the thought of Gregory of Nyssa in this regard. I am referring to the excellent study of the thought of Gregory of Nyssa by Paulos Mar Gregorios in his "Cosmic Man, the Divine Presence".

All that exists can be divided into two: Created and uncreated existences. The created existence exists within the limits of time and space, but the uncreated existence has no such limits. Thus, the uncreated existence is infinite, but the created existence is finite. Because the uncreated existence is infinite, the created existence exists within it. Because the created existence changes according to time and space, it depends on the uncreated existence, which is changeless. Because the created existence is finite, there is an unbridgeable gap between the created and uncreated existences, viewed from the side of the created existence. But viewed from the side of the uncreated existence, no such gap exists. In our everyday language, the uncreated existence is called God, and the created existence is called world. Such a division exists only when viewed from the side of the world; from God's view, nothing exists apart from God, because God is infinite, and the world is finite.

### God as Trinity

Viewed from the side of the world, God appears to be a separate reality from the world. Because of this, God also appears in three forms with three different functions. But viewed from the side of God (uncreated existence), God is one. Father is the absolute standard and source. Son, born from the Father, incarnates, taking upon himself the limits of time and space, thus identifying with (or becoming) the created existence. The Holy Spirit, generating from the Father, guides the Son (thus, the created existence).

The Holy Spirit was conceived as the third person in God after father and son. All the functions and role of the breath of God was transferred over to the Holy Spirit. Giving life to all living beings was considered the general and primary function of the breath of God. The Nicene Creed describes the primary role of the Holy Spirit as the giver of life to all. The Nicene Creed also describes another role of the Holy Spirit as speaking through prophets.

God's role in relation to the world has always been identified as a dynamic creative agent. This role as a creative agent couldn't be given to God when God was seen as transcendent in the geocentric worldview. When a second person of God was identified as the sum total of all the principles and laws that govern the world (Son), this role couldn't be ascribed to him either. That is perhaps why the Holy Spirit had to be added as a third person with this role as a creative agent. Father represents the ultimate reality, who is transcendent, infinite, and incomprehensible. The Son and Holy Spirit represent the two ways in which the ultimate reality is related to the world, as it appears to humans.

It is possible that in the early centuries, various Christian communities gave primacy to either the Son or to the Holy Spirit. Some communities saw God primarily as the Son, the personification of the sum total of all the principles and laws that govern the world. But some communities saw God primarily as the Holy Spirit, the creative and driving force behind the world. Behind all the diversities in God, Father, who is transcendent, infinite, and incomprehensible, served as an integrating principle, for we think of God, ultimately, God is incomprehensible to us.

The finitude of the created existence involves a possibility and potential for change and growth. The Father represents the fundamental and stable principle and standard upon which everything else happens, but the Son represents endless growth and development. The finitude of the world is not something apart from God, but something that happens within God.

The human presence makes the created existence conscious. The limits of time and space give Man the potential for endless growth. His growth is not automatic; he has to choose to grow. He also has to choose the path of his growth. His growth is self-directed. This privilege gives man a special responsibility; he has to take care of the rest of the world as his own body.

The limits of time and space is like a blindfold for man. He can't see the future at all. Also this makes him enter the world with no knowledge at all. He has to toil to keep himself alive through time. He has to fight against the forces of death for a bare survival. But he is not without help. Always available is the support and guidance of the Holy Spirit. Thus human life is a journey toward the Father, along with the Son (or as the son), with the guidance and support of the Holy Spirit. This is the view of God as Trinity as presented in the Nicene Creed.

God is presented as Trinity in the Nicene Creed, and it seems to be the best God-view evolved in the Christian tradition. Although it has been recited by most of the Christians in their worship for the last one and a half millennia, it is doubtful whether it has served as a meaningful foundation to the lives of most of them. Instead of seeing it as an example of an excellent God-view, it was fossilized, literally believed, and was transferred from generation to generation. Thus most of the Christians all over the world learned it by heart, and recited it faithfully almost every day without knowing what it is all about. It was easier to fall into the trap of staying hooked into it rather than developing a more sophisticated creed for their own context.

Christianity could evolve such a brilliant God-view because of its openness and willingness to learn from others. It was willing to revise its worldview by including the insights it received from the Philosophy and Science of the Greco-Roman world. Such willingness to adopt and adapt was probably what eventually made Christianity the dominant religion of the Roman Empire. Modern-day

Christianity needs to learn a lesson from this. If it is open, and is willing to learn from others, it has a future. If it remains a closed community unwilling to learn from others, its survival is unlikely. Christianity may want to see the variety of God-views available through other religious traditions as an opportunity to learn and grow. Such willingness to learn from others will make its own God-view much deeper and stronger. Even within Christianity, the God-views vary in the various traditions such as Orthodoxy, Catholicism, and Protestantism. Instead of each group trying to prove that they are right and the others are wrong, they all need to be willing to learn from each other. Such willingness to learn and grow will enable Christianity to evolve a much more sophisticated God-view than that of the Nicene Creed.

**Conclusion**

I have tried to explain what a God-view is, and why we need one. Then I have shown how the Jewish God-view evolved further to become the Christian God-view as presented in the Nicene Creed. I have argued that although this God-View is a very brilliant one, the Christian tradition still needs to remain dynamic in order to remain alive and meaningful.

# 14. What is our World Like?

What is our world like? If I address this question to ten different people, I will get ten different answers. Whenever I have asked this question to myself, my own answers have varied from time to time. When I searched for an answer to this question in the ancient scriptures and classics, I found that the answer to this question has varied from time to time and from place to place. When farming was the primary means of living for most of the people in the world, the world was seen as a huge farm. When there were kingdoms all over the world, the world was seen as a huge empire. In the industrial age, when people invented machines, the world was seen as a humongous machine. Later in the age of networked computers, the world has been seen as a huge network in which everything is connected to everything else. There is something in common with all these metaphors. They unanimously assert that the world is one system with all its parts working together.

Recently I addressed this question to myself again, and the novelty of the answer that surfaced in my mind surprised me. It also challenged me to radically transform my own life. What is our world like? My answer was this: It is like a moving electric train. I can see raised eyebrows. Let me briefly explain what I mean by this.

A train has several bogies, but they are connected together, and so it can move forward as one vehicle. The world consists of so many different component parts, but they all work together as one system. This idea is very well expressed in the above-mentioned metaphors. But this metaphor of the moving train goes beyond all those metaphors.

The word "moving" is significant here. I have related the world to a moving train, not to a stationary one. Our world is never stationary; it keeps moving. Its existence in space-time is what makes it move. Movement in space-time is expressed as changes in form. Nothing in the world is free from change, and this process seems endless. Did this process begin anytime? We just don't know. Human mind cannot conceptualize endlessness. We ourselves are within this moving train, and we cannot go out of this train and look at it objectively. Our mind is conditioned with this movement, and all our thoughts are relative to this movement.

But the movement of this train depends on two stationary things. One is the rails underneath and the other is the electric power line that goes above it. The world also depends on two stationary things. The world, which constantly changes according to space-time, depends upon a set of laws that do not change according to space-time. This set of laws is like the rails on which the train runs. The world cannot function without laws. The power line above gives a constant supply of energy for the train to keep moving. Without a constant supply of power, the train cannot move. The world keeps moving in time with all its changes because of a constant power supply. All the energies such as light, heat, electricity, magnetism, gravity, and life are the diverse forms of this power supply. The world cannot keep moving without these energies. Our sciences are our attempts to discover the various laws that govern the world and the various forms of energy that activate the world.

Now we come to the special role of humankind. Being a part of the world we share the same characteristics of the world. We are within space-time limit, and not free from change. So we have birth, growth, decay, and death. Our existence is also governed by laws. The laws applicable to the rest of the world are applicable to us too. We are also sustained by energies like the rest of the world, especially by life energy.

One may wonder if life can be called an energy like the rest of the energies. The truth is that we haven't found the true nature of life yet. I read somewhere that life may be better called an energy-processing mechanism. Here I am placing it along with energies because it shares certain characteristics of other energies. It is the presence of life that makes one alive like the presence of electricity makes a bulb lit. Life appears in various forms of plants and animals like electricity appears in various forms through different kinds of machines.

We know that the continued existence of the world depends upon the laws that govern it and the energies that sustain it. The world that appears to our eyes seems to be the expression of the invisible energies limited and governed by laws. But what lies behind the laws and the energies? Where do the laws and the energies come from? We don't know. It seems we can never know the answer to this question. Our ignorance does not mean that a source doesn't exist. A source of laws and energies exists, but human mind doesn't have the ability to conceptualize it. Whatever we think and verbalize can't be true about this Super Source.

However, without this piece, the puzzle won't be complete. Although the Super Source behind the laws and energies remains unknown, we may create a symbol to represent it so that we can complete the puzzle, and have a view of all that exists. It is like using an X for an unknown variable in an algebraic equation.

Humankind exists in a very special relationship with the Super Source and with the rest of the world. Humankind is similar to the rest of the world in most of the aspects, and it is also similar to the Super Source in certain aspects. This similarity to both the Super Source and to the world places humankind in between them in the role of a link or a mediator. Coming back to the metaphor of an electric train, humankind is like the driver of the train. The driver is a part of the moving train. However, unlike the remaining parts of the train, the driver has the freedom and the responsibility to run the train and make decisions about it. Humankind is similar to the rest of the world in that it is subject to all the laws that govern the world, and it needs the energies that sustain the rest of the world. However, unlike the rest of the world, it can consciously choose its path. While the rest of the world automatically follows the laws, humankind can choose to obey them or disobey them. Whatever humankind chooses to do, its consequences will be shared by the rest of the world as well. Wise choices will lead to beneficial consequences, and unwise choices will lead to unfortunate consequences.

Humankind has the responsibility to drive this world in such a way that the world will continue to move on smoothly. This responsibility is entrusted to humankind by the Super Source. In order to do this, humankind needs to know the laws that govern the world, and needs to be aware of the energies that make the world run. Humankind also needs to be very well aware of its own place in the world and the special role it has to play.

What does this picture of the world mean to us as individual human beings? Each individual is a driver of his own world, and the way he drives it affects his world. The choices he makes can be beneficial or harmful to his world. He needs to drive according to the laws and he is given energies to move on. He is entrusted with the responsibility to drive his world at the best of his knowledge and ability.

### The Role of Science and Religion

Science seems to be primarily an extension of our rationality, our left brain, and religion seems to be primarily an extension of our right brain. They are complementary, not contradictory. We need both, not one or the other. They help humankind perform its duty as the driver of the world.

Science explores the laws that govern the world. The Greek word Logos originally stood for the sum total of all the laws and principles that govern the world. Accordingly, the word Biology, made of bios + logos, would mean the laws that govern the living beings. Science also explores the nature of the various energies that make the world run. However, science limits itself to the observable phenomena, and remains silent about whatever that cannot be observed. Science remains silent about the Super Source behind the laws and energies of the world. Science can't say anything about the role and responsibility of humankind as well.

This is where religion comes to our aid. Where science stops, religion begins. Religion does not claim to know what science doesn't. It merely helps us to live our life meaningfully in spite of our ignorance. By the word 'religion' I mean the true religion, how religion ought to be, not the corrupted forms of religion we see around. Religion helps us create a meaningful worldview and a view of life on which we can build our life. It helps us create hypotheses, metaphors, and symbols where information is lacking, and facts and evidences are unavailable. Whereas science keeps silent about the Super Source, religion creates a symbol to represent it, so that we can have a picture of all that exists. This picture helps us answer the basic questions of existence, and build up a meaningful life.

Religion deals with beliefs, opinions, hypotheses, metaphors, and symbols unlike science, which mostly deals with facts, theories, and observable phenomena. Therefore it is almost impossible to keep religion from getting corrupted. Whereas science universally stays as a coordinated movement, religious movements keep splitting, which seems unavoidable. It takes sustained, conscious effort to keep the true religious spirit alive and active without getting corrupted. Corrupted religion endangers the existence of humankind. The solution is to strengthen the true religious spirit and fight against the corruption, not to get rid of religion itself. Getting rid of religion is even more dangerous to the existence of humankind because without it we wouldn't know what we are and why we live.

But how do we identify a corrupted form of religion from an uncorrupted form? A lot of people make a quick and naïve judgment: *my own religion is the true and uncorrupted religion, and all the others are corrupted*. This view makes a follower of a certain religion look down upon the followers of every other religion. Once we manage to transcend such naivety, we will look for a standard to distinguish between corrupted and uncorrupted forms of religion. The only standard I can think of is this: a form of religion that stands for the well being of all creation is an uncorrupted form of religion. If anything less than that is the goal of a certain form of religion, it is a corrupted form. We need to ask ourselves if our own form of religion is corrupted or not. This is a call for self-examination. Let us look for the beams in our own eyes instead of seeking the specks in the eyes of others.

### Insights from my own religious tradition

One might wonder how I developed this worldview. Let me explain. I have got the insights to develop this worldview from my own form of religion—the Eastern Orthodox Christianity. This is not to claim that this particular form of religion is an uncorrupted form of religion. Far from it. There have been a lot of corruptions in this form as well. However, if one digs deep enough through the piles of corruption, one can discover an uncorrupted form of religion in the life and work of the fourth century church fathers. This writer lacks the necessary competence to make such an excavation by crossing the linguistic and cultural barriers of this ancient civilization.

I heavily depend upon the work of Metropolitan Paulos Mar Gregorios, who excavated precious pearls of wisdom from the fourth century fathers. His doctoral dissertation, later published as *Cosmic Man*[1], is an in-depth study of the thought of Gregory of Nyssa, a fourth century Christian philosopher. In the introduction he sates: *The theme of this book focuses on humanity's two basic relationships—to the source and ground of its being on the one hand, and to the created world in which the humanity is placed on the other.* P. viii

Mar Gregorios asserts that it is fatal for humanity to ignore these two poles. Equally fatal are both an other-worldly mysticism, that ignores humanity's existence in history, and a secular humanism, that ignores the ground and source of the cosmos.

### Conclusion

Here I have made an attempt to present the worldview of Paulos Mar Gregorios and of Gregory of Nyssa as I understand it in a very simplified form. I have managed to avoid the technical/theological terms as much as possible to make it palatable for the ordinary readers. The purpose of writing this is to encourage others to join me in this study.

I have tried to present a picture of all that exists using the metaphor of a moving electric train. First I explained how the world is related to God. The world experiences this relationship in three different modes: the laws on which it exists (Logos), the energies that keep it alive and active (Spirit), and the Super Source of these two (the Father). Then I explained how humankind is related to the world. Though it is a part of the world, it shares some characteristics of God. Humankind has the responsibility to stand as a link between God and world, and manage the smooth functioning of the world on behalf of God.

# 15. What is Wrong with Secularism?

Secularism is one of the major topics dealt with by Metropolitan Paulos Mar Gregorios. He was never tired of explaining how harmful secularism is in a number of his books and in numerous research papers. Here I am making an attempt to introduce in a few words what Mar Gregorios was trying to tell us through these books and papers. *Enlightenment East and West[1]*, *A Light Too Bright[2]*, and *The Secular Ideology[3]* are the three major works that deal with this topic. About the first two books, he says in his autobiography:

THE SECULAR IDEOLOGY
AN IMPOTENT REMEDY FOR INDIA'S COMMUNAL PROBLEM

Paulos Mar Gregorios

> More recently I have done some significant non-theological writing. The Indian Institute of Advanced Study gave me a study fellowship which enabled me to write my Enlightenment: East and West published by that Institute and favorably reviewed in India. The State University of New York Press wanted to publish it jointly with the Institute, but the latter was not willing for some reason. In any case, the Shimla book had been written with an Indian readership in mind, pointing out that the great Founding Father of our nation, Jawaharlal Nehru, was primarily a child of the European Enlightenment, and not a promoter of the Indian heritage. For SUNY Press, I decided to write another book on the same theme, this time with the western readership in mind. That came out in 1992 under the title A Light Too Bright: The Enlightenment Today. Reviews so far have been favorable, though not raving.

The *Secular Ideology* is a collection of essays which were put together by Mar Gregorios toward the eve of his life. However, it could be published only in 1998, two years after his passing. This book deals with secularism in the specific context of India. Also he dealt with this theme in the *Dudley Lectures* at Harvard. He says:

> I gave the Dudley Lecture at Harvard University in 1979, questioning the then prevailing thesis that secularization was an irreversible process. I saw then that religion had to come back into public life in some new form, and would do so fairly soon. That was an unfashionable view for the establishment, and Harvard Theological Review, which had agreed in advance to publish my lecture, regretted their inability to abide by the agreement.

Although his lecture was not published as such, a report of his lecture appeared in the Divinity Bulletin of the Harvard Divinity School.[4]

### What is Secular?

Mar Gregorios traces the meaning of this word from the beginning of the Christian era. The Latin word Saeculum meant world. When a lot of people renounced the world (saeculum) and adopted a life of monastic rule (regula), a distinction developed as religious (monastic) and secular (non-monastic). During the French revolution, a property under the control of a monastery was taken away from its control and brought under public ownership. This process was called secularization.

A few centuries ago Christianity was the state religion in Europe. In those days an organized church controlled the state as well as all the political, economic, academic and cultural institutions of society. It took a very long process, both revolutionary and evolutionary, to liberate the state and the institutions of society from the control of the church. This process was called secularization.

What do we mean today when we say that India is a secular state? It means India is not like its neighboring state, Pakistan, which has adapted a particular religion as its state religion. Non-Muslims are second class citizens in Pakistan. For example, a non-Muslim cannot witness against a Muslim. In India, all people are given equal rights regardless of their religious affiliation, resisting the very strong pressure from the majority religious community belonging to Hinduism to make it the state religion.

### What is Secularism?

Although the word secularism sounds related to secular, it has a very different meaning. Mar Gregorios asserts that secularism belongs to the category of religions. It is an ideological system of concepts and values. Here is a definition of secularism from a 19th century American orator.

"Secularism is a religion, a religion that is understood. It has no mysteries, no mumblings, no priests, no ceremonies, no falsehoods, no miracles, and no persecutions. Secularism is the religion of humanity; it embraces the affairs of this world; it is interested in everything that touches the welfare of a sentient being; it advocates attention to the particular planet in which we happen to live; it means that each individual counts for something; it is a declaration of intellectual independence; it means that the pew is superior to the pulpit, that those who bear the burdens shall have the profits and that they who fill the purse shall hold the strings." Robert Green Ingersoll, (1833-1899) 5

Secularism seems to be a full-fledged ideological system developed in revolt against the domination of Christian church in Europe. It is very important to distinguish between secular and secularism because they are not the same. India is a secular state, but not a state of secularism. If India adopts secularism as its state religion, it will be another nation like Pakistan, and it won't be secular any more.

It seems that the religion of secularism is slowly bringing the entire world under its control. In *Saving Leonardo*, Nancy Pearcey makes a compelling case that secularism is destructive and dehumanizing. Pearcey reveals the goal of the book at the outset: "to equip you to detect, decipher, and defeat the monolithic secularism that is spreading rapidly and imposing its values on your family and hometown."6 Like Europe was controlled by the church in the Middle Ages, this new religion has already taken control of the whole world. It looks like the world is in need of another secularization to get out of the control of secularism.

Secularism is fine as long as it stays as one of the religions, but we don't want it to become the state religion or ideology. What we want is a secular state like the one we have in India, not a state controlled by secularism.

### The Context in India

The unity of the nation is in danger due to communal conflicts. The solution being suggested by so many intellectuals is the adoption of secularism. They seem to make such a suggestion primarily because they do not distinguish between secular and secularism. Mar Gregorios suggests that secularism is a religion, and it can coexist with other religions in India, but it should not become the state religion. Jawaharlal Nehru and Sarveppalli Radhakrishman represent two different approaches to secularism.

Nehru, as the first prime minister of the free India, had a very difficult task, and he suggested a secular and scientific approach for India's development. In Discovery of India he wrote:

"The modern mind ….. is practical and pragmatic, ethical and social, altruistic and humanitarian. … It has discarded the philosophical approach of the ancients; their search for ultimate reality, as well as the devotionalism and mysticism of the medieval period. Humanity is its God, and social science it religion."[7]

This is the view followed by a lot of intellectuals in India today. Although Nehru had a vision of India, the truth is that he did not lay down any proper intellectual foundations for his secular scientific approach. If we are faithful to his vision, we have to honestly question some of his assumptions. We will be dishonoring his vision if we take his assumptions as dogmatic truth.

We don't need to go very far for a correction to Nehru's view. S. Radhakrishnan, the president of India and a close friend to Nehru, had a very different view from Nehru. Although western-educated like Nehru, his vision was not grounded on the western secularism or a scientific view; his was firmly grounded on the traditional Upanishadic view of life. He believed in the unity of all that exists. He recognized as early as 1940s that a purely secular materialist Marxist movement, however revolutionary and creative it may at first appear to be, could not but come to grief.

## How do we face the threat of Secularism?

The best way to deal with secularism might be to find the roots of secularism and try to eliminate them. The primary root of secularism seems to lie in the false dichotomous worldview that divides the world into natural and supernatural. Such a worldview existed in the western Latin branch of Christianity since fourth century. Nature according to this false view is what we can experience and understand without revelation. It is a self-contained realm operating by its own principles different from the realm of revelation, grace, and super-nature. God can occasionally intervene in the realm of nature causing supernatural events of grace, revelation, and miracles.

Nature, according to this view, is far away from the supernatural and from God, which makes it evil. Salvation is for man to escape from this realm and enter the supernatural realm. Christ came down from the supernatural realm to the natural realm to save the human beings who were to be saved. Church is the group of the saved people eagerly waiting to get out of this miserable place and get transported to the realm above. Church members are definitely superior to the nonmembers. This view made the Christians look down upon others and rule over them.

People started revolting against this dichotomous worldview by denying the existence of a supernatural realm. If there is no supernatural, all that is left is our natural realm that we see around us. There is nothing beyond what we can perceive with our five senses, and whatever exists can be studied by our science. This is the creed of secularism, and it empowered the philosophical movement called European Enlightenment.

Secularism has been successful in helping people break free from the dichotomic worldview. However, it has not been successful in providing a functional meaningful alternative. It saved us heroically from the false dichotomic view, but it failed in providing us a view on which we can build up our life. It fails to answer so many of our basic questions about our life. Our questions such as what we are, why we live, and how we are related to each other have no answers from secularism.

If secularism cannot be an alternative to the dichotomic worldview, what else can be the alternative? The dichotomic worldview is the product of the western Latin branch of the Christian church with its primary theologian, St. Augustine of fourth century. The eastern branch of the Christian church did not share this worldview. The Cappadocian fathers such as St. Basil, Gregory of Nyssa, and Gregory of Nazianzus were the primary Greek theologians in fourth century.

The thought of Gregory of Nyssa has been studied in depth by the scholarly world in our time, and the results have been exciting. Gregory calls all that exists Ta Panta in Greek. Gregory does not divide Ta Panta into natural and supernatural. But he divides Ta Panta into created and uncreated. The uncreated existence is infinite (beyond the limits of time-space) but the created existence is finite. Such a division exists when viewed from the perspective of the created existence; but viewed from the side of the uncreated existence, even such a division disappears. If the uncreated existence (God) is infinite, the created existence (world), which is finite, cannot stay apart from it. This idea goes along with what St. Paul said to his audience in Athens, "In Him we live and move and have our being".

Traditionally all that exists was denoted by the expression "heaven and earth". In the beginning God created the heaven and the earth. Gen. 1:1. The Nicene Creed also uses the same expression. "I believe in one God, the Father Almighty, Maker of heaven and earth, and of all things visible and invisible." Made during the time of Gregory of Nyssa, this statement reveals an important division within the created world—visible and invisible. It is true that the Eastern Greek Christianity made such a distinction of visible and invisible, but it is not the same as the division into natural and supernatural.

Salvation for the eastern Greek Church was theosis, which is for the whole creation growing to the likeness of God; not some people escaping from this world and going to the supernatural world. Church was seen as the visible body of the invisible Christ, and its role was to serve and not to be served. The church members did not see themselves superior to nonmembers. The church assembled on Sundays to intercede on behalf the whole world because the church saw itself as a part of the humanity.

Paulos Mar Gregorios did an excellent study of the thought of Gregory of Nyssa in his doctoral dissertation, which was later published as Cosmic Man.[8] He says about this book in his auto biography:

> My doctoral dissertation submitted to Serampore University was published in 1980 by Sophia Publications, New Delhi, under the title Cosmic Man. It dealt with the relation between God, Humanity and World in the 4th century Eastern Christian Father St. Gregory of Nyssa. It was later republished under the same title in 1988 by Paragon, New York. It is a work that I had expected to be well received, but that has not been the case. I hope it will be studied more seriously by people in the future, for it deals with one of the fundamental problems of Christian Theism. People who believe in God often simply take it for granted that God, Humanity and World are three entities, while Gregory of Nyssa had already seen the philosophical problem of seeing the Creator and the Creation as two entities distinct from each other. The Hindu *Advaita Vedantin*'s point was recognized as basically sound and legitimate, though formulated and explained differently, by this ancient Asian writer from Cappadocia in Asia Minor (present-day Turkey). Gregory of Nyssa lived and wrote three or four centuries before Sankara in India.

### Conclusion

Secularism is a new religion which is only about four centuries old. It did a great service to humanity by saving it from the domination of western Christian church. It made sense to a lot of educated people throughout the world, who have renounced their original religions and embraced this new religion. As long as it stays as one of the religions, it is not a threat to humanity. We don't want to question the freedom of people to get converted from one religion to another one. But it becomes a great threat if it takes control of the governments and institutions of education as the western Christian church did in the medieval Europe. It does this under the guise of something other than a religion.

This reminds me of the old story of a fox becoming a king of animals. Once a fox fell in a bucket of white paint, and he looked very different. All the animals began to respect him and obey his orders. One day the fox instinctively howled when he heard another fox howling at a distance, and immediately the other animals realized his real identity and jumped on him. Today secularism is able to gain control of governments and institutions of educations because it doesn't appear a religion outwardly. It is a religion, and nothing more than a religion. Once people all over the world realize the true identity of secularism, it can't retain its power. What we need is a secular world; not a world dominated by secularism.

# 16. What is Interreligious Dialog For?

Paulos Mar Gregorios was a pioneer in Interreligious Dialog in our times. He was one of the prominent leaders of interreligious movement at global level for a quarter of a century till he passed away in 1996. What follows is a brief examination of his vision of religion and interreligious movement in the light of today's view and understanding of interreligious dialog and learning. [1]

**What is religion?**

Mar Gregorios is not comfortable with the word religion because it acquired a very different meaning from its original one in the 19th century. The original meaning is found in the Latin word *religio* which meant a life bound by a rule of life or *regula*. It is something that serves as the very foundation of human existence. But the cultural movement known as the European Enlightenment cast away this corner stone of life as a worthless stone. It placed man on the throne of God,

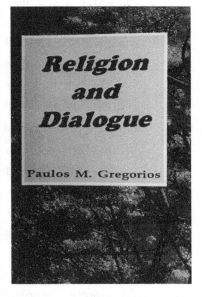

*Religion and Dialogue*

Paulos M. Gregorios

and treated human rational power as the only reliable means of knowledge. It declared that man has attained adulthood, and so he does not need religion any more. Thus in human growth or evolution to adulthood, religion, which was useful once, became a useless appendix that occasionally gives us trouble, and can be surgically removed. Thus religion, which was once seen as the head of a community or culture or human life, was demoted to the status of a useless and trouble-making appendix.

If the word religion is used, the listener or reader will understand it as a useless appendix of human life rather than as the head of human life. Therefore, Mar Gregorios prefers the Sanskrit word *Dharma*, which retains the original meaning of religion.

*Dharma* involves four aspects: understanding, self-discipline, worship, and compassionate service.

> 1. Understanding: This is the awareness of the truth of existence. Dharma means that which holds or sustains the reality. The awareness of the unmanifest reality that holds the manifest reality is fundamental. Based on a Dharmic understanding, a life-style will be developed in relation to oneself, to the Ultimate, and to the fellow beings.
> 2. Self-discipline: We practice Dharma in relation to ourselves mainly in the form of self-discipline. We have to learn to control our senses, passions, drives and desires.
> 3. Worship: We practice Dharma in relation to the Ultimate as unconditional surrender and obedience to the ultimate. The highest honor will always be given to the Ultimate.
> 4. Compassionate Service: We practice Dharma in relation to our fellow beings by unconditional love and service to our fellow beings. We will honor every human being as a dwelling place of the ultimate.

This view of Paulos Mar Gregorios might have been influenced by contemporary scholarship in various disciplines. The anthropologist Clifford Geertz (1926–2006) saw religion as a cultural system. In his seminal work *The Interpretation of Cultures*, Geertz described culture as *a system of inherited conceptions expressed in symbolic forms by means of which people communicate, perpetuate, and develop their knowledge about and attitudes toward life.* He defined religion as *a system of symbols which acts to establish powerful, pervasive, and long-lasting moods and motivations in men by formulating conceptions of a general order of existence and clothing these conceptions with such an aura of factuality that the moods and motivations seem uniquely realistic*[2].

The idea of Mar Gregorios that today's limited sense of the word *religion* is a product of Enlightenment is reflected in the present-day scholars such as Timothy Fitzgerald and Daniel

Dubuisson. Fitzgerald explains how with the Enlightenment religion became a personal feeling or emotion rather than a universal social attitude.[3] Dubuisson explains how religion emerged as a category separate from culture and society in the 19th century.[4]

### What is Interreligious Dialog for?

Interreligious dialog is basically communication among people. It happens globally as well as locally. Its purpose is to enhance understanding among people so that they can live together peacefully. Unity in diversity is the primary condition of a dialog. If the parties of a dialog have the same view of life, there is 100% unity, and there is no need of any dialog. If there is 100% diversity between two parties, there cannot be any dialog between them because there has to be some kind of unity in something between them to begin a dialog. This is usually referred to as a common ground. Various common grounds have been suggested such as the ultimate truth of life behind what appears true to us, the mystical experiences common to all religions, and the healthy and meaningful existence of humankind.

This situation can be understood better if we use the analogy of medical systems. Let us imagine that someone is severely ill, and physicians belonging to various medical systems such as Homeopathy, Ayurveda, Naturopathy, Acupuncture, and English medicine arrive to treat the sick person. They use diverse ways to diagnose and treat the sickness, and they do not even understand each other. What if they make an attempt to communicate with each other? Where do they begin? What is common for them? They are all healers and they are trying to heal the same sick person. If they are open to each other, they can learn from each other, and create new knowledge by integrating the insights from diverse medical systems. Religions are healing systems. In spite of their diversity, they are trying to heal the same sick humanity. If they can communicate and learn from each other, very valuable knowledge and information that will contribute to the well being of mankind can be generated.

Inaugurating the centenary celebrations of the Parliament of World's Religions in Chicago in 1993, Paulos Mar Gregorios made his view of the goal of interreligious dialog crystal clear.5 The unity of humanity with cultural diversity without any domination by any one part of humanity is the ultimate goal of interreligious dialog. Absolute loyalty to the parts of humanity such as tribes, races, religions, and nations is antihuman, and so we need to rise above and beyond such loyalties in pledging allegiance to the humanity. Each religion is like a healing system with centuries of rich experience behind it. It has to develop in its own way without merging with others. However the existence of a religion should not be more important than the existence of humankind. Religions exist for the wellbeing of humankind. Nothing short of the unity and wellbeing of humankind can be the goal of interreligious dialogs. Religions will be able to do this only if they regain their original status which was lost due to the European Enlightenment.

### How is Interreligious Dialog Done?

Once the unity of humanity is set as the goal of interreligious dialog, Mar Gregorios asserts that what we need is a global concourse of religions in which various religions flow together supporting and learning from each other and working together for the good of humanity. He suggests the name "A Global Concourse of Religions" instead of "A parliament of World Religions" because he thinks that religions need to flow together keeping their identity rather than occasionally meet to talk with each other. Religious people need to cooperate with nonreligious people in creating a just and peaceful world with a life-supporting environment. The problems of injustice, war, and environmental deterioration were caused by our immaturity and greedy handling of the earth and in our relationship with the human beings in it. The religions have to work together to redeem humanity. "We do not abandon our particular religious loyalties; but we shall deepen them in dialog and concourse with other religions in order to find those deeper roots in each religion which affirm the unity of global humanity and which affirm the transcendent love in which we all live and move and have our being."[6]

Interreligious dialog is to enhance understanding among religions. The quality of understanding depends upon the willingness to understand. Paul F. Knitter gives an excellent introduction to interreligious learning in his book, *Theologies of Religions*.[7] In the four parts of his book, he presents four models of the Christian attitudes toward interreligious dialog: replacement, fulfillment, mutuality, and acceptance. In the first one, the Christian willingness is 0%. The willingness increases in the next models, and finally, it becomes 100% in the acceptance model.

When one party is not willing to listen to the other, there cannot be a dialog, but only a monolog. Thus the willingness to listen and understand from each other has to be seen as the primary condition of an interreligious dialog. If we want to seek a solution to this problem, we need to find out why someone or a group of people is unwilling to listen to and understand from the others. Religions deal with how we view life. Our views of life vary from culture to culture. The phenomenon of existence is so mysterious that we are like the blind men who examined an elephant. If we identify our view to be the absolute truth, we will be unwilling to listen to the others. However, if we realize that ours is just one view of the reality, we will be willing to listen to the others as well.

Those Christians with 0% willingness to listen and understand others believe that they have the absolute truth in their custody, and they seek to convert others to Christian religion. The Christians who are partially willing to listen to others are willing to admit that the others may have a part of truth in their custody too. These Christians are like a physician who claims that only he is in custody of the cure of a certain sickness while other physicians may have the diagnosis of the sickness. Those with 100% willingness to listen to others believe that no religion is in custody of the absolute truth. All are like the blind men who tried to understand an elephant.

Mar Gregorios narrates in his autobiography the attempts he made in the WCC for an interreligious dialog. He speaks about a Christian bishop with 0% willingness to listen to others.

> At the Nairobi Assembly of 1975, we invited a select number of observers from the great religions of the world and devoted a whole section of the Assembly to interreligious dialogue, in the hope that along with the environmental issue being highlighted at Nairobi, the issue of cultural pluralism and interreligious dialogue would move from the margins of the WCC agenda to its centre. I was asked to chair that section on dialogue, with our distinguished non- Christian friends present.

> Our hopes were soon to be dashed on the hard rocks of European cultural parochialism. In response to my presidential remarks, a friend of mine, a Norwegian Lutheran bishop, asked me, "In what sense does the Chairman find the revelation in Jesus Christ so insufficient that he has to go the non-Christians to learn the truth?"

> I was offended, but being in the chair, could not retort in my usual rude manner. So I responded, "In this sense that the Chairman is not as fortunate as his friend the bishop from Norway, who seems to have so mastered the revelation in Jesus Christ, that he is so totally self-satisfied and does not feel any need to learn from others." I doubt that the barb got through. But my non-Christian friends saw for themselves the shameful narrow mindedness of European Christianity. They were hurt, but kept their cool and continued to be polite.[8]

Mar Gregorios proposes three ways of interreligious dialog to match with the three ways of dealing with reality: *Practical handling of reality, verbal conceptualization and communication, and various ritual expressions of meaning though dance, music, gestures, and liturgical actions*. These three ways may be summarized using the Sanskrit words that denote the three ways of yoga: *karma, jnaana, and Bhakti*. In the words of Mar Gregorios, they are practical level, theoretical level, and symbolic and ritual level.[9] He further elaborates these levels as follows:

1. Dialog on common social or economic problems and about common projects and practical collaboration
2. Dialog on the theoretical or theological aspects of religion

*3.* Dialog in which a and b are transcended into the realm of entering into each other's spiritual experience and group worship.[10]

The first way is to talk about or work together in a common existential problem such as poverty, violation of human rights, etc. The second one is to talk about how they are similar and different in their views of life. For example, in a dialog between Christians and Muslims, Christians will have to explain what they mean when they say "the son of God", and how the belief in trinity does not violate monotheism. The third one is to try to establish a bond at the level of the unconscious by common worship.

These are three different ways to do dialogs, and whichever appropriate is to be chosen according to the context.

1. The first one is the most appropriate for the common people, who lack theological training. People need to collaborate everywhere to tackle common existential issues. This is a level at which religious people can collaborate with nonreligious people.

2. The second way is appropriate only for those few people who are sufficiently trained in theology. Theologians who are well-versed in their own religion and scriptures may come together willing to explain and to learn from others how they view life. Religious people may enter into dialog with nonreligious people as well at this level.

3. The third way is appropriate only in very few situations when an interreligious community is made ready for it through the first two ways.

### Interreligious Learning

Interreligious dialog leads to interreligious learning, which takes various approaches. Francis X. Clooney, a Jesuit priest and a professor at Harvard, lists the various approaches in his book, Comparative Theology.[11] The approaches may be simplified and illustrated as follows:

1. Comparative Religion --The learner takes an outsider view of the religions compared.

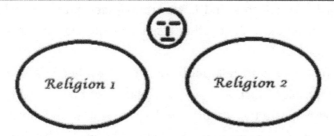

2.        Theology of Religions – The learner takes an insider view of one's own religion, but takes an outsider view of other religions.

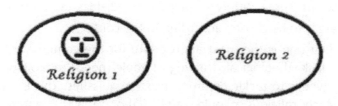

3.        Comparative Theology – The learner takes an insider view of one's own religion as well as of the religion that is compared.

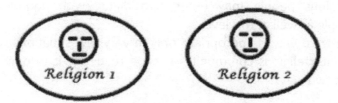

It seems that Mar Gregoios used the approach of Comparative Theology when he learned the other religions. He tried to learn various religions not from the perspective of a Christian but from the perspective of someone inside those religions. Here is what Kabir Saxena, a Buddhist, says about him:

> Father once gave a talk on Dharmakirti and Dignaga at our Tushita Meditation Centre in Delhi. It was stimulating to say the best. Here was an ostensibly Christian Father, discoursing on the intricacies of Buddhist madhyamaka philosophy with flowing gusto.

Here is what Dr. Mohinder Singh, a Sikh scholar, says:

> I once accompanied him to the Gurdwara Bangla Sahib in New Delhi. While taking him around I told him about the Gurdwara and the history connected with it. While coming out there is a tradition that we all take Prasad and the holy water. Whenever I take non-Sikh guests with me I explain the significance of the two but do not insist that they partake the same. What surprised me was the fact that even before I could explain to him about these he had already partaken the Prasad and the holy water like a devout Sikh.

What Mar Gregorios says in his autobiography also illustrates this:

> I need to learn from all, and have indeed learned from many. My major liberation in life has been from thinking that the Western way of thinking, with its specific categories and modalities, is the only way to think and to know. Now that I know a little bit about the Yin-Yang polarity-complementarity way of thinking and knowing in the Chinese Tao, I do not have to be a slave of the Western subject-object mode of thinking, and the logic of the excluded middle. From my own Indian tradition I have learned the principle of Ekam advitiyam or One without a Second; I know now that all diversity and difference ultimately find their unity in the One without a Second; that One is more ultimate than the many. My own Eastern Orthodox tradition has confirmed that there is no creation other than God or outside God, because the Infinite Ultimate has neither outside nor other.
>
> I have learned from the Jains the great Anekanthavada, which holds that all statements are conditional and qualified truth, which have to be supplemented and completed by other truths; that our Ahimsa or non-violence should extend to other ways of thinking, and not just to other beings.
>
> I have learned from Buddhists that all epistemology is finally without basis; that our perceptions of all things, including the world, are but mental events that happen when our kind of mind -sense and whatever is out there come into contact with each other; that this world which the secular mindset takes to be some kind of ultimate

reality is neither real nor unreal, and should be taken seriously, but not so absolutely.

And I have learned much from Jews and Arabs, from Sikhs and Zoroastrians, from Adivasis and Aborigines, from Africans and from the indigenous peoples of America. And I hope I am still learning and will continue to do so until the end.[12]

## Conclusion

Being an extraordinary genius, Mar Gregorios had a very clear vision of religion and interreligious dialog. By organizing and participating in global interreligious forums, he devoted his time and energy to create a united humanity and a peaceful world. The world will greatly benefit if his vision becomes a reality.

# 17. What is the Mission of the Christian Church?

What is church, and what is its mission? This question can be answered from the view of an outsider or an insider. An outsider view, a sociological one, would describe church as an institution or as a voluntary organization of Christian believers. This approach will certainly yield valuable information about the churches today, but not very helpful in defining the mission of the church. The question of the mission of the church can be meaningfully answered only from an insider view, which is theological. Paulos Mar Gregorios approaches this question extensively as an insider in a number of his published papers and books.[1]

The role of the church is explained in the New Testament using a number of metaphors such as a family, a kingdom, a building, a body, an army, a flock of sheep, etc. The one metaphor Paulos Mar Gregorios uses the most meaningfully is that of a body. He is never tired of repeating over and over that the church is the body of Christ. Christ, who is invisible to us, continues his mission today through his visible body, the church. Before attempting an examination of the view of Mar Gregorios, we may trace the evolution of this metaphor in the New Testament.

### The Evolution of a Metaphor

At the very beginning of the Church, it understood itself as the new Israel, traveling to the Promised Land. The church claimed that the old Israel proved irresponsible to God, so it was replaced with the Christian church, the new Israel. Jesus was seen as a new Moses, saving people from the captivity of Satan. Salvation begins for an individual when he/she joins the church. One has to stay with the church growing in holiness. Finally, one enters the Promised Land (heaven) when he/she dies. But one cannot be certain whether he/she will reach heaven. Under the leadership of Jesus, the new Moses, the church has claimed freedom from sin and death. However, as long as they are in the world, of sin and death, they are like the Israelites who were in the desert on their way to the land of Canaan. Their salvation begins when they join the church, they are being saved while traveling as a part of the church, and they will be fully saved when they reach the heavenly Canaan.

But how did the world happen to be enslaved to sin and death? The story of Adam and Eve, seen as a historical incident, answered this question to their satisfaction. It was believed that the sin of Adam and Eve in the Garden of Eden marked the fall of humanity.

However, there has never been a consensus about what salvation involves. If humanity had a fall in the Garden of Eden, salvation must be a restoration to the original state. For some others salvation is from the captivity of Satan, like from the Pharaoh for Israel. For some others it is from the capital punishment of God.

As a development to this thought, Jesus was seen as a new Adam in contrast to the first Adam. Adam was the beginning of a human race that disobeys God; in Jesus starts a new human race that obeys God. *Just as through the disobedience of the one man the many were made sinners, so also through the obedience of the one man the many will be made righteous.* (Rom 5.19) *And that ye put on the new man, which after God is created in righteousness and true holiness.* (Eph 4:24) *For neither is circumcision anything, nor uncircumcision, but a new creation.* (Gal 6:15) Someone becomes a new creation when Christ lives in him and he lives in Christ. Thus this model of new creation, which evolved naturally from the previous one, was found much more meaningful.

How are those who have become new creation related to each other? If Christ lives in them, and if they all live in Christ, obviously they are related to each other as the organs of the same body. Thus there evolved the concept of church as the body of Christ. *Now you are Christ's body, and individually members of it.* (I Cor. 12: 27). As the members of a body, the members of the church are supposed to live and work together in perfect unity. Thus this metaphor, which naturally evolved from the previous ones, seems to be even more meaningful.

Paulos Mar Gregorios claims that the Eastern Orthodox Churches, with their central emphasis on the Eucharist, have always seen church as the body of Christ.[2] The Roman Catholic Church has been willing to accept it as its official view in the Second Vatican Council.[3] The Protestant Churches, however, haven't yet understood the significance of this model; they still seem to be operating with the previous models.[4]

### Church as the Body of Christ

Mar Gregorios has elaborated on this topic primarily in a series of Bible studies given to the staff of the World Council of Churches (WCC) in Geneva, which was later published in a book namely, the *Meaning and Nature of Diakonia* [5]. Mar Gregorios argues that being the body of Christ, the mission of church is to continue the mission of Christ, and the role of WCC is to assist the church in performing this mission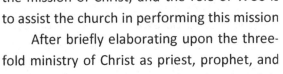

After briefly elaborating upon the three-fold ministry of Christ as priest, prophet, and king, Mar Gregorios asserts that the church has the same three-fold ministry. As a priest, Jesus Christ gave himself as a sacrifice to the Father, and He rose again, victor over sin and death. We celebrate this sacrifice and victory in the Eucharist, in which, we get united with Christ, and we sacrifice ourselves to the father.[6]

### Humanity as a Mediator

This picture of the church having the same mission of Christ needs to be seen in the context of a wider framework which spells out how church is related to the humanity, and how the humanity is related to God and creation.

Mar Gregorios would define church as a human community that performs the role of a mediator between the creator and the creation. Following Mar Gregorius of Nyssa, Mar Gregorios equates God with all that exists. Viewed from God's side, God is all that exists, but viewed from the side of the creation, it exists apart from the creator (God). The creator is infinite, but the creation exists within the limits of time and place.

The creation is multiple in form, and the capacity of each form to respond to God varies. Inorganic matter responds less freely than the plants and the trees; the animals are more conscious, and mankind even more than the animals, but the church is more aware of the creator than mankind in general.[9]

Mankind is a part of the creation-- the most conscious part. Being the most conscious part of the creation is a position of privilege indeed; it is a position of great responsibility as well. Although the privilege of being aware of God is open to all mankind, only a part of them actually rise to the level of such awareness. Those few people do not feel superior to the rest of the people who do not rise to such awareness. Instead they would humbly serve them, and would represent them before God. The church sees itself as that part of mankind.

The church has the privilege to be aware of the goodness of God. God's wisdom gives the knowledge of the good, God's freedom chooses the good, and God has the power to perform it, which is expressed as love or as self-giving. This awareness of God's love makes the church respond by similar self-giving love to God. This response takes the form of adoration and unconditional surrender and obedience. As a result, the church becomes the visible image of the invisible God for the rest of the creation. Actually the whole of mankind is called to be the visible image of God; those few who respond become the church. The church does this in union with Christ, and following his lead. Thus the mission of church is nothing but the mission of Christ-- uniting with God in unconditional surrender representing the creation, and manifesting God's goodness to the rest of the creation.

The church can perform such a mediator role between the creator and creation only by constantly engaging in self-disciplinary practices and exercises. The mysteries (called sacraments in the west) are effective ways of self-discipline. The Eucharist is the supreme mystery of the church symbolizing church's uniting with Christ. The Eucharist dramatizes the events in Christ's life, and by taking part in this periodically, the church internalizes Christ at the subconscious level, and becomes one with Christ. Baptism makes one a member of Christ's body. Christmation or Anointment lets one share the anointment of Christ as king, priest, and prophet. The liturgical year lets the church participate in the saving events in Christ's life.

The living church, performing such a role, will be a community united by love to each other. It will appear as the visible image of God's unconditional love to the world. The members of this community will always be driven by the motivation to serve, and not to be served by others.

### The State of the Church Today

What we have already seen is how the church is supposed to be, not how it really is. The reality is far from the ideal. In the first few centuries of its origin the church spread to the Roman Empire in the west, and to Persia, India, and China in the east. In spite of its global growth, the church has failed in its role as a mediator between the creator and the creation because it has lost its vision of its true mission, and its focus has been upon preserving the church and its tradition.

A false understanding of mission as the assimilation of other people into a culture dominated by a special race of Christians distorted the proclamation of the gospel in the world.[10]

Without a vision that keeps us united for our mission, the church has broken into so many pieces.

As early as the fourth century, there arose a controversy about the Holy Trinity. Some Christians who relied on a literal interpretation could not give the Son and the Holy Spirit the same status as the Father, and they expressed this belief in their doxology, *"Glory be to the father through the son by the Holy Spirit"*. A doxology is a verse or sentence that glorifies God. This was rejected as a heresy, and the church accepted the doxology, *"Glory be to the father, to the Son, and to the Holy Spirit"*. Thus the church called itself orthodox to mean those who glorify God in the right way, combining orthos (right) and doxadzein (glorifying God).11

Soon there arose another controversy regarding the Holy Trinity. The western Christendom, headed by the Pope of Rome, claimed that the Holy Spirit proceeds from the Son also in addition to the Father, and modified the Nicene Creed accordingly, but the eastern Christian world continued with the earlier belief. Moreover, the Pope's claim of superiority over all the other patriarchs and bishops elsewhere added fuel to the division between the west and east. The churches in the East, headed by the patriarchs of Constantinople, Alexandria, Antioch, and others refused to accept the superiority claim of Rome, and came to be known as the Eastern Orthodox Church, whereas the Roman church became known as the Catholic Church. The corruption in the Catholic Church led to the Reformation movement in the 16th century, which led to the formation of numerous Protestant Churches.

A controversy regarding the divine-human nature of Christ led to a split among the Eastern Churches in the fifth century. The church of Constantinople (Byzantine) claimed it to be two, whereas the others claimed it to be one. The two sides called each other *Diophysites* and *Monophysites*. The Byzantine cultural domination over the others fueled the split.

The primary reason for these controversies and splits in the church is the claim of the custody of truth. Addressing the Parliament of World's Religion in Chicago in 1993, Mar Gregorios said,

> "In each religion there are two levels. One level is exclusivist, and expansionist. That is to say, each religion says, we have the truth and if you want to have the truth, join us. That is the exclusivist, expansionist, lower type of religion. All religions have that lower type. But in religions there is also a higher type, a type which is universal in its orientation, which is all-embracing in its love, which is non-discriminating between members of its own community and those outside."[12]

Paulos Mar Gregorios asserts that claiming the custody of truth is lower type religion. It makes people narrow-minded, unwilling to listen to and learn from others. Although he made the above statement about religions, it can be applied to the various groups within a religion as well. How could these churches claim the custody of the truth about the incomprehensible God? If the churches are honest and open-minded to admit that God alone is in custody of the absolute truth, they will forfeit all claims of the custody of truth, willing to learn from each other and even from other religions.

When the church was slowly emerging, St. Paul proclaimed, *"There is neither Jew nor Greek, slave nor free, male nor female, for you are all one in Christ Jesus"* (Gal 3:28). Ethnicity, class, and gender have been the three primary criteria that erected walls of separation among humans, and Paul claimed that because Christ has broken all walls of separation, perfect unity has to be the goal of the church. The first major conflict in the church was caused by ethnicity – there were Jews and Greeks in the church. Having two separate churches for them might have been an easy way out, but Paul fought fiercely to keep the church united overcoming the wall of ethnicity.

Unlike the western churches, the eastern churches are very much bound by ethnicity. Mar Gregorios cites an interesting example from the situation in the US.

> The Yugoslavians and the Russians have the same faith, the same liturgy, and the same liturgical language. But in the same town you find a Serbian Orthodox Church and a Russian Orthodox Church. Why is it not possible for them to merge into one church? Simply because the communal loyalty is stronger than the loyalty to the church as the Body of Christ.[13]

This is a shameful situation for the orthodox churches. Mar Gregorios further asserts,

> We became closed communities rather than churches open to all people. Our concern is less with Jesus Christ and his righteousness than with the glory and honor of our community.[14]

Mar Gregorios advises the orthodox churches to make a conscious attempt to break the wall of ethnicity following the example of the western churches.

Orthodoxy holds the pure tradition of the ancient undivided church. But because of its ethnic group egoism, it remains incapable either of enjoying their rich spiritual heritage or of sharing it with others... There may be Eucharistic communion between the Greeks and the Russians, for example, but very little love.[15]

In a Bible study conducted at the headquarters of the World Council of Churches in Geneva based on the Gospel passage in which the sons of Zebedee send their mother to Jesus to request a special privilege, Mar Gregorios asserts,

Nothing has been so divisive of the churches as the ambitions, the jealousies, the power struggles among the Christian workers and leaders. Quite unconsciously we fall a prey to that perennial temptation—for power and position, for worldly glory and honor. So long as that is our basic orientation, the church cannot be united.[16]

Mar Gregorios asserts that disunity is a violation of the true nature of the church. It is the failure of love that leads to disunity. God is love, and the church has to reflect that nature.

Where there is no love, the spirit of God is not at work. The Church may work all day and night, and yet it may catch nothing (Jh 21:3). Sociologically the church may be growing in numbers, wealth, and institutions; but it is all hay and stubble, that the fire will destroy.[17]

### Conclusion

Paulos Mar Gregorios paints a clear picture of how the church must ideally be by using the metaphor of the body of Christ, and shows us how it really is. The churches all over the world need to heed the wisdom of this sage, and strive for the ideal.

# 18. What is the Meaning of the Eucharist?

Paulos Mar Gregorios developed his view of Eucharist in the context of the initiative of the Second Vatican Council for liturgical reformation. In a paper read at the Hammersmith Christian Unity Conference in May 1966 evaluating the Council of Vatican II, he said,

..the liturgical constitution, which not only liberates the Catholic Church from the impoverishment of uniformity of language, but in fact paves the way-- by disrupting patterns of worship which established for centuries, have carried the people without always engaging their minds-- towards a total revision of the recent liturgical practices of the Western Catholic Church. Enrichment of worship cannot come merely from the introduction of the vernacular into the Roman rite or from unsystematic experiment. But the introduction of the vernacular is a necessary first step to the discovery of its inadequacy or unsuitability for large segments of the Catholic population. The liturgical constitution's major contribution, however, will, I suggest, lie neither in the theologically dubious innovation of the priest facing the people throughout the entire liturgy, nor in the vernacular transformation of an austere Latin liturgy, but rather in the stimulus it has given to fresh thinking on the centrality of the Eucharist in the life, mission and unity of the Church.[1]

He wrote a full-length book on Eucharist, about which he writes,

My first major published book dealt with some of the specifics of Eastern Christian worship. Associated Press in New York and Lutterworth Press in London jointly published-- *Joy of Freedom, Eastern Worship and Modern Man*[2], in 1967.

## Introduction

In making this study, I humbly acknowledge my indebtedness to the scholarly work of Paulos Mar Gregorios, the spokesperson of Eastern Orthodox Christianity. The primary purpose of this study is to direct the readers to the work of Mar Gregorios. There is no claim of any inerrancy or authority to the information and opinions presented here. I earnestly request the readers to make further study of this topic and verify the information and opinions found here.

### Food as a Symbol

Taking a bath and eating food are two of the most common things we all do in our daily life. They have become two of the most important symbolic rituals in the life of Christian church as in most of the other religions. From the bath evolved baptism, the ritual of entrance to the community, and from eating evolved Eucharist, the ritual that keeps the community in existence. Just like Eucharist, baptism also appears with diverse names, forms, and meanings across the Christian world. *Baptism, .. now saves you, not as a removal of dirt from the body but as an appeal to God for a good conscience.* (I Pet. 3: 21). The regular bath has the purpose of removing dirt from the body, but the purpose of baptism, which is a ritual bath, is not at a physical level at all. Similarly Paul makes a distinction between eating for hunger and eating the Lord's Supper, a ritual meal. *If anyone is hungry, let him eat at home, so that you will not come together for judgment. (I Cor. 11:34).*

Eating has had symbolic meaning in sacrifices and harvest festivals in the ancient societies all over the world. Passover, the primary festival of Judaism, was celebrated by eating together. Eating gained symbolical meaning in Christianity as well. Now the questions we consider here are: What is the symbolic meaning of food and eating together? What meaning did Jesus give to eating together? What meaning did the early Christianity give to this? What meaning did the later Christianity give to this?

Food has been a powerful symbol of life in the traditional cultures, which explains why food is respected and not wasted by them. Those from the traditional cultures give thanks to God before they eat because they see God as the source of life, which reaches us through food.

Sharing food is sharing life. A mother nursing her baby is sharing her own life with the baby. In a family, when parents share food, the fruit of their sweat, with their children, they actually share their very life with them. Family members eat together, which serves to keep its bond. If you eat with someone outside your family, it means that you are willing to treat that person as a family member. People normally wouldn't share table with someone belonging to a different class. In all traditional communities, one usually eats with someone he/she is close to. In order to share table, we have to transcend the differences of color, class, race, and gender.

### Meaning of Eating Together for Jesus

When Jesus traveled in Galilee and Judea with his disciples, eating together was an act of great significance for him. Pharisees at the time of Jesus strictly followed the religious purity rules, and avoided the people who did not follow those rules. However, Jesus and his disciples did not care much for the purity rules. Also they ate with those people who neglected the purity rules—the ones who were avoided by Pharisees. The Pharisees accused Jesus of being a drunk and a glutton. Jesus' miracles and teachings often involved food and feasting. He instructed his apostles to eat with the people that they preach to and heal. In the gospels we read how Jesus eats together with his disciples the day before he gets crucified. Also after the resurrection, Jesus meets with his disciples and eats with them.

Pharisees followed their religion according to letter. They tried to preserve and promote their religion at the expense of everything else. Jesus also followed his religion, but not according to letter as Pharisees did. He knew that religion was for the well-being of humanity, and he declared that Sabbath is for man. Jesus tried to re-establish the essence of his religious tradition by opposing the literalness of the Pharisees. He saw God as father and people as God's children. This makes the world a family and the people brothers and sisters to one another. The role of religion is to create and maintain these relationships, not to break them. On the other hand, Pharisees broke human relationships using their religion. They stayed away from some people in the name of religion. Their religion made them see some people sinners and untouchables.

Therefore Jesus made it a point to eat with the sinners and tax-collectors and other similar people avoided by the Pharisees whenever he could. That is probably why Jesus asked for water to drink from a Samaritan woman and why he went to the home of Zacchaeus. By eating with them, Jesus was accepting them as his brothers and sisters. He was also letting them know that they were God's children too.

Jesus proclaimed the gospel of the Kingdom of God. He encouraged the people to address this king as their father. In the prayer he taught, he asked them to pray, *Our father.... Let they kingdom come*. Although God is the king of the world, God is father to human beings. People are supposed to love God as their father, and submit to His will willingly. Jesus proclaimed this gospel not only by word, but also by his deeds. Eating and drinking with all kinds of people was one of the primary ways through which Jesus conveyed his message across.

Jesus taught them to pray, *Give us this day our daily bread*. This prayer acknowledges that God is the source of food. If food comes from God, nobody can monopolize it; it belongs to all people. Like the manna from the sky, it is for each day for all people to eat, and not for some people to store for another day while others remain hungry.

### Meanings of Eucharist in the Early Church

At the earliest stage of Christianity, Christians saw themselves as belonging to Judaism, and continued to go to the temple and synagogues on Sabbath. However, they also met informally on other days, especially on Sundays, and they ate together when they met. We read that they broke bread on Sundays. A better translation would be that they shared food with one another. They probably attached the same meaning that Jesus attached to eating together.

Eating together seems to have evolved in two separate directions in the early church: as the Lord's Supper and as the Agape Feast. The Lord's Supper started as a meeting of Christians alone and the original purpose was probably to strengthen their bond. They probably brought their own food and ate together like a modern pot-luck dinner. St. Paul speaks about this in his letter to Corinthians. (11: 17-34). Agape feast (Jude 1:12) was a feast organized by Christians for all people – rich and poor, Jews and gentiles, male and female. The Lord's Supper eventually got transformed into a symbolic, ritual meal consisting of bread and wine with a lot of meanings attached to it. Agape Feast could continue only as long as the community was small, and there were people willing to spend their resources for it. As the church grew larger, the Agape Feast died out.

The meanings attached to the Lord's Supper depended on how the early Christians viewed themselves-- their self-identity. Now we will see how the early church understood Eucharist, and how this understanding was directly based on their understanding of the church. Then we will see how their understanding of Eucharist evolved with their new understanding of the church.

### 1. As the New Passover

As the followers of Jesus Christ increased in number, and as the local synagogues began to see them as extremists and heretics, the Christian community began to evolve slowly as an independent movement. It started as a reform movement within Judaism, but as the Jewish religious authorities remained stubborn, the reformers had no choice but to leave their community and be on their own as a new religious movement.

When they were cast out of Judaism, instead of taking it negatively with self-pity for themselves, they took it positively, and developed a self-identity as the true Israel. They explained that the old Israel proved irresponsible, and so God had fired them from their job, and appointed a new Israel. Paul elaborated this idea in his epistle to Romans (ch.11), and as a major idea promoted by

Paul's movement, it gained momentum. This served as a very powerful foundational idea upon which they could build up further details, and answer many of their questions.

Judaism had two celebrations related to its formation and self-identity: Passover and the feast of the unleavened bread[3]. Both of them commemorated their escape from slavery in Egypt. Passover commemorated the escape of their firstborns from death, and the feast of the unleavened bread commemorated their hurry departure from Egypt. Although they were celebrated separately first, eventually they were celebrated together with the name, Passover.

In the gospels of Matthew, Mark, and Luke, we see Jesus celebrating Passover with his disciples the day before his death. While passing out the bread and the wine to his disciples, Jesus said, *This is my body, and this is my blood.* By this Jesus probably implied that he was the lamb that would be slain for the liberation of the new Israel.

Thus Eucharist began to be associated with the last supper of Jesus and with the Jewish festivals of Passover and unleavened bread. The bread in the Lord's Supper represented the feast of the unleavened bread and the wine (blood) represented Passover. Some churches specifically use unleavened bread for Eucharist even today.

When the church viewed itself as the new Israel, it saw the crucifixion and resurrection of Jesus Christ as the specific event in history that marked the birth of the church. They related this to the specific event that marked the birth of Israel from Egypt. Thus when the church was seen as a new Israel, Eucharist was seen as a new Passover. As Passover became a celebration of freedom for Israel, Eucharist became a celebration of freedom for the new Israel.

### 2. As the Participation in the New Covenant

According to Paul (I Cor. 11: 23) and the gospels, Jesus also says in the Last Supper, *"this cup is the new testament in my blood."* This refers to the covenant (testament) made between Israel and Yahweh at Mount Sinai on their way from Egypt with Moses as the mediator (Ex. 24). They offered an elaborate peace offering to Yahweh, during which they made an agreement that they would remain obedient to Yahweh even at the price of their life. To sign this agreement, Moses sprinkled half of the blood of oxen on the altar, and the other half upon the people.        Later        Prophet Jeremiah said,

> This is the covenant I will make with the people of Israel after that time," declares the LORD. "I will put my law in their minds and write it on their hearts. I will be their God, and they will be my people. Jer. 31: 31-34.

The author of the Epistle to Hebrews argues that Jesus established a new covenant as prophesied by Jeremiah. (Heb. 8:7-13). Thus the early church saw Jesus as a new Moses, establishing a new covenant with God on behalf of the new Israel at Mount Calvary instead of Mount Sinai. Jesus used his own blood to sign the agreement instead of the blood of oxen. And the Holy Eucharist was seen by the church as a celebration of this new covenant with God to be fully obedient even at the price of life. Each time a community celebrates the Eucharist, they take part in the original covenant undertaken through Christ, thus reinforcing it in their lives. They renew their commitment to live according to the will of God.

### 3. As the New Manna

The Israelites were given manna from the sky, in the desert, on their way to the Promised Land. (Exodus 16; Numbers 11:6-9)[4]. As Christians saw themselves as the new Israel, they found this metaphor very meaningful, and Eucharist was related to manna.

Although the synoptic gospels elaborately describe the last supper, John's gospel, which was written much later, does not include last supper at all. But Eucharist appears in John's gospel as new manna.

> I am the bread of life. Your forefathers ate the manna in the desert, yet they died. But here is the bread that comes down from heaven, which a man may eat and not die. I am the living bread that came down from heaven. If anyone eats of this

bread, he will live forever. This bread is my flesh, which I will give for the life of the world (John 6:48-51).

In John's gospel, Christ uses manna as the type and symbol of the Eucharist, which is true "bread from heaven", and "bread of life", i.e., life-giving bread, in a far higher sense than the manna of old (John 6). St. Paul in calling the manna "spiritual food" (1 Cor.10:3), alludes to its symbolical significance with regard to the Eucharist as much as to its miraculous character. The church saw in Eucharist a new manna which strengthens them on their way to the promised land.

All these three meanings of Eucharist (Passover, covenant, manna) were closely related to how the early Christians saw themselves. They saw themselves as pilgrims engaged in an adventure trip toward a promised land. The first one reinforced their self-identity as the true continuation of Israel, the second one reinforced the need to be fully obedient to God, and the third one reinforced their willingness to accept divine providence gratefully.

### Meanings of Eucharist in the Imperial Church
### 1. As a Cosmic Drama of the Christian Worldview

At the beginning of the fourth century CE there was a radical shift in the status of the Christian church—it became the official imperial religion of the Roman Empire. Until then it was just one of the several religious movements competing for a bare survival in the empire. It was often frowned upon by the rulers. Many of them were persecuted and even brutally killed. The edict of Milan (313 CE) changed everything; Christianity replaced the existing imperial religion. People and wealth began to flood in. Basilicas began to rise. The leaders of the church became imperial dignitaries, and began to be dressed like Roman senators.

This changed status in the fourth century radically altered the self-identity of the church. Church had finally gained the freedom it had always sought for. It was no more in slavery, but it was ruling the world. During this time, Eucharist also changed radically in form and meaning. Christians were no more meeting in their homes, and they didn't have their love feasts any more. They started meeting in their basilicas, and they were having elaborate ceremonial Eucharist on Sundays.

A shallow and easy-going view was gaining ground that the Kingdom of God was already on earth. They didn't feel like pilgrims any more. There was a general feeling that they had reached the Promised Land. The goal was achieved. The emperor of Rome was ruling on behalf of Christ, and all that was left for Christians to do was to rule the world along with Christ.

Although there was a general feeling that the Kingdom of God was already on earth, there were a few who were not fooled by the appearances. They refused to believe that the Roman Empire was the same as the Kingdom of God. They took it as a temptation to overcome. Many of them turned to monastic movement. They left social life and lived in isolation. This was in revolt against the utter foolishness with which people in general faced the new situation.

Eventually some others developed a better vision of the role of the church. Instead of running away from social life, they decided to face the temptation staying right in the midst of the society. Running away from social life and living in isolation was seen escapism by them. They asked themselves what Christ would do in this changed situation. Would Christ run away from everybody else into a deserted place? Of course, he went to the deserted place for a short while, and that was to gain some strength to come back. Christ's mission was right in the middle of the people. They decided to live in the very midst of the society as the embodiment of Christ. They took upon their shoulders the mission of Christ.

They saw the church as the visible embodiment of the invisible Christ. Church had been related to the body of Christ by Paul long time ago. He used this metaphor to tell the church members that they have to act in perfect cooperation like the members of the same body. This metaphor gained a renewed sense in the fourth century-- Christ was viewed as living in the world through His body, the church. Paulos Mar Gregorios clarifies the situation in his book, *The Faith of our Fathers*:

The official approval of Christianity by Emperor Constantine in 313 has sometimes been deplored by historians as the beginning of the decline of Christianity. It is true that the Christian Church was no longer persecuted and therefore there was no more opportunity to become martyrs. But martyrdom is not the only way of expressing the Christian faith. Constantine's Edict of Milan placed the Church in a position where it had to take this world more seriously. Today we live in the same situation. It is not sufficient to think about the other world alone. We have to give expression to our faith here and now, in this world. The Church was forced to take an active and responsible role in politics, in culture and in education because of the Constantinian settlement. Previously the Church could condemn the Roman Empire as Babylon the harlot, which persecutes the faithful. Now the Empire was in the hands of the Church, so to speak[5].

The great leaders of the church who developed this sophisticated view were the church fathers. They refused to run away and live in isolation, but lived in the midst of the society. They saw church as the embodiment of Christ-- not as the Christ who rules the world, but as the suffering Christ. They encouraged Christians to live like Christ. It was not easy to change the mindset of the people. Some of them were excellent orators. Sunday after Sunday they taught people how to live like Christ. Some of them were excellent writers. They wrote essays, hymns, Bible commentaries, parables, and prayers.

The church fathers developed Eucharist as a mystical act that strengthens the bond between the invisible Christ and the church, the visible body of Christ. So many scholarly and saintly church fathers contributed their liturgies to make Eucharist as meaningful and engaging as possible. They developed it into a form of art that combined literature, music, dance, and painting. The liturgies they developed incorporated the various meanings of Eucharist. Eucharist was developed like a drama in the sense that everything in it represented something else. A church building represented the world, which includes both heaven and earth. The community that worships in a church building represented all the Christians of all times and places, both the living and the departed. This cosmic community was understood as the embodiment of the invisible Christ. In the Eucharist all the participants together acted out the cosmic divine drama of incarnation, crucifixion, and resurrection of Christ. The story of this cosmic drama may be elaborated as follows:

The people on earth lead a life of disobedience and alienate themselves from the king of heaven and earth (God). The prince of heaven (Christ) descends to the earth as a mediator. Born as a human child, the prince identifies himself with the people on earth. The rebelliousness of the people on earth makes them reject the prince as well. The prince gives himself to be killed – a self-sacrifice. Being the son of God and a son of man simultaneously, with the role of a mediator, the death of the prince gets more than one meaning. It becomes an expression of the unconditional love of the king of heaven toward the people on earth. It also becomes an expression of the obedience on behalf of the people on earth. This self-sacrifice thus bridges the gap between God and the people on earth. The prince rises from among the dead, victorious over the forces of evil. The prince goes back to heaven and assumes the position of the primary counselor of the king of heaven. Also the prince sends a counselor to the earth from heaven to continue his work. In the present time, Christ is at the presence of the king of heaven mediating on behalf of the people on earth. The counselor he sends to earth is constantly working with the people on earth on behalf of the King of heaven. As a result of the work of Christ and the counselor, more and more people get reconciled to the king of heaven, and Christ continues to be present on earth through them. The community of these people acts as the embodiment of Christ. Sometime in the future the gap between heaven and earth will be fully bridged, and all people on earth will live according to the will of God. Then the prince will return to the earth as its ruler.

Although Eucharist enacts all the events of this drama, the self-sacrifice of Christ (prince) is its central event. Christ as a priest sacrifices himself as a lamb. In the Eucharist, a priest plays the part of Christ as priest. The bread and wine represent Christ as the lamb. The congregation plays the part of the whole church, which consists of all Christians of all places and times, and which identifies with Christ. Thus the priest as well as bread and wine on the altar represent not only Christ but also the church.

This cosmic drama served as a window to the reality of existence behind the appearance. As they acted out this drama over and over and week after week as a community, the reality sank deep into their subconscious, and this made them capable of thinking, feeling, and acting at a far higher level than those who perceived only the appearance. It cleansed them of all the dirt in their minds, strengthened their bonds with one another, and it made them one with Christ, so that they could represent Christ out in the world as one cosmic visible body of the invisible Christ.

What is Eucharist for? Paulos Mar Gregorios, asserts that in Eucharist the church as the embodiment of Christ performs the high-priestly function of representing the creation before the throne of God.

> The continuous act of offering the Eucharist is the church's fulfillment of her own priestly role. .. The church does so on behalf of the whole of humanity, and also of the whole of animate and inanimate creation[6].

Such an understanding makes Eucharist a part of the regular life of the church. Eucharist is a natural output of the very nature of the church. It is not a means to get anything.

## 2. As a Means of Grace

Christianity spread to the east, west, and south from Palestine though we read in the Bible only about the spread of Christianity toward the west. Paul was the primary apostle to the west, and Thomas was the primary apostle to the east. We don't know exactly who took Christianity to Africa.

In the west, where Paul spread Christianity, Greek became its primary language even in the first century. Although Latin was the language of the Romans, it was not used by any Christian writer until the beginning of the third century. Tertullian (160 - 220 CE) was the first Christian writer who wrote in Latin. Eventually there were more writers such as Cyprian, Ambrose, Jerome, and

Augustine. Thus Greek Christianity was already three centuries old when Latin Christianity was born. Some of these Latin writers were also fluent in Greek, but not all of them. Augustine, the one known as the primary architect of Latin Christianity, didn't know Greek. Thus he didn't have the advantage of acquiring the rich Greek Christian heritage. Augustine's views deviated sharply from the views of the Greek fathers in several aspects. The way the Latin Christianity saw the role of the church and meaning of Eucharist deviated from the traditional understanding of the Greek fathers.

A shallow and easy-going view that the Kingdom of God was already on earth seems to have become the primary view in Latin Christianity. The emperor of Rome was viewed as ruling on behalf of Christ, and all that was left for Christians to do was to rule the world along with Christ. This view was rejected by the Greek fathers as silly and shallow, but it gained deep roots in the Latin world. Since the time Constantine moved his capital to Constantinople, the bishop of Rome was seen as a replacement of the emperor in Rome. The Latin Church saw itself as the embodiment of the King Christ, and was ruling the world on behalf of Christ, and the bishop (pope) of Rome began to execute this power as the vicar (representative) of Christ.

Eucharist was seen as a means to receive the divine power to stay in the privileged position of authority representing Christ. St. Augustine, the primary Latin father, defined a sacrament as the visible means of an invisible grace, and grace was understood by the Latin Church as a power that comes from God. This may be related to the third meaning of Eucharist given by the early church—as manna. It seems that this meaning gained emphasis in the Latin Church over against the other two meanings.

While the Greek Christianity saw Eucharist primarily as a covenant that we make with God, the Latin Christianity saw it primarily as the providence we receive from God. Thus while the Greek Christianity stressed our responsibility, the Latin Christianity stressed our privileges. While the Greek Christianity thought about what we can give, the Latin Christianity thought about what we can get.

It seems that the Latin Christianity lacked the ability of the Greek Christianity to handle metaphorical language. The Latin Christianity had difficulty understanding the metaphors and symbolism in the scriptures and in the liturgy. As a result they tend to make the mistake of interpreting metaphorical language literally. Forgetting the simple truth that everything in Eucharist (the building, the people, the things, the actions, the words and the sounds) represents and symbolizes something else, the Latin Christianity has had centuries of arguments and fights over whether Christ is really present or symbolically present in Eucharist. This lack of ability to understand metaphorical language might have been another reason for the Latin Christianity to really usurp political power for the church. They probably assumed that Christ was literally ruling the world through them. When they went for crusades with the Muslims and when they imprisoned Galileo for claiming that the earth was round, and when they burned William Tyndale for translating the Bible to English, they were misusing their power from a false and literal understanding.

As a result of this understanding, Eucharist became something that a priest could do by himself. When a priest uttered the correct Latin words, the spirit of God descended, and the bread and wine magically transformed to the body and blood of Christ. This made the priests extraordinary people with extraordinary power upon the Spirit of God, and the common people had to depend upon them to connect with Christ and to obtain salvation. This widened the gap between the priests and the laity, and eventually the ignorant laity was widely exploited by the unscrupulous clergy.

It was claimed that the Holy Eucharist provided an opportunity to the people to be present at the scene of crucifixion by asserting that Christ was really made present on the altar and the breaking of bread was really the crucifixion of Christ. All the participants would accept the Eucharist from the priest as a symbol of accepting Christ and his salvation. Not accepting Eucharist meant that they were rejecting Christ. This understanding made all the participants accept

Eucharist, and it continues even today. Thus Eucharist was seen as a means of grace and salvation. It clearly divided people into those who accepted Christ and those who did not.

The Latin Christianity grew to become a very powerful institution which had its own laws and lands. It also imposed taxes. It accepted gifts of all kinds from people who wanted special favors or wanted to be certain of a place in heaven. The power of the Church grew with its wealth, and it was then able to influence the kings and rulers of Europe. Opposition to the Church resulted in excommunication, and the excommunicated ones could not attend any church services or receive the sacraments, and as a result, they would go straight to hell when they died. In order to suppress heresy, the church employed Inquisition—burning to death. Many famous medieval people were accused of heresy and were subject to an inquisition.

This made a **reformation** essential in the Latin Christianity in the 16th century. The numerous protestant churches that were born as a result have been protesting against the corruption in the Latin Christianity for the last four centuries. The big chunk of the church that stayed without splitting away as Protestants continued to be known as the Roman Catholic Church. As the Catholic Church elevated the Eucharist as a means of salvation, the Protestants demoted it to a very insignificant level. In many protestant churches, a podium replaced the altar, for listening to the word of God replaced Eucharist as the means of salvation for them. Someone could get saved by faith, and faith occurred by listening to the word of God. A preacher represents Christ for Protestants. If you attend a Sunday worship in a Protestant church, you will notice that a sermon is the peak point of the entire service there.

Recently the Catholic Church has had the good sense to correct some of its mistakes. Pope John Paul, the head of the Catholic Church, went around the world apologizing for the centuries-old mistakes and errors committed by his Church. The second council of Vatican (1962-65) was a major attempt to correct some of the errors in the Catholic Church. One of the major corrections made by the Vatican council was in its understanding of the Eucharist. It had the willingness to be open to the understanding of the Greek fathers regarding the church as the body of the suffering Christ and of Eucharist as a mystical act that bonds Christ and church. The Second Vatican Council's document, the Constitution on the Sacred Liturgy (1963), emphasized the Eucharist as an ordered celebration of the whole community led by the priest and called for the full, conscious, and active participation of all the faithful.

**Eucharistic Hospitality** is a topic hotly debated in the ecumenical circles today. The Roman Catholic Church does not normally offer Eucharist to non-Catholics. The protestant churches protest against it and ask the Catholic Church to be willing to be hospitable to non-Catholics as well. If the Holy mass is a means of God's grace, the Catholic Church has no right to limit it to the Catholics; it belongs to all. This is how the protestant churches argue their case.

Neither do the Orthodox churches offer Eucharist to the non-Orthodox, but for a different reason. For the Orthodox, Eucharist is not a means of grace. It is not something that God gives us. It is a sacrifice that the church offers to God, it is a covenant that the church makes with God, and it is a mystical act that unites the church with Christ. There is no question of hospitality here. Paulos Mar Gregorios has clarified this point.[8] Moreover, the Orthodox worship is highly symbolic, and an uninitiated person wouldn't make any sense of it at all. What is the body of Christ for the initiated would be nothing but a piece of bread for the uninitiated.

### A Comparison of the Greek and Latin Understanding
To have a clearer picture of the difference between the Greek and Latin approaches to Eucharist, compare these two scenarios.

Imagine that you are an Orthodox Christian and you are participating in the Holy Eucharist. You enter into the presence of God in the church, which represents the heaven and earth. You are no more an individual but a part of a community, which is the body of Christ--the embodiment of the invisible Christ. The people inside the church building represent the complete body of Christ of all times and places. Here you transcend the limits of time and space, and participate in the incarnation of Christ. Christ, as both the priest and the lamb, sacrifices himself. The bread and wine on the altar represent the body of Christ. As the priest places the body and wine on the altar, you, along with the entire body of Christ, sacrifice yourself to God. Thus you participate in the self-sacrifice of Christ. Only those people who have prepared their body and mind by fasting and prayer will come forward to accept Eucharist. Not accepting Eucharist does not mean rejecting Christ.

Now imagine that you are a Catholic and you are meaningfully participating in the Latin mass. When the priest pronounces certain words, the bread in his hands transforms into the body of Christ. When the priest breaks the bread, the crucifixion happens. This lets you transcend the limits of time and space, and have the opportunity to be an eye-witness of the saving event that happened two thousand years ago. When you accept the bread from the priest, you actually accept Christ into you, and accept the salvation he gives you through his sacrifice on the cross. You realize that you are among the people who are saved. All people in the congregation go to accept the Eucharist from the priest, because if you don't, it is like rejecting the salvation offered by Christ.

How are they similar and different? Both are symbolic, and both let you transcend time-space limitations. But there are differences. In the second you are a mere spectator, and you are a passive recipient of the grace and salvation you are offered. In the first, as a part of the body of Christ, you sacrifice yourself to God.

|  | Latin | Greek |
|---|---|---|
| Church building | Place of crucifixion | Heaven and earth (The whole world) |
| Congregation | Witnesses of crucifixion | Represents the whole church, which is the body of Christ |
| Bread & wine | Becomes Christ | Represents Christ |
| Purpose | To receive grace | To participate in Christ's high-priestly vocation of representing the creation before God. |

## Eucharist in the Indian Orthodox Church – An Example

This author belongs to the Orthodox Church in India, which has been on the side of the Greek Church. It has been in existence in India since the first century CE. Toward the end of sixteen centuries of its peaceful existence came the missionaries from the Latin Church in the west. They exhibited their aggressive and uncivilized manner here by forcefully bringing the church in India under their control for a short period. They burned the precious literary wealth of this community. During the fifty years of captivity under them, they managed to change most of our indigenous ways to suit their Latin ways. They infused the corrupt Latin views and rites into this community in fifty years. Today though we are no more under their control, we are still struggling to overcome the shock, and struggling to get rid of the corrupt views and rites.

The Orthodox Church in India today seems to be operating with the false notion that church is the embodiment of the King-Christ. This false assumption makes it misuse its power to rule just like the Latin Church in Rome did. Similarly the Orthodox Church in India seems to be under the impression that Eucharist is a means of grace which would keep us in our privileged position of power.

Credit goes to Metropolitan Paulos Mar Gregorios for identifying the presence of such corrupted beliefs in our church. Tirelessly did he preach that church is the body of Christ, whose throne is a cross, and the mission of the church is to manifest this suffering Christ. He also spent a great deal of his time and energy to tell us that Eucharist is not a sacrament as the Latin Church saw it, but a mystery as the Greek church understood it. Mar Gregorios explains this idea in his books, *Joy of Freedom* and *Introducing the Orthodox Churches,* and in numerous papers. Fr. M. C. Kuriakose has elaborated on this in his paper, *The Concept of the Sacraments in the Writings of Paulos Mar Gregorios and its Relevance.*[9]

## Concluding Remarks

The Latin Christian world, which includes both the Catholic Church and the protestant churches, needs to modify its understanding of church and of Eucharist. The Greek Christian world, which was heavily influenced by the Latin world, also needs to make the modification. Three areas that need modification are listed below:

1.  The Christian world can continue to believe that church is the embodiment of Christ, and Christ is king. But they need to make a minor correction in their view of the nature of the kingship of Christ. Christ's kingship and his kingdom are not like the ones we see in this world. As Paulos Mar Gregorios points out, Christ's throne is his cross. It was on the cross that we see the inscription, *The King of the Jews*. He rules his kingdom of love from his cross.

2.  While the Latin Church saw Eucharist as a means of grace primarily by relating it to the manna from heaven, the Greek Church understood it primarily as the covenant made with God. Once this difference is recognized, there can be better understanding between the two tributaries. They can learn from each other and move on together.

3.  The Christian world needs to learn to understand and use metaphors. When we keep on arguing whether Christ is really present in the bread, we are with Nicodemus who asked how he could get into his mother's body again. Although Nicodemus was an educated person and belonged to the higher strata of his society, he lacked the simple ability to understand metaphors. If the Christian world is willing to gain this ability of decoding metaphors, the world can be a more peaceful and healthy place.

With this altered understanding of Christ, Church, and Eucharist, the Christian church all over the world can once again become a truly visible image of Christ.

My purpose here is not polemical. I am not attacking the west standing on the side of the east. Actually the east and the west belong to our past, and today we are all together in this small global village. We can stand together hand in hand and look at our past to identify the specific ideas and events that separated us, so that we can be fully one in Christ.

# 19. Science for Man or Man for Science?

Is the origin of the universe accidental or planned? This was the topic of a seminar in Houston, and the presenter was Mr. Philip Thekkel, a High School Science teacher. He concluded that the origin of the universe is accidental, and not planned by any external force. The participants listened with great interest to all the scientific information he presented and they were fully in agreement with all

of them. However, they couldn't wholeheartedly agree with his approach toward science and its role in human life. To the pointed question by a participant whether he was a theist or an atheist, he evaded giving a direct response, and said that the question itself was irrelevant. When he was asked by another participant how he would relate scientific knowledge to the life of humanity, he responded that science evolves as a result of human curiosity, and it helps us raise our standard of living, but beyond that he couldn't see any other connection between science and human life. Asked about his worldview, he didn't have anything to say; even the term worldview sounded unfamiliar to him.

Underlying the approach of Mr. Thekkel, there is a loaded question-- is science for man or man for science? He seems to believe that man is for science. Science for him is the only reliable and unprejudiced pursuit of truth, and it exists for its own sake. The well-being of humanity cannot be a goal of science. The motto must be science for science, not for man. If mankind understands this, it will be free from superstitions that inhibit human development. This belief that man is for science is supported by secularism, empiricism, and naïve realism. Secularism is a view that religion and religious considerations should be ignored or excluded from social and political matters. Empiricism is the epistemological principle that all ideas and categories are derived from sense experience and that knowledge cannot extend beyond experience. Naïve realism is the ontological view that what appears to our senses is what really exists.

Two thousand years ago Jesus Christ asserted that man is not for religion (Sabbath), but religion is for man. Whenever religion gets corrupted and becomes a dehumanizing force, a reformer or a reform movement arises with this message. Protestantism was such a reform movement in response to the corruption in the western Christianity. But it is very little known that secularism and Marxism were also reform movements against the corruption in Christianity. Although these movements do have value as reform movements, they do not provide a comprehensive worldview as a replacement. Secularism emphasized the role of science to revolt against religion, but it overemphasized this role to the extent of asserting that man is for science. Today we need another Jesus to assert that science is for man, and not man for science.

Paulos Mar Gregorios points out three different attitudes toward science in our world.

1. A blind faith in science
2. A blind rejection of Science
3. A balanced view

According to the first, Science and technology are potentially capable of solving all the problems of mankind. This view is popular in the developing countries. According to the second, Science is good for nothing because it has been lionized out of all proportion by the necessities of urban-industrial life and by the political opportunism of the technocracy. This counter-culture view is popular in advanced industrialized societies. According to the third view, Science is a useful tool, which helps us to predict certain aspects of reality and therefore to control them. It may also help us partially to understand the nature of reality, but cannot give us an adequate picture of it. This is the view of the philosophers of science from the English-speaking world.

The approach of Mr. Thekkel seems to be a blind faith in science. He represents the general approach of the developing countries. This blind faith in science seems to have developed in revolt against a blind rejection of science in the name of preserving the culture or of counter-culture. But what we need is a balanced view of science. Science is one of the ways in which we seek knowledge, and it is a very useful way indeed. But placing science in the seat of God will jeopardize human existence.

### Science on the Seat of God

Paulos Mar Gregorios has explained clearly why human existence can be in jeopardy if science occupies the seat of God. What follows is a summary of his argument.

Modern Science is comparatively new in the history of humanity, only a few centuries old. Science had once to fight for survival against the unjust onslaughts of the dogmatic western Christianity. That period is now happily over. Science has overcome the resistance from religion and it can stand on its own. However, Science itself had been tempted to claim certain dogmatic certainties for itself in the light of some of her spectacular achievements in the last century.

Medieval European society unquestioningly obeyed the Roman Catholic Church as the ultimate arbiter of truth in all fields. The notorious medieval dictum: *Roma locuta est, Causa finita est* (Rome has spoken, the matter is settled) represented this unquestioning obedience. A revolt against the medieval church's authority occurred in several stages. First there were the pre-Renaissance protests of simple peasants against the exploitation and domination by the Church as major landholder. Then came the European Renaissance which counter-posed the authority of ancient Greek philosophers and Classics as an alternative to the authority of the church, especially in art, music and literature. Then came the Protestant Reformation which lifted Scriptural authority against Papal authority. Finally, the French Revolution and the European Enlightenment of the 18th and 19th centuries fully repudiated the authority of King and Priest, of Church and Tradition, and set up human rationality as the final arbiter of truth. Man became the measure and centre of all things, with Humanism, liberal and Marxist, becoming the dominant ideology. This is the context in which Modern Science developed and flourished.

Medieval priests in their black robes and Cross in hand have been today replaced by Modern Scientists in their white smocks and computer at hand. The uncritical devotion of both scientists and lay people to Modern Science and Technological Rationality as the ultimate arbiter of truth is similar to the uncritical obedience of the medieval Europe to the Roman Catholic Church. Today the dictum has become: *Scientia locuta est, Causa finita est* (Science has spoken, the matter is settled).

The scientific rationality assumes dogmatically and unscientifically the given-ness of a self-existent entity called 'Nature'. It also assumes that things are what they appear to be. This assumption is called Naive Realism, which refuses to ask questions about the ontological status of phenomena due to the inability of science to answer those questions. Worst of all, it assumes that man, the knowing subject, can stand outside the nature, and objectify, know, and manipulate it. By overvaluing objectivity and underplaying subjectivity, this approach has distorted human personality; disciplining oneself to be always objective renders human beings very inhibited in their subjective human relations.

There have been so much faith and hopes upon Science. Once it was thought by some at least that Scientific Rationality would provide us with the right morality. Every attempt so far has failed to yield the desired fruit. Again, once it was thought that scientific reasoning would open all the doors to all knowledge. We now know that science has its limits, and that much of what we know does not come from science, but from other forms of experience, including human relations, art and music, literature and drama, pain and pleasure, and perhaps even from religious experience. Many of us believed that scientific knowledge is objective and therefore true, while other convictions, which are subjective, are prone to error. Today we know that totally unsubjective objectivity is unattainable, for subjectivity is an essential aspect of all knowing. And we know that current scientific knowledge is subject to revision in the light of future knowledge, and that there is no "finally proved" status to any scientific proposition.

A ridiculous dogma was held by the 19th century European Positivists that all human knowledge passes through three stages: theological, metaphysical, and scientific. It was held that the scientific is the only true knowledge which supersedes the two previous stages, which are the infant and adolescent stages of human evolution. This dogma concluded that science makes all theology and metaphysics obsolete. Today this is recognized as a dogma produced by the European Enlightenment of the 18th and 19th centuries.

Most of the philosophers of science see science as a way of seeing our world using paradigms. The paradigms are in a process of constant revision and change, not in accordance with any rational law, but almost randomly. These philosophers agree that Science is not proven knowledge, but only a way of seeing reality, a very successful way indeed. But no infallibility can be claimed for science, nor can it be given any monopoly over human knowledge. Such a modest evaluation of science is common among the Philosophers of science today. Toward the end of the last century, dogmatic scientism was slowly becoming outdated and unfashionable.

The revolt against scientific rationality has only begun. The protest will take at least several decades to mature and gain sufficient momentum to compel attention. When the protest matures, the foundations of a new civilization will also come to light.

### Science-Technology Needs to Become a Tool for Doing Good

There was a time when pure science was distinguished from applied science, but today more than 95% of science is applied. Scientific research is so bound up with improving technological capability that the distinction between science and technology is difficult to maintain. Scientific research is no longer an open possibility for all societies because the cutting edges of scientific research are tied with unaffordable high technology. There was a time when scientific knowledge was public, open to experimental confirmation or refutation by any competent scientist. This is no longer so. The world scientific community today is divided into two classes: One class of scientists are employed by defense or military establishments and the other by large profit-oriented corporations, who are sworn to secrecy and are not allowed to share their scientific knowledge with others, for security reasons or for monopoly considerations.

As a result, war and profit-oriented establishments corner the best scientific talent in the market by paying them extra incentives. The cutting edge of current scientific research thus looks for greater killing capacity or greater profit and power for the few. Science is thus prostituted and misused. Not much scientific research is available for humane purposes like healing, healthy and economic housing development, unmonopolizing and non-chemical food production, and for good education in a healthy environment.

Science/technology itself has become a commodity and private property. Since high-tech is much in demand by all people, its high marketability becomes a new tool of exploiting and oppressing the poor. Patenting and copyright laws make knowledge itself a commodity for trade, profit making, exploitation, and enslavement. The commercialization and prostitution of science and technology for mass murder and easy profit is a deviation from its original nobility.

Modern science and technology have immensely increased the capacity of humanity for good and evil. Such an increase is a challenge to the human will to direct its abilities towards the good and not towards evil. This is a demand for greater moral and spiritual effort, but unfortunately, we let ourselves morally disintegrate, by choosing a culture of meaningless affluence and instant gratification of all urges. Even religion and its leadership, instead of setting high standards, seem to fall below the prevailing moral standards of ordinary people. Scientists themselves had at one time an enviably high moral level, in their commitment to the truth and in their pursuit of knowledge. The link between science and integrity seems to grow weaker day by day.

### Conclusion

This has been a quick overview of the various attitudes and approaches toward science in our time. In some parts of the world, Science is placed in the seat of God and is seen as a panacea for all human existential problems. In some other parts, science is placed in the seat of Satan and is seen as the cause of all human existential problems. But fortunately, in many other parts of the world, science is neither divinized nor demonized, but is seen as a tool. Those who see it as a tool are in two camps: those who want to use it for the good of mankind and those who want to use it to destroy mankind. Which side are we? Do we choose the path of life or of death?

# 20. Can Christian Faith Contribute to Global Peace?

Can Christianity still be an agent of unity and peace in spite of its long history of internal divisions? It seems very unlikely. But a young priest of the Oriental Orthodox Church answers it affirmatively in his recent book, *Christian faith and Global Peace*[1].

In this book, which is his doctoral dissertation, published recently by CSS Books in India, Father Bijesh Philip evaluates the contribution of two towering theologians of the last century toward global peace—Hans Küng and Paulos Mar Gregorios. Bringing them together, Father Philip claims that in Hans Küng and Mar Gregorios, the western and eastern Christian traditions converge with the single purpose of bringing about peace in the world. Hans Küng and Mar Gregorios, who have been giants in the world of thought, have so much in common although they have come from the two diverse tributaries of Christianity. The common goal of peace and justice has made the differences between them insignificant.

What is the most authentic form of Christianity with which all the other forms of Christianity can be measured and evaluated? This is the point at which Hans Kung and Mar Gegorios apparently disagree. As the most authentic form of Christianity, Hans Küng views Jesus Christ and the New Testament church, whereas Mar Gregorios gives due importance to the Holy Tradition as a whole. If we compare the Holy Tradition of the church to a stream, its source is Christ and His gospel, and its record is the Holy Scriptures, with the writings of the fathers, creeds, and liturgy as its subsequent expressions. Even though both Hans Küng and Mar Gregorios take this into consideration, Hans Küng's focus is more on the source of this stream whereas Mar Gregorios takes the stream as a whole seriously.

By peace they both mean *shalom*-- all humanity existing together maintaining right relationship with the environment (nature) and with the transcendent. We do not have peace today because all these relationships are disrupted. We do not maintain a right relationship with God; in fact, we live our life based on a worldview that does not even have a God. Instead of taking a responsible role in relation to the nature, we keep on exploiting it. Instead of making peace with our fellow beings and living together as a family, we spend a good part of our resources to develop ways to annihilate each other.

The Godless worldview which originated in the European enlightenment and spread all over the world is seen by both as the primary reason behind the mess our world is in today. Although the European enlightenment helped us to see the world in a better way and helped develop the modern medicine, education, science, and technology, it blinded us from seeing the transcendent ground of everything. This Godless worldview is the root cause of the uncontrolled exploitation of nature and of mounting moral crisis leading to violence in global scale. The irresponsible misuse of authority by the Christian church in Europe is what originally led to such a development. The solution today is to adopt a worldview that affirms God's existence. We need to turn to our rich God-affirming religious resources with an open mind, which can enrich our medicine, education, economics, science and technology, paving way to a much better and more meaningful way of life for mankind.

There can't be peace without justice. How can there be peace and justice where there is slavery and exploitation? Global peace cannot be established or maintained without a conscious and united effort of the humanity to establish justice in the world. Religious people must have the willingness to join hands with the nonreligious people in this mass movement for justice and peace.

Although Hans Küng and Mar Gregorios are well-rooted in their own religious traditions, they extend their arms to hold the entire human race. Their religious faith does not prevent them from working for the wellbeing of all; on the contrary, their faith empowers them to do so. Thus from their own life, they set this as an example for all the religious people in the world. They advice all people to be well-rooted in their own religious traditions, but stretch their arms to include all the fellow beings without excluding any. Such an attitude and approach can root out fundamentalism and communalism.

Although they have unshaken faith in God, neither of them does the mistake of trying to contain God within their own religious community or tradition. They both believe in a God who transcends all limits and barriers. They see God's presence wherever there is good, and they challenge their fellow Christians to see God in other religious communities and even among nonreligious people.

Father Philip begins this study with a biographical note of Hans Küng and Mar Gregorios. After presenting a detailed study of their commitment to the Christian faith and to global peace in several chapters, a comparison of their thought and work is made in the last part. Father Philip has made it readable for all by avoiding the theological jargon as much as possible and by providing appropriate explanation and translation wherever needed.

The work of father Philip is a contribution to ecumenism as well as to global peace. Hope and pray that this work will serve as a stepping stone to further studies on this topic.

# 21. What is the Role of Science and Faith?

What is the role of science and faith in the future of humanity? I am addressing this question with the help of two books published in the eighties-- The Cosmic Code[1], a book by Heinz R. Pagels, the associate professor of Theoretical Physics at the Rockfeller University, and The Cosmic Man[2], a book by Metropolitan Paulos Mar Gregorios, the principal of the Orthodox Theological Seminary in India.

### The Cosmic Code

"I think the universe is a message written in a code, and the scientists' job is to decipher that code," Dr Pagels writes. The book deals with the incredible progress of physicists in revealing the nature of the universe. Our age is witnessing a revolution in Physics, which has radically altered our world view. The revolution began with the theory of relativity by Albert Einstein, and the quantum theory by several eminent physicists of our time.

Just two decades ago, the steady state model of the universe was accepted widely. According to this model, the universe has no beginning and no end. Aristotle, the ancient Greek philosopher, thought of the universe in this way. This model has been replaced by the standard big bang model in our own time. According to this model, the entire universe originated in an enormous explosion. All matter was once concentrated into a very hot soup of quarks, leptons, and gluons. This soup expanded rapidly and exploded. Then it cooled down, enabling nuclei, then atoms, and finally galaxies, stars, and planets condensed out of it. This explosion is still going on. It has been observed that the universe is expanding.

Where did the primordial soup of quarks, leptons and gluons come from? Dr. Pagels answers this question without the slightest doubt -- from vacuum. What is vacuum? The modern quantum theory has a surprisingly novel idea about vacuum, that vacuum is not empty. The vacuum actually consists of particles and antiparticles being spontaneously created and annihilated. Space looks empty only because this great creation and destruction take place over such short times and distances. Everything that ever existed or can exist is already potentially there in the nothingness of space. A quantum that goes in and out of reality is called a virtual quantum. It could become a real quantum, an actual particle, only if it had sufficient energy to do so. Well, what will happen to the universe ultimately? The universe will probably go back to where it came from -- to vacuum.

The discovery of modern Physics is very exciting indeed. However, Dr. Pagels warns us against an easy -going optimism. The discovery of the cosmic code is a major challenge to our civilization according to him. It can annihilate us or give us a better existence. Dr. Pagels prescribes the way to face the challenge as follows,

> The challenge to our civilization which has come from our knowledge of the cosmic energies must be met by the creation of a moral and political order which will accommodate these forces or we shall be destroyed.

Dr. Pagels thinks that both knowledge and faith are indispensable for healthy existence.

> Our capacity for fulfillment comes only through faith and feelings. But our capacity for survival must come from reason and knowledge. They are different resources of human life. Both impulses live inside each of us; but a fruitful coexistence sometimes breaks down, and the result is an incomplete person.

Unfortunately, people often deviate to extreme attitudes. Knowledge without faith, faith without knowledge -- both are extremes. Dr. Pagels is especially concerned with the latter kind of extremity. As an example he tells about a poet he happened to meet. She belonged to a community which rejected the use of machines. She wore handmaid dress, and wrote with quills. The poet explained the reason for her behavior as follows:

> A demonic spirit inimical to humanity came upon the earth 300 years ago. It captured the best minds among the scientists, philosophers and political leaders. Soon the monsters of science, technology and industrialism were loose upon the land.

Dr Pagels thinks that the problem is really misunderstanding.

People like this poet see reason as the tool of the devil, an instrument for the destruction of life and simple faith. They see the scientist as a destroyer of the free human spirit, while the scientist sees the poet's allies as blind to the material requirements of human survival.

He further says,

Science is not the enemy of the humanity but one of the deepest expressions of the human desire to realize the vision of infinite knowledge". "But, knowledge must be tempered with justice, a sense of moral life and our capacity for love and community.

### Cosmic Man

As Metropolitan Paulos Mar Gregorios says in the introduction, Cosmic Man analyses the problem of human existence in relation to the writings of Gregory of Nyssa, a fourth century Christian philosopher.

Every civilization has at its basis a cosmological-anthropological structural perspective, which answers the basic questions of existence such as how man is related to the world, and how world is related to God. The structural perspective is so decisive that a slight distortion in it can lead to major errors of judgment in shaping lives. In short, a strong basis is essential for the healthy existence of mankind.

Mar Gregorios argues that our contemporary civilization has a distorted basis. Dante's Divine Comedy is replaced by Russel's human tragedy of an objective world where standing "on the firm foundation of unyielding despair," modern man can worship only "at the shrine that his own hands have built". Alienation has so caught up with us that we dread this shrine which we have built, for it may at any time collapse bringing the roof down over our head.

Why do we say that the basis of our civilization is distorted? In the cosmology of our civilization, man is pushed aside to a marginal position. The objective nature, open to our science and technology, occupies the central position, and God has no place at all in the structure.

The very existence of the humanity depends upon digging out the distorted basis and putting a new basis which doesn't have the drawbacks of the present one. It is in search of an alternative basis that Mar Gregorios goes to the fourth century philosopher. Gregory of Nyssa was well grounded in the classical philosophy and in the Christian tradition. He was also well acquainted with the contemporary schools of philosophy and sciences.

Though the teachings of Gregory were widely accepted in the Eastern Christendom, they were misunderstood in the West. Mar Gregorios blames the Western Christendom for its inability to understand the thought of Gregory of Nyssa in the right way.

> Loaded with categories like original sin and supernatural, the baggage accumulated through centuries of alienation from the authentic tradition, theologians have lost the ability to see straight, and to look at the profundity of a thinker like Gregory, who does not operate within that framework.

Nevertheless, Mar Gregorios doesn't advocate a slavish adoption of the structural perspective of Gregory of Nyssa.

> Our own cosmology will have to be much more sophisticated than Gregory's because we know much more about the structure of the universe, of matter and energy, of cells and life, and of sub-atomic particles than Gregory could know in his time.

Gregory's cosmology consists of God, man, and the world. Man is a part of the world, which exists within the limits of time and space. However, God exists beyond all such limits. Therefore, God exists without any change although the world goes on changing. As God exists beyond the limits of time and space, God is incomprehensible to man. Human thought and language are limited to what exists within the limits of time and space.

Gregory makes a distinction between the *ousia* and *energia* of God. The *ousia* (essence) of God is totally incomprehensible to us. The world depends upon the *energia* (operation) of God for its existence. It is from non-being, which merely appears to exist, that God, the true being, has brought the world into existence.

According to the western Christian thought, which originated in Augustine, the essence of man is his sinful nature. Man is originally sinner. Gregory cannot agree with this idea. If man is sinner by nature, how can he be blamed for doing sin? According to Gregory, the essence of man is nothing but the essence of God. Man is the visible image of the invisible God. The original and the image differ in that the original is self-existent and remains unchanging whereas the image depends upon the original, and moves from beginning to end. Man is absolutely free as God is free. However, man is in a state of growing-- growing up to the perfection of God. As man is in need of growth, he is immature. Immaturity often makes man misuse his freedom. This is what Gregory calls evil or sin. Whatever in our attitude and behavior that hinders the perpetual growth towards the perfection of God is evil.

It is the whole of humanity at every place and time that is the visible image of God. As humanity is a part of the world, and the image of God, humanity has a mediating role -- between God and world.

What is history? Gregory would say that it is the kindergarten of mankind. When *chronos* (time) ends, *aion* (created eternity) begins. The whole of humanity in all time and place will be co-present there. Life in history is like a seed of corn. The seed dies and the plant comes out. The shape and size of a full grown plant cannot be predicted from the shape and size of its seed.

Paulos Mar Gregorios repeatedly asserts that we need a new science and technology that gives central place to mankind, as mediator between God and world. He further asserts that we need a new politics, a new economics, and a new social education. Mar Gregorios concludes the book saying that cosmic man becomes the divine presence in creation by a transformation of individuals, societies and of the whole of humanity.

### Concluding Remarks

The lines of thought presented in these two books are major contributions to laying a strong foundation to a new civilization. Can there be a new civilization without science? This is the question Dr.

Pagels addresses. His answer is an emphatic 'No'. Science is basic to the existence of the humanity. However, Dr. Pagels cautions us about the possibility of misusing science. He tries to make it clear that the problem is not in science itself but in the absence of right faith and morality. The solution to the problem is not to avoid the use of science, but to use it properly. Dr. Pagels strongly advocates the co-existence of science and faith. One without the other is fatal to mankind.

Mar Gregorios takes these issues and goes to the root of the matters. He is never tired of saying that we need a new science-- a science based on faith in the centrality of Mankind, a science based on faith in the existence of God. He digs deep down into fourth century to put a strong basis to the new civilization. The thought of Gregory of Nyssa, the fourth century philosopher, is astoundingly relevant in our age of quantum physics. That the world has come out of vacuum is basic to Gregory's thought. It is from non-being that the world is brought into existence by God, the true being. As Mar Gregorios says, our own Cosmology must be more sophisticated than that of Gregory because we have a much better knowledge of the world as revealed to us by science. According to the modern Quantum Physics, the world exists at two levels-- the world made of virtual quanta (vacuum), and the world made of real quanta (material world). The latter exists within time and space, whereas the former exists unaffected by time or space. Our visible world of real quanta came out of the invisible world of virtual quanta. We have to think of how we can put together the new knowledge brought to us by science and Gregory's cosmology. Can we equate the vacuum, made of virtual quanta, to Gregory's non-being? Gregory says that non-being is a kind of existence that doesn't really exist, but only appears to exist.

These questions make us aware that the attempt to put a strong foundation to a new civilization has only started. The major part of the work is yet to be done. Let scholars from every cultural background ask the basic questions of existence, and dig deep down to discover hidden treasures just as Mar Gregorios did.

# 22. What is Wrong with the European Enlightenment?

What is wrong with European Enlightenment? This is the question addressed in the book *A Light Too Bright, The Enlightenment Today*[1]. It was first published by the State University of New York Press in 1992. As the subtitle states, this book is an

assessment of the values of the European Enlightenment and a search for new foundations. The title of the book compares the European Enlightenment to the sunlight, which makes our world clearly visible, but at the same time makes a deeper level of the world invisible. We have to wait for the Sunset to see the star-filled sky.

In the preface, Mar Gregorios wants us to know that this book is not an academic work as it does not fit into any academic disciplines in the western world, but it is a plea to examine the foundations of human existence in this world. He also tells us how and where he happened to write this book. He did half of the work at the Isthmus Institute in Dallas, Texas with a three-month fellowship, and did the other half at the Indian Institute of Advanced study in Shimla with another three-month fellowship. Introducing this book, Harold G. Coward of the University of Calgary says that the author has a special talent for bringing together vast amounts of material and for summarizing them in clear and insightful ways. He thinks that the approach taken here in the critique of the European Enlightenment is unique, for it came from a non-European.

Encyclopedia Britannica defines European Enlightenment as a European intellectual movement of the 17th and 18th centuries in which ideas concerning God, reason, nature, and man were synthesized into a worldview that gained wide assent and that instigated revolutionary developments in art, philosophy, and politics. Central to Enlightenment thought were the use and the celebration of reason, the power by which man understands the universe and improves his own condition. The goals of rational man were considered to be knowledge, freedom, and happiness. Agreeing with this definition, Paulos Mar Gregorios proceeds to make an evaluation of its nature and its role in creating or present civilization. Mar Gregorios applauds this movement for liberating the world from ignorance and superstitions to a great extent and for elevating the living conditions throughout the world. But he also warns that the spectacular blessings of this movement should not make us so blind as to ignore the curses it has brought about, which will become clear if we are willing to examine the living conditions of the humanity today.

### The Living Conditions of the Humanity Today

Writing immediately after the Gulf war of 1991, Mar Gregorios begins this book asserting that we live in a sea-change period of world history. He says, "As ancient values crumble, time-honored institutions of social living disintegrate without new ones ready to take their place." Then he explains how the Gulf war radically altered the power configuration of the world. In 1990, right after the collapse of the Soviet Union and right before the Gulf war, the world had three major systems of political economy contesting for dominance: the temporarily triumphant western liberal democracy, the defeated Marxist-Leninist socialism, and the Pan-Islamism. But after the war, the US emerged asserting the uncontested global leadership. The world became a global market economy including almost all countries in the world with the US as the general manager. The UN, which was a major force before the war, was "captured and domesticated" during and after the war. Mar Gregorios calls for a new international alliance for global justice to counter this new unjust power structure and to seek justice, peace, dignity, and freedom.

In addition to this conflict, we have several other conflicts in our world-- feminist struggle, the conflict between national loyalty and ethnic identity, conflict among US, Europe, and Japan for world economic leadership, conflict due to the local cultures resisting the road roller of technological civilization that claims to be universal, and conflicts between those who want to make a fast pile and those who want to maintain a healthy environment for life.

Mar Gregorios presents the living condition of the humanity very clearly in his *Human Presence* as follows:

1. The poverty of billions of people perpetuated by economic injustice and exploitation. We failed in producing essential goods and distributing them equally, which makes us fight and even kill each other to possess the resources.

2. A sense of meaninglessness and boredom among the affluent, raising fundamental questions about the values of the consumer society and the civilization based on it.

3. Challenges to human existence posed by scientific-technological culture such as resource depletion, pollution, possible nuclear war, and possible misuse of artificial gene mutation.

In short, our civilization is "too destructive of human potential and has become capable of destroying itself and humanity in one blow".

## The Role of the European Enlightenment

European Enlightenment (EE) has been a very powerful cultural movement which could make the entire humanity flow together by merging the national and regional streams. The world has become one united interdependent market place because of EE. In order to understand this situation better, let us imagine the following scenario:

A few animals of different species are kept in a building in a zoo—the same kind in each room. No species comes in direct contact with any other one-- they have separate lives. One day a zoo manager removes the separation between the rooms of these animals so that the building becomes one big room. This is a challenging situation. It will take a while for the animals to adjust with the new situation. The transition can be painful. During the transition, the weaker ones might get eliminated or cornered.

This picture seems to be very similar to our present world. We have been living within our separate national and regional boundaries. Then comes this powerful cultural movement from Europe with its science and technology eliminating the boundaries with faster means of communication and transportation. This elimination of boundaries, often called globalization, raises a challenge to the human survival on the planet. Although the physical walls are disappearing, the invisible mental walls are still there. If we fail to learn to live together, the chances are that we may eliminate each other, and human race as we know it might become a part of history. We don't have the option of going back and reinstalling the boundaries that separated us. The only option left with us now is to demolish the mental walls as well. If we fail to do so, we will be risking our very existence.

The western liberal democracy, the Marxist-Leninist socialism, and the Pan-Islamism were living in their own separate worlds. With the boundaries collapsed, the weaker ones are cornered, and are facing the threat of elimination. Although they stay cornered for the time being, they will always be looking for an opportunity to jump upon the powerful.

The EE has had the power to eliminate the physical walls, but it does not have the power to eliminate the mental walls. It has also created new mental walls and also strengthened some of the existing ones. We need to look elsewhere for ways to demolish the mental walls. This is the context that encourages Mar Gregorios to look for what he calls "Other Enlightenment" (OE).

EE has been successful in demolishing the existing civilization, but it has been a failure in building up a new one its place. As a rebel it did a very good job by dethroning the existing power structures of humanity. But once it was enthroned to be in charge of a new civilization, it proved a failure. The civilization it replaced was entrenched in superstitions and irrationality. EE demolished this civilization using the powerful weapon of rationality. Rationality served as a good weapon, but it couldn't serve as a new foundation for a new civilization.

### The Worldview of European Enlightenment

The answers given to the three fundamental questions of existence by EE are inadequate as a dependable foundation for a new civilization. The questions are: what exists, how do we know, and why do we know. The chapter entitled *Reason's Unreason* examines the answers given by EE.

### 1. What exists?

Naïve realism, the fundamental belief of EE, is the assumption that there are subjects and objects, that subjects can know the objects as they are, and what cannot be known is unreal. Enlightenment rationality has no notion of transcendent knowledge that overcomes the opposition between the knower, the known, and the knowledge. Reality, both at microphysical level and at the megacosmic levels is not visualizable or conceptualizable. The concept of object can exist only at the macro level of our perception. When we speak of the universe as a mega object, we are transferring a category that applies only at the macro level. Really, the universe cannot be made an object of our thought or perception.

The self-dependence of the universe is an unexamined dogma of EE. God is thus an unnecessary hypothesis. But insights into things like Multiple Possibility Universe, dark matter, and other cosmic phenomena raise a big question here. Non-western and so-called primitive cultures have produced better models to understand the reality of the universe.

Secularism absolutizes time-space reality as the only kind of reality that we can deal with. But the ancient question whether they exist independent of our consciousness or whether they are just products of our mind is gaining currency in scientific circles. We need to understand it as window through which we can get to a transcendent apprehension of a higher level of reality.

EE sees the universe as a machine. However, the cosmos seems to act like an organism, which has both memory and personality. The effort to absolutize the world open to our senses as the only possible world and to deny its dependence on the transcendent can only lead to desperation.

### 2. How do we know?

The ultimate truth is assumed in EE to be an object or an idea about an object. However, Truth is a quest, not a concept. It is a state of being, not a statement of fact. Truth is what is, not what is stated. A valid proposition about truth can be a help in the quest, but is itself not the object of the quest.

Language is seen as the vehicle of truth. Enlightenment has overplayed the roles of language and conscious mind. Symbol, myth and ritual have been qualified as irrational. Truth lies beyond language and logic, and we need to seek liberation from the prison that enlightenment rationality has fortified.

Epistemology or theory of knowledge has been used in modern scientific disciplines as the guarantor of truthfulness. Every attempt in modern western thought to impose an epistemology as an absolute validation criteria falls under the criticism that no epistemology can be validated by itself. Epistemology is an arbitrary absolutization. The attempt to absolutize epistemology as an unquestionable first, and then make it the unshakable foundation of all knowledge, seems doomed from the start.

Conscious reason is seen by the Enlightenment as the instrument of knowing. But there are other ways and levels of knowing like the one we receive through meditation.

Causality is seen as an explanation for everything. Modern science depends on causality, and once we question the principle of causality, the whole scientific enterprise becomes shaky. Science looks at the world as a machine with interconnected and interacting parts. Causality is unable to explain the behavior of quantum phenomenon. But in non-western religions like Buddhism, there are different logical ways of explaining reality without idolizing causality. The Jungian "synchronicity" is an example from the west itself.

Precise measurement is seen as a way to truth. Measurement works in the macro level of the universe, but when it comes to micro level, it doesn't work.

### 3. Why do we know?

Traditionally, knowledge has been an end in itself, but EE made it a means to an end. Following Plato's notion of theoria, classical theory sought after ontology of the whole as the true, the good, and the beautiful. In order to find that ontology, the contemplative mind has to move away from the surface appearances. What lies behind and beyond the phenomena is the goal of the classical quest. All that exists was held together by nous or logos as an interconnected system. Classical theory also had an elaborate technology for rising from the temporal to the eternal, and these techniques were taught in Plato's academy and Aristotle's school. Mathematics was taught not to prepare them for engineering or accounting but to help their mind move higher to abstraction. But the real ascent of the mind was achieved by purification and illumination. The mystical tradition as it is called in the west is a series of practices that lead to the beatific vision or the mystical union. The classical tradition values practice only for the sake of theory. In the modern European Enlightenment, theory is ancillary to practice. Knowledge equips you to action. Knowledge gives the power to control, manipulate and dominate.

### The Overall Religious-Cultural Outlook

OE, compared to EE, has been universal. In the west, it has been called mysticism or spirituality or religion. All these are misnomers that dangerously distort the real sense to mean a department of human activity, a personal choice, an optional interest of certain individuals. In the absence of a better name, Mar Gregorios calls it "overall religious-cultural outlook". OE may be philosophically expressed. Aspects of this may be expressed through the various art forms. A community may express it through myth and rituals. A great soul like Buddha, Christ, Mohammed, or Lao-tze might be seen as an embodiment of this. Mar Gregorios cites several examples of OE from within Europe such as the ancient religious heritage, classical philosophical heritage, neoPlatonic heritage, Christian heritage, and its esoteric heritage. Before European enlightenment and the resulting process of secularization, religion was the all-pervasive basis of human existence. It is now reduced to something simply useful, functional, a utility for social integration, identity and maintenance and crisis confrontation.

The world is a global village today, but the humanity has not become a community yet. In order to create a global community, we need to go beyond the worldview held by EE. Those who hold the worldview of EE have to open up their minds in order to engage in a dialog with those who hold the view of OE. They need to forfeit their blind faith that what we see is all that exists. If they are willing to admit that what appears to our senses is different from what truly exists, they will have the opportunity to learn from all the other expressions of OE that are available to us, and we will witness not only the unity of humanity but also a tremendous advancement for humanity.

Religious world views are diverse and incompatible with each other, but they all agree in rejecting the naïve realism. Where science openly agrees that scientific knowledge is only operational, and that it has no access to the ultimate nature of reality, religion and science can co-exist peacefully. However in our civilization, science has taken the seat of authority. Many people think that science has the last word on everything. Religions need to be open and willing to listen to science and its rationality. Neither science nor religion should occupy the seat of authority. They need to seek the mystery of existence hand in hand.

### Hegel's Insight

Hegel is a child of European Enlightenment rather than a founder of it. However, instead of slavishly following the enlightenment view, he criticized it, and he introduced the transcendentalist point of view. In Hegel we see a view of religion that is classical and that represents the human tradition in a more adequate way than the later enlightenment concept of religion as a private matter. Hegel perceived the conflict between science and religion clearly. Religion distrusts finitude; science distrusts totality and the transcendent. Feeling and reason are alienated from each other. Hegel sought a reconciliation of science and faith, which he thought was the true function of philosophy. The conflict between science and faith for Hegel is a normal stage in the dialectical development of the spirit, and the polarities of thesis and antithesis have to be resolved at a higher level of synthesis.

According to Hegel, Philosophy and Religion are concerned about the meaning of the whole. The difference between them is in the method used. Philosophy uses thought, and this, according to Hegel, makes it superior to religion. According to Mar Gregorios, Hegel's overconfidence in the capacity of thought is misplaced. Thought, he says, cannot comprehend truth, but can only illuminate it. This does not mean that thought is undervalued by Mar Gregorios. He affirms that thought should be an essential part of all human activity, including religion.

Although religion uses thought, feelings, convictions, moral rules and worship, the primary method it employs is ritual. A ritual is a participatory symbolic act of a community to express and inform itself the transconceptual reality of human existence. A community expresses the meaning of its existence through rituals that can be transmitted from generation to generation.

European enlightenment expressed itself as naturalism and materialism in France, empiricism in Britain, and moralism in Germany. Basic to all these was the Cartesian dualism of Being and Thinking or of the world and the consciousness. However, it did not treat consciousness as having a separate identity, and it was also explained in terms of mechanical laws of causation, function, behavior, and laws. Hegel, however, saw the world and consciousness as the dialectical poles of a single reality—poles that have alienated from each other and in need of reconciliation.

Following the logic of thesis, antithesis and synthesis, these two poles will eventually get reconciled to each other at a higher level.

### Does "A Light Too Bright" Ignore Christ?

Brian McDonald, a former Presbyterian pastor but now a member of the Romanian Orthodox Church (OCA) in Indianapolis, Indiana, has written an interesting review of this book[2]. Being a convert to Orthodoxy from Protestantism, he certainly values Orthodoxy. That is probably how he happened to read a book by Paulos Mar Gregorios, an Orthodox bishop. However, contrary to his expectation, the view of Paulos Mar Gregorios does not fit his picture of Orthodoxy. Although he begins his review in a positive tone, soon it turns negative. He thinks that being an Orthodox Bishop, Mar Gregorios should have presented the theme of this book differently. He concludes that Mar Gregorios deviates from the ideals of Orthodoxy by being more in line with ecumenism and pluralism.

The disagreement occurs when Mar Gregorios suggests considering the other enlightenments in human history. There has been enlightenment in many traditions and cultures. Many cultures in the past and many current so-called undeveloped areas are poorer but wiser than our own. And this wisdom is based on an entirely different view of knowledge. Mar Gregorios cites examples from the Buddhist and Hindu traditions. Then he gives examples from the European tradition itself. At this point McDonald expresses his disappointment at the too brief treatment given by this Eastern Christian bishop to his own faith—the eastern Christianity. Mcdonald thinks that the view of the bishop is similar to the Hindu belief in many different roads leading to the ultimate goal. McDonald describes it a failure and an intellectual tragedy:

> The failure of Bishop Gregorios to present his Lord as the Light Universal for those walking in darkness is more than a deficiency in this book. It is almost an intellectual tragedy. What our world cries out for today is the kind of mind that can do in our era what the patristic thinkers did in theirs. There can be few individuals better placed by education, ability and

historical position than Gregorios to address modern-day seekers in the idiom of their various traditions. But it is a task that the bishop has apparently declined to do. Do not look to find a new Gregory of Nyssa here. Rather look to find beneath the mitre and robes of the Christian bishop the heart and soul of a World Council of Churches ecclesiastic, dedicated rather to "pluralism" and "inclusivism."

He concludes his review as follows:

I find myself asking how a Christian bishop could have any other desire in writing a book about the Enlightenment than to draw people into communion with the One who said that he was "the Light of men." This book is about light, but it is not about Christ. And that may leave its Christian reader feeling that they have been left sitting in the dark.

Brian Mcdonald is very upset about this Christian bishop for being too pluralistic and inclusivistic as to ignore his own religious tradition. He would have been so happy if this bishop presented Orthodoxy as the true and right way, and Christ as the only light. Contrary to his expectation, this bishop did not even one time mention in his book the Lord who proclaimed, "I am the light of the world." He calls it an intellectual tragedy.

It is true that Jesus made the proclamation, "I am the light of the world." However, this statement does not claim any uniqueness for Jesus because Jesus also said to his disciples, "You are the light of the world." Moreover, Mar Gregorios believed that all that is good in the world comes from God in spite of which channel it comes through. Thus the light that the world received through Mahatma Gandhi, or Buddha, or even the atheist, Karl Marx, is originally from God. However, people like McDonald believe that only the light seen through Jesus is the true light, and all other lights are false or misleading. McDonald blames Mar Gregorios for being ecumenical. He does not realize that Mar Gregorios transcended even ecumenism when he asserted his allegiance to the entire humanity. While he had his feet firm on his own inherited tradition of Orthodox Christianity, he embraced with his arms all that exists.

It is true that Mar Gregorios does not talk much about Jesus in this book. But what he says in this book seems to be what Jesus might say if he were living in our world. Mar Gregorios' exposure of the fallacies of EE reminds me of Jesus' exposure of the fallacies of the Pharisees' teachings in Matthew's Gospel. Jesus asked his generation to overcome the righteousness as taught by the Pharisees and go back to the true righteousness expressed in the traditional laws of Moses. Similarly Mar Gregorios is asking today's generation to overcome the values of the European Enlightenment and embrace the values of the universal and traditional enlightenment.

## Conclusion

Our modern human civilization, which began a couple of centuries ago, has been very successful in elevating our living conditions. However, it has also elevated the possibility of the extinction of human species from the planet. While holding on to the contributions of this civilization, we need to address the increased risk of our extinction. In *A Light Too Bright*, Paulos Mar Gregorios is addressing this issue, and suggesting a solution. EE needs an open mind regarding the basic questions of existence: what, how and why? EE thinks that only what our senses perceive exists, we know only with our ability of reasoning, and that we gain knowledge for the purpose of gaining mastery of the world. If we open our minds willing to listen and learn, we have a chance of survival. We need to know that the world is more than what we perceive, that rationality is only one way of knowing, and that knowledge is not a means to an end but an end in itself.

# Notes and References

**Chapter. 1**
1. Gregorios, Paulos. (1997). Love's Freedom The Grand Mystery: A Spiritual Auto-Biography. Kottayam: Mar Gregorios Foundation.
2. Thomas, Joseph E. (2001). Dr. Paulos Mar Gregorios, A Personal Reminiscence. Kottayam: Roy International.

**Chapter. 2**
1. Gregorios, Paulos. (1968). The Gospel of the Kingdom. Madras: Christian Literature Society.

**Chapter. 3**
1. http://paulosmargregorios.info/vatican_ii.htm
2. Gregorios, Paulos. (1976). What do the Orthodox believe? Introducing the Orthodox Churches. (1999) New Delhi: ISPCK.

**Chapter. 4**
1. Gregorios, Paulos. (1969). The Faith of Our Fathers. Kottayam: MGOCSM.
2. Gregorios, Paulos. (1968). The church fathers in the fifth Tubden from the Annual Report of the Orthodox Theological Seminary, Kottayam.

**Chapter. 5**
1. Gregorios, Paulos. (1988). The Meaning and Nature of Diakonia. Geneva: WCC.

**Chapter. 6**
1. Gregorios, P. (2000). Religion and Dialogue. Kottayam: Mar Gregorios Foundation

**Chapter. 7**
1. Gregorios, Paulos. (1997). Love's Freedom, The Grand Mystery. Kottayam: MGF.
2. Gregorios, Paulos. (1978). Science and Our Future. Madras: CLS.
3. Gregorios, Paulos. (1978). Human Presence. Geneva: WCC
4. Gregorios, Paulos. (1980). Science for Sane Societies. Madras: CLS.
5. Gregorios, Paulos. (1997). Love's Freedom, The Grand Mystery. Kottayam: MGF.

**Chapter. 8**
1. Gregorios, Paulos. (1995). Healing- A Holistic Approach. Kottayam: Mar Gregorios Foundation.
2. Heurman, Tom & Olson, Diane. Worldviews. http://www.amorenaturalway.com

**Chapter. 9**

1. Gregorios, Paulos. (1995). Education for a New Civilization in the New Millennium.
http://paulosmargregorios.info/English%20Articles/education.html
2. Verghese, Paul. The Impact of Western Educational Styles on India's Struggle for Development and Justice: Some Reflections.
    http://paulosmargregorios.info/English%20Articles/Impact_of_western_education.html


### Chapter. 10
**1.** Gregorios, Paulos. *(1976). Quest for Certainty: Philosophical Trends in the West: A Sample Survey of Later Twentieth Century Western Thought for the Average Indian Reader.* Kottayam: Orthodox Seminary.


### Chapter 12
1. Gregorios, Paulos Mar. (1987). Human Presence. Amity House: NY.
2. Gregorios, Paulos Mar. (1992). A Light Too Bright, The Enlightenment Today. Albany: State University of New York Press.
3. Verghese, T. Paul. (1970). The Freedom of Man. Philadelphia: The Westminster Press.
4. Verghese T. Paul . (1974). Freedom and authority. Madras: CLS
5. Varghese, T. Paul. (1971). Sanyaasajeevitham enthinuvendi?
6. izhakkambalam: Bethlehem St. Mary's convent souvenir. Sneham, Swaathanthryam, Puthiya Maanavikatha (2006). P.628.
7. A Letter to friends (1969). Retrieved from Paulosmargregorios.co.in


### Chapter. 13
1. Gregorios, Paulos (1980). Cosmic Man. New Delhi: Sophia Publications
2. Riley, Gregory J. (2001). The River of God. HarperOne
3. Lossky, Vladimir. (1976) The Mystical Theology of the Eastern Church. New York: St. Vladimir Seminary Press , p. 77


### Chapter. 14
1. Gregorios, Paulos. (1982). Cosmic Man. The Divine Presence. New Delhi/Kottayam: Sophia Publications.


### Chapter. 15
1. Gregorios, Paulos. (1989). Enlightenment East and West: Pointers in the Quest for India's Secular Identity. Shimla: Indian Institute of Advanced Study/New Delhi: B. R. Publishing Corporation.
2. Gregorios, Paulos. (1992). A Light Too Bright. Albany, New York: State University of NewYork Press.
3. Gregorios, Paulos. (1998). The Secular Ideology: An Impotent Remedy for India's Communal Problem. Kottaym: MGF/New Delhi: ISPCK.

4. http://paulosmargregorios.info/English%20Articles/Dudlean_lectures.ht ml

5. http://www.infidels.org/library/historical/robert_ingersoll/secularism.ht ml

6. http://www.bhpublishinggroup.com/savingleonardo/about-saving-leonardo.html.

7. Nehru, J. (1946). Discovery of India, Calcutta: Signet Press. P.680

8. Gregorios, Paulos. (1982). Cosmic Man. The Divine Presence: New Delhi/Kottayam: Sophia Publications.

## Chapter. 16

1. Gregorios, Paulos (2000). *Religion and Dialogue*. New Delhi: ISPCK. P.81

2. Geertz, Clifford (1973). *The Interpretation of Cultures: Selected Essays*. New York: Basic Books.

3. Fitzgerald, Timothy (2007). *Discourse on Civility and Barbarity*. Oxford University Press. pp. 45–46.

4. Daniel Dubuisson. "Exporting the Local: Recent Perspectives on 'Religion' as a Cultural Category", Religion Compass, 1.6 (2007), p.792.

5. Gregorios, Paulos (2000). *Religion and Dialogue*. New Delhi: ISPCK. P.116

6. Gregorios, Paulos (2000). *Religion and Dialogue*. New Delhi: ISPCK. P.124

7. Knitter, Paul F. (2002) *Introducing Theologies of Religions*. NY: Orbis Books.

8. Gregorios, Paulos. (1997). *Love's Freedom: The Grand Mystery*. Kottayam: MGF.

9. Gregorios, Paulos (2000). *Religion and Dialogue*. New Delhi: ISPCK. P.171

10. Gregorios, Paulos (2000). *Religion and Dialogue*. New Delhi: ISPCK. P.164

11. Clooney, Francis X. (2010) *Comparative Theology: Deep Learning Across Religious Borders*. Wiley-Blackwell.

12. Gregorios, Paulos. (1997). *Love's Freedom: The Grand Mystery*. Kottayam: MGF.

## Chapter. 17

1. The M*eaning and Nature of Diakonia*. Geneva: WCC, 1988. P.33

2. *Introducing the Orthodox Churches*. Kottayam: MGF / New Delhi: ISPCK, 1999. P. 7-8

3. "Vatican II: Gains, Hopes and Hurdles." Address delivered at Third Hammersmith Christian Unity Conference, May 1966

4. *Introducing the Orthodox Churches*. Kottayam: MGF / New Delhi: ISPCK, 1999. P. 3

5. *The Meaning and Nature of Diakonia*. Geneva: WCC, 1988

6. *The Meaning and Nature of Diakonia*. Geneva: WCC, 1988 p. 37

7. *The Meaning and Nature of Diakonia*. Geneva: WCC, 1988 p. 42

8. *The Meaning and Nature of Diakonia*. Geneva: WCC, 1988 p. 43

9. *Introducing the Orthodox Churches*. Kottayam: MGF / New Delhi: ISPCK, 1999 p.49

10. *Cosmic Man. The Divine Presence*. New Delhi/Kottayam: Sophia Publications, 1982. P. 233

11. *Introducing the Orthodox Churches*. Kottayam: MGF / New Delhi: ISPCK, 1999 p.5

12. http://paulosmargregorios.info/English%20Articles/Vision%20Beckons. htm

13. *Introducing the Orthodox Churches*. Kottayam: MGF / New Delhi: ISPCK, 1999 p.59

14. *Introducing the Orthodox Churches*. Kottayam: MGF / New Delhi: ISPCK, 1999 p. 61

15. *Introducing the Orthodox Churches*. Kottayam: MGF / New Delhi: ISPCK, 1999 p.54

16. *The Meaning and Nature of Diakonia*. Geneva: WCC, 1988 p. 3

17. *The Meaning and Nature of Diakonia*. Geneva: WCC, 1988 p. 36

### Chapter. 18

1. ttp://paulosmargregorios.info/English%20Articles/vatican_ii.htm.

2. Gregorios, Paulos. (1967). *The Joy of Freedom: Eastern Worship and Modern Man*. London: Lutterworth Press & Richmond, Virginia: John Knox Press.

3. According to the Encyclopedia of Food and Culture (http://www.ebook3000.com/Encyclopedia-of-Food-and-Culture--3-Volume-set-_93677.html) p. 41, the Passover sacrifice and the feast of unleavened bread are Spring festivals that predate the Exodus. Pesach, a pastoral holiday during which animals were sacrificed and eaten, probably as a propitiatory measure to protect the flocks; and Hag Ha'Matzoth, an agricultural festival associated with the beginning of the barley harvest, during which unleavened bread was eaten. (Lev. 23:5–6; Num. 28:16–17) Eventually these two festivals were observed together and were later identified with the commemoration of a historical event, the Exodus. According to the biblical account of the Exodus, God visited ten plagues on the Egyptians to persuade them to release the Israelites from bondage. Before the last plague, during which the firstborn in each household would be slaughtered, God told Moses to tell the Israelites to slaughter an unblemished lamb and smear the blood on their two door posts and lintel so their homes would be passed over and their firstborn spared. The Israelites, as instructed, roasted and ate the animals just before leaving Egypt but were in such a hurry that their bread had no time to rise (Exod. 12:1–28).

4. Manna fell during the night in small white flakes or grains which covered the ground and presented the appearance of hoar frost. These grains are described as resembling coriander seed and bdellium, with a taste like

"flour with honey", or "bread tempered with oil" (Exodus 16:31; Numbers 11:7-8)

5. Gregorios, Paulos. (1969). *The Faith of Our Fathers*. Kottayam: MGOCSM.

6. Gregorios, Paulos. (1999). *Introducing the Orthodox Churches*. New Delhi: ISPCK. p. 49

7. Gregorios, Paulos. (1969). *The Faith of Our Fathers*. Kottayam: MGOCSM.

8. http://paulosmargregorios.info/English%20Articles/Euchasristic_Hospitality.html.

9. http://paulosmargregorios.info/Gregorian%20Vision/Kuriakose%20thesis.pdf

## Chapter. 19

1. Gregorios, Paulos. *Science, Technology, and the Future of Humanity*.
http://paulosmargregorios.info/English%20Articles/science_technology_future.htm

2. Gregorios, Paulos. (1993). The Role of Science in Society.
http://paulosmargregorios.info/English%20Articles/The%20Role%20of%20Science.html

## Chapter. 20

1. Philip, Bijesh. (2010). Christian faith and Global Peace. Tiruvalla: CSS.

## Chapter.21

1. Pagels, Heinz. (1982). The Cosmic Code, Quantum Physics as the Language of Nature. NY: Simon & Schuster.

2. Gregorios, Paulos. (1982). Cosmic Man. The Divine Presence: New Delhi/Kottayam: Sophia Publications.

## Chapter. 22

1. Gregorios, Paulos. (1992). *A Light Too Bright: The Enlightenment Today*. NY: State University of New York Press.

2. McDonald, Brian. Blinded by Light? Touchstone, A Journal of Mere Christianity. http://www.touchstonemag.com/archives/article.php?id=06-04-030-b#ixzz1RREEnDcd

# A List of Books by Paulos Mar Gregorios

The Joy of Freedom: Eastern Worship and Modern Man. London: Lutterworth Press/Richmond, Virginia: John Knox Press, 1967; Madras: CLS, 1986.

The Gospel of the Kingdom. Madras: CLS, 1968.

Date of Easter and Calendar Revision of the Orthodox Churches: A Preliminary Study, Addis Ababa: The Standing committee of the Conference of Oriental Orthodox Churches, 1968.

The faith of Our Fathers. Kottayam: MGOCSM, 1969/Kottayam: Bethel Publications. 1996.

The Freedom of Man. Philadelphia: Westminster, 1972.

Be Still and know. Madras: CLS/Delhi: ISPCK/Lucknow: The Lucknow Publishing House, 1974.

Freedom and Authority. Madras: CLS/Delhi: ISPCK/ Lucknow: The Lucknow Publishing House, 1974.

Quest for Certainty: Philosophical Trends in the West: A Sample Survey of Later Twentieth Century Western Thought for the Average Indian Reader. Kottayam: Orthodox Seminary, 1976.

The Human Presence: An Orthodox View of Nature. Geneva: WCC, 1978/Madras CLS, 1980/New York: Amity, 1987/ New York: Element Books, 1992.

Truth Without Tradition?. Tirupati: Sri Venkateswara University, 1978.

Science for Sane Societies: Reflections of Faith, Science and the Future in the Indian Context. Madras: CLS, 1980/ New York: Paragon, 1987.

Cosmic Man. The Divine Presence: An Analysis of the Place and Role of the Human Race in the Cosmos, in relation to God and the Historical World, in the thought of St. Gregory of Nyssa (ca 330 to ca 395 A.D.). New Delhi/Kottayam: Sophia Publications, 1982.

The Indian Orthodox Church: An Overview. New Delhi / Kottayam: Sophia Publications, 1982.

The Meaning and Nature of Diakonia. Geneva: WCC, 1988.

Enlightenment East and West: Pointers in the Quest for India's Secular Identity. Shimla: Indian Institute of Advanced Study/New Delhi: B. R. Publishing Corporation, 1989.

A Light Too Bright. Albany, New York: State University of New York Press, 1992.

A Human God. Kottayam: MGF, 1992.

Healing: A Holistic Approach. Kottayam: Current Books/ MGF, 1995.

Love's Freedom The Grand Mystery: A Spiritual Auto-Biography; All Uniting Love with Creative Freedom in the Spirit, As the Grand Mystery at the Heart of Reality - One Man's Vision. Kottayam: MGF, 1997.

The Secular Ideology: An Impotent Remedy for India's Communal Problem. Kottaym: MGF/New Delhi: ISPCK, 1998.

Global Peace and Common Security. Kottayam: MGF / New Delhi: ISPCK, 1998.

Disarmament and Nuclear Weapons. Kottayam: MGF / New Delhi: ISPCK, 1998.

Introducing The Orthodox Churches. Kottayam: MGF / New Delhi: ISPCK, 1999.

Religion and Dialogue. Kottayam: MGF / New Delhi: ISPCK, 2000.

The Church and Authority. Kottayam: MGF / New Delhi: ISPCK, 2001.

Worship in a Secular Age. Kottayam: MGF / Thiruvalla: CSS, 2003.

Made in the USA
Middletown, DE
22 October 2023

41265910R00137